D0554422

ORDER AND REASON
IN POLITICS

UNIVERSITY OF HULL PUBLICATIONS

ORDER AND REASON IN POLITICS.

*Theories of Absolute and
Limited Monarchy in
Early Modern England*

ROBERT ECCLESHALL

Published for the UNIVERSITY OF HULL *by the*
OXFORD UNIVERSITY PRESS
1978

Oxford University Press, Walton Street, Oxford OX2 6DP

OXFORD LONDON GLASGOW
NEW YORK TORONTO MELBOURNE WELLINGTON
IBADAN NAIROBI DAR ES SALAAM LUSAKA CAPE TOWN
KUALA LUMPUR SINGAPORE JAKARTA HONG KONG TOKYO
DELHI BOMBAY CALCUTTA MADRAS KARACHI

© *University of Hull 1978*

British Library Cataloguing in Publication Data

Eccleshall, Robert

Order and reason in politics.
1. Monarchy   2. England – Kings and rulers
I. Title
321.6'0942   JC385   77–30452

ISBN 0–19–713431–9

*Printed in Great Britain by
Cox & Wyman Ltd,
London, Fakenham and Reading*

ACKNOWLEDGEMENTS

THE ADOLESCENT phase of this project was a Ph.D. thesis submitted in the University of Hull. Any merit the book possesses owes much to the friendly and stimulating atmosphere of that place. Dr. Bhikhu Parekh is responsible for taking hold of me as a raw student and awakening an interest in political ideas, while Dr. Robert Berki supervised the thesis in his typically shrewd and kindly manner. Their bestowal of time and friendship has been supererogatory. As an undergraduate, I was fortunate in attending the last series of lectures in Political Thought given by Dr. W. H. Greenleaf before he left Hull for a chair at Swansea. It will be evident how much I have gleaned from his own work on the period; and he was instrumental in persuading me that the thesis was worth reworking into a book. Finally, in agreeing to sponsor the book, my *alma mater* has supported me in a more tangible fashion. And that is no small measure of generosity in these days of financial stringency. I must also thank the Queen's University of Belfast for having been helpful in this respect.

One justification for the work is that it brings to bear on political thought the conclusions of other scholars engaged in a study of the period; the text will reveal the abundance of my debts. In addition, I have received encouragement from Dr. J. B. Morrall of the London School of Economics, Dr. D. O. Thomas of University College, Aberystwyth, and Dr. Leslie Clarkson of the Queen's University of Belfast.

Ms. Hazel Bond's typing of the final manuscript was exemplary. The book was completed in a battered city where the question of why the thoughts of the dead should take precedence over the sufferings of the living lurks like a shadow: it would be churlish not to thank friends, colleagues and students for providing sustenance in a variety of ways.

Belfast
December 1976.

CONTENTS

I

INTRODUCTION

MY THEME is the emergence, prevalence, and eventual decline of two predominant styles of political thought in early modern England. Characteristic of one was a tendency to mystify political activity by removing it from the range of normal human competence. This was done through the suggestion that political matters were ultimately disposed of in heaven by a benevolent deity who had bestowed upon his temporal deputy certain unique and communally advantageous gifts. In the other, politics was brought down to earth in that it was conceived as an essentially human activity to be undertaken by organized members of the corporate community. So far from being the prerogative of one standing apart from the community, politics was envisaged here as a co-operative enterprise in which the nation attained direction from the combined wisdom of its assembled members.

In more familiar language we are dealing with two distinct theories, those of absolute monarchy or the divine right of kings and limited monarchy or mixed government.[1] Put like this, the question arises as to why it is considered desirable to re-chart fairly well-trodden territory. The answer is that the two theories

[1] I intentionally conflate the phrases 'limited monarchy' and 'mixed government' throughout the text. Strictly speaking, limited monarchy implies constitutionally limited monarchy, whereas mixed government suggests a judicious mixture of the three basic forms (monarchy, aristocracy, and democracy) in a balanced constitution. The distinction became significant during the Civil War when some writers conceded that the king was constitutionally limited, though not that he was a more or less equal partner in a form of mixed government. For most of the period, however, the distinction was practically irrelevant. Those who described English government as mixed, as well as those who emphasized the institutional limitations to the exercise of the royal prerogative, were united in one fundamental respect; specifically, that English public practices were informed by objective standards of justice because the legislative process was a co-operative activity in which the monarch was constitutionally obliged to associate with representatives of the community. In conventional usage, the two terms were practically synonymous. To use them interchangeably highlights the shared assumptions of those who perceived the necessity of institutional safeguards to the common good, as compared with those who relied on an extra-communal guarantee of sound government.

are usually wrongly contrasted as though they exhibit a tussle between two patterns of belief, the Christian Aristotelianism of the feudal world and the individualism of an unfolding age. The theory of absolute monarchy is frequently presented as a hangover from a dying culture, while that of limited monarchy is said to embody the values of an ascendant era. In fact, both evolved from, and were contained comfortably within, an established system of assumptions that was to hold sway until the middle of the seventeenth century. Only with the coming of civil war was that system to be challenged by individualist assumptions, which were appropriated simultaneously by royalists and parliamentarians. The reason why an epistemological revolution in political thinking did not occur before this is not difficult to grasp. It is that both theories reflected the Tudor experiment in power sharing between the crown and the propertied classes by means of which the political nation was created. Had they issued from a squabble for power or had the defenders of limited monarchy been intent on making radical demands on behalf of groups excluded from the political process, one side or the other might have been forced to ground its thinking in an alternative set of assumptions. But this is speculation. As it was, each group of writers continued to elaborate certain well-worn medieval themes. Each refined and adapted them to its own conception of political legitimacy.

The general failure of historians to identify an adequate context of understanding derives partly from the fact that they still tend to treat early modern political thought in a perfunctory fashion, regarding it as the product of an intellectual dark age that was squeezed between the architectonic splendours of the Scholastic era and the analytically rigorous contract theories of the mid-seventeenth century. Seeing the period as the prologue to a time of intellectual fervour in which there was a proliferation of novel and exciting ideas, commentators have indulged in an orgy of retrospection. The unwitting authors of the period have been consequently fathered with the ideological conflicts of the English Civil War and beyond. Even Richard Hooker's work, which can lay legitimate claim to being the most systematic and philosophically sophisticated piece of political writing produced in the sixteenth century, has been shamelessly plundered in a bid to elicit from it the embryonic version of practically every modern doctrine. Mediated through the interpretative frameworks of various historians, *Of the*

Laws of Ecclesiastical Polity is reduced to a rag-bag of contradictions.

Not that lesser writers have fared any better, especially the theoreticians of mixed government who are usually seen as the inaugurators of a new age. The scholarly Christopher Hill, for example, implies that they were in some sense the carriers or spokesmen of emerging bourgeois values.[1] The implication is that their thinking constituted a radical devaluation of more traditional beliefs, which it did not. There seems to lurk in this case that spectre of economic reductionism which Hill has been careful to exorcize on other occasions. Indeed, far too many historians seem reluctant to extricate themselves from a once hallowed straitjacket, a simplistic identification of royalism with a reactionary feudal class and parliamentarianism with a progressive bourgeoisie. Marxists and non-Marxists, says Hexter, 'have joined in the dreary game of "Button, button, where is the bourgeoise?"'[2] They have selected the early modern period as a perfect playground for the game on the assumption that it offers an initial glimpse of a cleavage that was to dominate the English scene for several centuries, the protracted struggle between a declining aristocracy and a rising bourgeoisie.

[1] Christopher Hill, *Intellectual Origins of the English Revolution* (Oxford, 1965), p. 7: 'Sixteenth-century middle-class Englishmen, encouraged in literacy so as to be able to read the Bible, taught at grammar schools which merchants had founded in order to free education from clerical control, grew up into a confusing world. Traditional ideas were in retreat, but no new synthesis had replaced them . . . The urban way of life, pragmatic, utilitarian, and individualistic, where things mattered more than words, experience more than authority, was in harmony with new trends in Protestant and scientific thought . . . The most striking feature, then, of the intellectual life of pre-revolutionary England is its confusion and ferment.' The context having been established, the intended implications of his brief remarks about the theorists of limited monarchy, pp. 270–1, become clear: 'A full account of the intellectual origins of the English Revolution would have to discuss the "liberal" constitutional ideas which descend from Fortescue through Christopher St. Germain, Thomas Starkey, and Sir Thomas Smith. The latter touches our story at many points. The son of a protestant sheep farmer, he himself purchased monastic lands, and disliked "conjurors and mass-mongers" . . . Smith was interested in astronomy, having Copernicus in his library, and making globes with his own hands; and also in astrology, navigation, alchemy, medicine, economics . . . Like Ralegh, Smith was a proponent of religious toleration, an admirer of the yeomanry, an advocate of colonization, as well as setting new architectural fashions. Like Bacon, Smith favoured a career open to the talents . . . Smith links the radicalism of the reign of Edward VI with the radicalism of the Revolution.'

[2] J. H. Hexter, *Reappraisals in History* (London, 1961).

Again, we are told that in the ideas of these writers is to be perceived an erosion of the significance of natural law and an incipient struggle for sovereignty that led inexorably to the eruptions of the seventeenth century.[1] One who reads the secondary literature of the period may be forgiven for supposing that Whig historiography is alive and healthy. American commentators, in particular, perhaps unconsciously importing to the English setting their own experience of a written and precisely delineated constitution, have been eager to establish a perspective that features a gradual yet irresistible attempt to construct a balanced constitution protecting the rights and guaranteeing the interests of everyone.[2]

In ways such as these the intellectual history of the period is endowed with a Cinderella-like quality, being written so as to disclose a teleological project in which the outcome of the final chapter is implicit from the start. Given it is a success story, the triumphant march of nascent capitalism or the spirit of liberal constitutionalism, the historian is content to search the rags of the sixteenth and early seventeenth centuries for clues as to the logical, though partially concealed, sequence of ideas which is said to accompany changing social and political practices. It is hardly a defensible pastime because prone to the sort of distortion which normally occurs when ideas are torn from context to

---

[1] George L. Mosse, *The Struggle for Sovereignty in England from the Reign of Queen Elizabeth to the Petition of Right* (East Lansing, 1950), p. 6: 'The ascendance of Henry Tudor to the throne of England in 1485 marked no break in the continuity of political thought. It was only gradually, during the Tudor period, that the idea of sovereignty rose to prominence. Even then, it was not yet the concept of a single agent, such as the monarch, endowed with absolute authority, but rather the sovereignty of the "King in Parliament". The actions of the king and the representatives of the people, jointly, were allowed to be sovereign in the name of the law of reason. This sovereignty of the "King in Parliament" antedated the struggle for sovereignty on the part of both king and the Parliament. Once the idea of sovereignty had supplanted medieval concept of a commonwealth, a struggle for power was almost inevitable.' Apart from being an odd interpretation of history in its location of the motor of historical change in the realm of ideas, this statement is pure retrospection in its false imputation of a doctrine of sovereignty to a theory in which no more was claimed than that the king in parliament was a competent institutional device for ensuring that human laws were framed according to divine standards of justice.

[2] Even such a fine piece of scholarship as Margaret A. Judson's, *The Crisis of the Constitution: An Essay in Constitutional and Political Thought in England 1603–1645* (New Brunswick, N.J., 1949), is marred by this sort of perspective.

be reconstituted through the conceptual apparatus of a later epoch.

Other historians have at least attempted to make the political thought of the period intelligible in its own terms by unravelling the network of background assumptions by which it was informed. Notable among these is W. H. Greenleaf whose *Order, Empiricism and Politics*, seemingly inspired by the Hegelian conviction that the world will assume a rational aspect for him who cares to look at it rationally, elucidates the basic premises of the contemporary world picture. His intention is to perform a salvage operation by illustrating that certain political arguments, though to modern minds apparently spurious, are rational in terms of criteria that were familiar to their authors. Greenleaf nevertheless falls into the same trap as other commentators, that of identifying the theory of limited monarchy with a novel empiricist style of thinking; in contrast with the theory of absolutism said to be associated with the traditional world view of order. Greenleaf's failure to provide what he terms 'an historically credible framework' derives, I think, from his reconstruction of the medieval world picture as a monolithic structure, a neat canopy of basic beliefs in which actual nuances of thought are obscured. Finding that certain writers cannot be accommodated in the over-tidy web he has woven, he has no alternative than to suggest that they represented another, as yet incipient, pattern of assumptions.

My purpose, then, is to provide an account of two contrasting styles of thought, each reflecting the differing intentions of their authors but not initiated by them as rival or mutually exclusive theories. In a transformed environment, the turmoils of civil war, we shall see that they were to be combatively deployed in an ideological battle. But it would be quite wrong to infer from this that buried somewhere within them is an anticipation of those conflicts which it is the job of the historian to uncover. They are to be understood, rather, as arising within the framework of the medieval world view, the conception of a rationally ordered universe, which was sufficiently flexible to meet the various ideological needs of dominant social groups who therefore felt no compulsion to develop the kind of political thinking usually associated with individualism. The fact that England, in Tawney's phrase, stood at 'the brink of an acquisitive society' does not provide sufficient basis for a supposition that there must have existed a corresponding body of intellectuals intent on eroding traditional beliefs in the light of their experience of social change. The prevalence of divergent trends of political thought does not necessarily imply the coexistence of radically opposed premises regarding the nature of social reality, nor even a time of intellectual confusion in which one world view was being superseded by another. Yet this is the mistake we shall make if we regard the thought of the sixteenth and early seventeenth centuries as a prelude to a later age, a Pandora's Box or treasure chest, according to one's perspective, in which is to be found an immature expression of what C. B. Macpherson aptly terms *The Political Theory of Possessive Individualism :* or if we treat a world picture as a tight system of assumptions yielding a single set of conclusions about a particular human activity. Given that an important function of a system of basic beliefs is to enable men to cope with the exigencies of a usually precarious reality by transposing the institutional order to a more enduring framework of significance, it is not difficult to understand why they should be reluctant to abandon the conceptual equipment familiar to them. It may take a political crisis, the sudden and dramatic breakdown of traditional patterns of social control, to open a floodgate of ideas which rapidly consolidate into a novel conceptualization of social and political realities.

The evidence suggests that the English Civil War performed such a role in precipitating individualist notions into most areas of thought. In 1644 Henry Robinson, London entrepreneur and advocate of imperialism, expressed impatience with those whose religious intolerance had generated a constitutional and ultimately military confrontation. Such matters, he indicated, detracted from the real purpose of life which was capital accumulation. Religion, he believed, was a piece of private enterprise so that no one could successfully entrust his salvation to an external authority.

In civil affaires we see by experience that every man most commonly understands best his owne businesse, and such as doe not, but rely upon the managing and foresight of others, be they of what calling or condition soever, in a few yeares run out at heels, to the utter undoing of themselves and whole families . . . (I)n spiritual matters it holdeth much stronger, and concerns men to be more circumspect and warie, as the good or ill thereof readeth unto eternity: wherefore since it is as possible for them or him to erre, who take upon them to conduct me to heaven, as I am selfe . . .; since if I miscarry through mine owne choice and will, I shall easier acknowledge my destruction to be from my selfe, and declare Gods judgments to be just; If I perish by mine own folly, tis the losse of one, but if misled by others, we all fall into the ditch together, with an aggravation of our condemnation, to me that relyed finally upon others in a businesse of the greatest concernment that possibly could befall me, without other possibility of assurance of doing well, than by an implicite faith; and to them that tooke upon them to be guide and pilote unto others in a coercive way especially, when they knew not how to save themselves . . . I desire every Christian heart . . . to consider . . . whether it be not a much safer way in spirituall affaires, for every particular man to understand his owne estate betwixt God and himselfe, and manage his own business. . . . It is usuall with gamesters to say they had rather lose their own money, then that others should lose it for them; and surely if we took as much delight in saving our soules, as gamesters doe in losing of their money, we would quickly chuse a hazard the losse of our owne souls our selves, rather than forgoe the present joy and comfort of endeavouring the salvation of them by our owne, and not by an implicate faith.[1]

In both material and spiritual concerns, Robinson is suggesting, the autonomous individual possesses the requisite capacities for successfully engaging in the business of life. Here is evidence enough that the emerging pattern of social relations had made an impression on the consciousness of at least some people. By the Civil War, then, the traditional picture of society as a hierarchical structure where each was enjoined to perform the duties of his ascribed role had been challenged, if not completely supplanted, by another conception in which society appeared as a collection of interacting individuals each of whom was legitimately engaged in the pursuit of private acquisition. But this is not sufficient reason for supposing that ideas articulated in the immediately preceding period were but a pale shadow of succeeding notions. And if the evidence points to the persistence of established beliefs, as well as revealing contrasting political standpoints within the orbit of those beliefs, it becomes necessary to shelve the conventional interpretation of the age as an arena in which opposing

[1] Henry Robinson, *Libertie of Conscience*, in William Haller (ed.), *Tracts on Liberty in the Puritan Revolution 1638–1647* (New York, 1965), III, pp. 155–7: cf. W. K. Jordan, *Men of Substance: A Study of the Thought of Two English Revolutionaries, Henry Parker and Henry Robinson* (New York, 1967), who takes a somewhat elevated view of Robinson as an exponent of the freedom of conscience doctrine.

assumptions were vying for attention in the minds of political thinkers.

Precisely why the advocates of both absolute and limited monarchy continued to find inherited notions serviceable is not hard to appreciate. It relates to the paradoxical nature of the Tudor State. Here political power was exercised by landed groups pursuing policies which simultaneously protected their interests and fostered developments ultimately to erode the economic basis on which the power of those groups depended.[1] In the interim measures which provided a spur to nascent capitalist activity—the centralization of political power, the massive transfer of land, the growth of commercial and colonial activities—were sponsored by landed groups because they were the immediate beneficiaries of these trends.[2]

In so far as ideas are rooted in the reproduction of material human life, it is probably safe to assume a coincidence between prevalent beliefs and the interests of dominant groups. Political thinkers do not constitute a flock of classless beings whose position in the world barely affects what they think; indeed, especially in an age when literacy is confined to the upper stratas of society, they are generally favourably disposed to the existing order. But this does not make it legitimate to infer that their views are a crude superstructural reflection of some mechanistically conceived economic base, which appears to prompt at least some of the attempts to detect in the theory of limited monarchy an incipient expression of bourgeois values. Underlying this form of restrospective history there seems to lurk the following assumption: given that socio-economic changes presupposed a gradual dissolution of a multitude of dissipated feudal rights and privileges, and their consequent concentration into the hands of the owners

---

[1] I am, of course, skirting the debate about the alleged rise or decline of the gentry. There now seems to be a consensus that both positions are deficient: cf. the editor's introductory remarks in Conrad Russell (ed.), *The Origins of the English Civil War* (London, 1973). But the two propositions essential to our argument, i. that political power was exercised predominantly by landed groups, usually referred to as the gentry, and ii. that it would be inappropriate to describe these groups as bourgeois, would now be generally accepted. Hexter, *Reappraisals in History*, p. 28: 'whether rising or not, the gentry did not stand to the peerage in the relation of a middle class to an aristocracy. Economically gentry and peerage were of the *same* class – the class that ordinarily drew the larger part of its income from the exploitation of proprietary rights in land.'

[2] For some enlightening remarks see the brilliant analysis by Perry Anderson, *Lineages of the Absolutist State* (London, 1974), esp. chs. 1, 2, 5.

of landed and commercial property—the facilitation, that is, of an exchange economy—individualist premises must have immediately registered themselves in all department of thought.

Yet it would be quite wrong to imagine that the existence in the early modern period of two significant political theories indicates a jostling between bourgeois and pre-bourgeois values, or a nascent form of class struggle, which at least until the outbreak of the Civil War it was not. Both the theories that concern us issued from a refinement of traditional ideational patterns because both derived from a single development: the emergence of a centralized nation in which the political power of landed classes was entrenched. Both theories lent weight to the privileges of such groups, which could be adequately accomplished without abandoning transmitted ideas. The fact that this single development generated two distinct theories of politics was due to various factors: the immediate context in which each theory was shaped, the types of audience to which each writer addressed himself and the predominant message which each tried to get across, the role of government censorship, the particular relation of each author with the government, and so forth.

I begin with an outline of those traditional patterns of thought within which the theories of absolute and limited monarchy were to unfold. In one sense, the continuity in the early modern period of medieval premises has been more than adequately documented.[1] Inspired by the publication of A. O. Lovejoy's seminal work *The Great Chain of Being*, numerous commentators have made use of his account of one 'unit-idea'. They have done so in order to reveal that reflection upon most forms of activity in early modern England was informed by the belief in a philoprogenitive deity who had been moved to manifest his beneficence in a proliferation of external forms that corresponded to the various layers in the scale of creation. Typical of this mode of thinking was a reverential appreciation of nature as the supposed source of a normative pattern for the regulation of human affairs. Associated with it was

---

[1] W. H. Greenleaf, *Order, Empiricism and Politics: Two Traditions of English Political Thought 1500–1700* (London, 1964); Michael Walzer, *The Revolution of the Saints: A Study in the Origins of Radical Politics* (London, 1966), ch. 5; E. M. W. Tillyard, *The Elizabethan World Picture* (London, 1963) and *Shakespeare's History Plays* (London, 1944); Hardin Craig, *The Enchanted Glass* (Oxford, 1960); Theodore Spencer, *Shakespeare and the Nature of Man* (New York, 1951).

a particular method of argument, the irresistible temptation to compare the political structure with other parts of the world, from the beehive to the structure of the universe itself, in order to underpin the need for integration within the human community. Seen in this context, that of a divinely patterned universe, the political thinking of the age appears as something other than a mingle-mangle of fanciful and superficial arguments strung together for the purposes of propaganda.

I only repeat the exercise of elaborating certain familiar themes in the belief that the interpretation of the thought of the period in terms of this overarching ideational canopy has led to the type of error Lovejoy himself warned against:

The study of the history of ideas is full of dangers and pitfalls; it has its characteristic excess. Precisely because it aims at interpretation and unification and seeks to correlate things which often are not on the surface connected, it may easily degenerate into a species of merely imaginative historical generalization.[1]

For the reconstruction of the medieval world view as a homogeneous web of assumptions has served to conceal the fact that from it might emerge contrasting images of political activity. By stating most cogently how he conceives the historical enterprise, Professor Greenleaf exhibits the strength and weakness of an approach which attempts 'to see the ideas of a particular period of the past on their own terms. This means looking at them as it were internally, as a living reality which can, historically speaking, be properly understood only by reference to their own standards of what is reasonable and logical.'[2] The error lies in the attribution of methodological priority to the conceptual framework equivalent to the established world view, rather than to the actual social processes and human practices that persuaded writers to operate with a traditional system of values. If a function of a world picture is to transpose discrete events and practices to a more stable framework of meaning, it follows that to place its retrieval at the forefront of the historical task is to be committed to uncovering a relatively integrated structure in which actual social tensions have been largely resolved. Believing that his sole task is to illustrate contemporary standards of rationality in order to eradicate from a set

---

[1] A. O. Lovejoy, *The Great Chain of Being* (New York, 1960), p. 21.
[2] Greenleaf, *Order, Empiricism and Politics,* p. 2.

of writings what later generations might see as inconsistencies, the historian easily slips into the idealist fallacy that inconsistencies are provisional things of the mind that are destined to disappear through mental effort. His task, he imagines, is complete once he has shown that the levels of argument used by various writers combined into a particular brand of that single theme which inspired all the intellectual patterns of a given period. The effect is to contract all the writings of an age into an undifferentiated unity in which differences of emphasis are obliterated. Each writer is not represented as a conscious social actor who developed intellectual traditions in an effort to deal with the problems of his world. He appears, rather, as the inhabitant of some abstract mental abode who was intent on exploring the logical implications of an internally consistent, disembodied system of assumptions as it manifested itself at a particular historical moment. Should writers be found putting forward contrasting views about some activity, it has to be supposed that we are dealing with different ideational worlds. But the world picture with which we are concerned was not as rigidly integrated as this approach would indicate. It did not preclude the emergence of contrasting conceptions of political activity.

Nature appeared in the medieval world picture as pulsating with teleological significance. Replete with evidence of the divine wisdom, it contained injunctions for the proper allocation of social functions and the distribution of rewards within human society. Ultimately, the dissolution of relationships into exchange values was to erode the assumption of a just correspondence between patterns of human authority and the structure of the natural world. Francis Bacon's conceptualization of nature was the initial statement of a line of thinking which was to divest it of inherent meaning. Nature was to be conceived as raw matter which, through scientific investigation and control, could be systematically transformed into objects of human need. But the traditional view, expressed by John Aylmer, a defender of mixed government which is supposed to indicate the undermining of traditional beliefs, was that 'Nature is nothinge els but God him selfe, or a diuine order spred throughout the whole world, and ingrafte in euerye part of it'.[1] The human imperative was to accommodate to the immutable

[1] John Aylmer, *An Harborowe for Faithfull and Trewe Svbiectes* (Strasbourg, 1559), sig. M.3.

structure which was everywhere in evidence. For as Thomas Starkey, another advocate of limited monarchy, said, nature was 'a glasse of the diuine maiestie' that reflected the infinite richness of God's creative wisdom. Order was the principle by which the world were consolidated, a symmetrical pattern in which all things were allotted their proper place. 'Consider all the order of Gods work,' preached John Pelling in a sermon delivered at Paul's Cross,[1] 'thou shalt see cause enough to praise God for all.'[2] Order was the product of a fecund deity who, being in Richard Hooker's words 'all-sufficient', was moved by 'that natural desire which his goodness hath to shew and impart itself' to reproduce himself by creating every conceivable type of being.[3] Thus, the universal pattern was that of a continuous hierarchy that ascended gradually from the lowest physical level to the spiritual plane. Order, therefore entailed inequality. The basic idea was clearly expressed by Sir John Fortescue, a late fifteenth-century writer and also a proponent of the theory of limited monarchy.

There is nothing virtuous and nothing good which doth not observe the law of order . . . And what is this order but a disposition of equal and unequal things assigning each to its proper place? And what is the proper place of a superior but the condition and degree by which a superior is set over an inferior? and what is the place of an inferior but the condition and degree whereby he is placed under the superior in the order of the universe? For it is true that God created as many different kinds of things as He did creatures, so that there is no creature which doth not differ in some respect from all other creatures, and by which it is in some respect superior or inferior to all the rest . . . So that there is nothing which the bond of order doth not embrace.[4]

There flowed from these few simple propositions regarding the nature of reality so much that is distinctive of the thought of the time. The product of a single creative wisdom, the design of the universe was said to be duplicated in its every aspect. This conviction that a repetitive structure was everywhere displayed led to a

---

[1] The Paul's Cross sermons provide a useful indication of contemporary beliefs. cf. Millar Maclure, *The Paul's Cross Sermons, 1534–1642* (Toronto, 1958).

[2] John Pelling, *A Sermon of the Providence of God* (London, 1607), p. 19.

[3] Richard Hooker, *Of the Laws of Ecclesiastical Polity*, V. App. I, p. 565, in *The Works*, ed. John Keble (3rd ed., Oxford, 1845).

[4] Sir John Fortescue, *De Natura Legis Naturae*, Pt. II, ch. lix, in *The Works*, ed. Lord Clermont (London, 1869).

certain method of argument. It was deemed appropriate to increase
knowledge about one segment of reality through analogy with
other parts. Argument by correspondence was 'a dominant characteristic of the age'.[1] The effort to perceive unity in plurality, the
discovery of correspondences between apparently dissimilar sections of reality, was considered a worthy occupation for the human
mind. Edward Forset was only voicing the conventional wisdom
when he wrote: 'It is the greatest miracle of Gods powerfull
wisdome, in the innumerable formes of things, to make so infinite
variation; Then it must needs be a great worke of the wit of man,
in such multiplicitie of difference to find out the well agreeing
semblances.'[2] The universe was stocked with signposts for humankind because everywhere was evidence of an imitable model. An
exploration of its essential features was thus a means of clarifying
divine intentions. How fortunate was man, Edwin Sandys re-
minded his congregation, in having 'so many schoolmasters' to
instruct him in regard to his communal arrangements.[3] The
appropriate organizational features of human society derived
necessarily from the conception of the universe as an ordered
hierarchy. Disorder within society was a frightening spectacle,
assuming cosmic dimensions because it seemingly undermined the
principle of universal cohesion. And a rightly ordered community
was a functionally differentiated structure of mutual interdependence and inequality. Society was consequently envisaged as a
fabric of affective ties and strictly delineated social roles operating
for the benefit of all. Anyone who attempted to vacate his ascribed
role was, in a real sense, acting impiously. There was no room here
for a conception of political institutions as an expedient set of
coercive arrangements designed to mediate between individuals
publicly enjoined to pursue their private interests. The political
realm was not a market-place where bargains were struck between
competitors with little to unite them beyond a common desire for
security and appropriation. The human community was to be

[1] James Winny (ed.), *The Frame of Order* (London, 1957), p. 14. S. L. Bethell, *The Cultural Revolution of the Seventeenth Century* (London, 1951), p. 45 comments that correspondences were 'part of an ordered and generally accepted
system of thought, not mere vagaries of the pious imagination or eccentric striv-
ings of minority apologetics'.
[2] Edward Forset, *A Comparative Discovrse of the Bodies Natvral and Politiqve* (London, 1606), 'To the Reader'.
[3] Edwin Sandys, *A Sermon Preached Before the Queen*, in *The Sermons*, ed. John Ayre (Cambridge, 1842), p. 98.

understood against the backdrop of the cosmic pattern, and political activity was a means of ensuring adjustment to it.

It was the peculiar position of the human species within the universal scheme that made it an object of so much intrigue and speculation. It was to man that Phineas Fletcher referred when he suggested that, at the time of creation, God had:

> cast to frame an Isle, the heart and head
> Of all his works, compos'd with curious art;
> Which like an Index briefly should impart
> The summe of all; the whole, yet of the whole a part.[1]

The belief that man's standing in the scale of creation was unique because he embodied the wider world on a smaller scale was reiterated continually.[2] In the first place, it was said that the human body consisted of the four elements, earth, fire, water and air, of which the natural world was composed. Corresponding to these were four humours, the mixture and predominance of which was thought to determine mental behaviour.[3] More important was the fact that he was held to bridge the great divide in the scale of creation, for he stood astride the two worlds of matter and spirit. Sharing physical existence with inanimate objects at the lower end of the scale, life with vegetative species, sensation with animals, and intellect with the angels, man alone supplied the crucial link that ensured the continuity of the chain of being. It was this pivotal position that made him at once a glorious and tragic creature, an almost schizoid figure who was constantly torn between the demands of reason and the promptings of passion. For sin, in the Christian view, inclined him constantly to yield to the yearnings of his sensuous nature. The paradox of the human microcosm was expressed by Humphry Sydenham in a funeral sermon delivered in 1625.

[1] Phineas Fletcher, *The Purple Island, Or The Isle of Man,* in Giles and Phineas Fletcher, *Poetical Works,* ed. F. S. Boas (Cambridge, 1909), II, p. 21.

[2] Examples are given in Marjorie Hope Nicholson, *The Breaking of the Circle: Studies in the effect of the 'New Science' upon seventeenth-century poetry* (London, 1960), ch. 1. For the history of the idea see G. P. Conger, *Theories of Macrocosms and Microcosms in the History of Philosophy* (New York, 1922). On a more systematic discussion of the theme see Rudolf Allers, 'Microcosmus: From Anaximandros to Paracelsus,' *Traditio,* II (1944), pp. 319–407. Also Leonard Barkan, *Nature's Work of Art: The Human Body as Image of the World* (New Haven and London, 1975).

[3] Elaborated in Lawrence Babb, *The Elizabethan Malady: A Study of Melancholia in English Literature from 1580 to 1642* (East Lansing, 1951), ch. 1.

Man, the masterpiece of [God's] designe and workmanship, the great miracle and monument of nature, not onely for externall transcendencies but the the glorie and pompe of inward faculties stampt, and engraven to the image of his God, through the righteousness of an immortal soule; besides, a body so symmetriously composed as if nature had lost its selfe in the harmony of such a feature. *Man,* the abstract, and modell, and briefe story of the universe,—*utriusque naturae viculum*—, the cabinet and store-house of three living natures, sensuall, intellectuall, rationall, the Analysis and resolution of the greater world into the lesse, the Epitome and *compendium* of that huge tome, the great *Manuscript* and work of nature, wherein are written the characters of Gods omnipotencie and power, framing it, disposing it, all in it, to the use and benefit of *man,* of *man* especially, of *man,* wholly; other creatures paying him an awfull obedience, as a tribute, and homage due to their commander in all things, so neere kinne to Deitie, that *Melancthon* makes him a terrestriall transitory God: having little to divide him from a – – Numan – –, but that one part of him was mortall, and that not *created* so, but occasion'd, miserably occasion'd, by *disobedience.*[1]

It was the additional gift of reason that elevated the human species above the animal world and was the source of human dignity. Hardly a work appeared in which the author did not allude to the fact. Instructing children in good manners, for instance, William Fiston saw fit to remind them that 'God hath not onely made thee a liuing creature, whereas thou hadst no beeing, but hath made thee a reasonable and euerliuing soule: euen a Semblance of Image of his owne excellent Maiesty, a partaker of reason and diuine knowledge in heauenly thinges, with the Angels'.[2] Whereas angels apprehended without the medium of the senses and animals instinctively gravitated towards objects which the senses found gratifying, the human being could subordinate sensory evidence to the discriminatory eye of reason. He had what has been called 'the power of mistaken choice',[3] or free will, because he was under no compulsion to perform any specific action. Subjecting the data which the senses received to rational evaluation, man was brought into contact with a transcendental reality. For reason might elicit norms which, far from being

[1] Humphry Sydenham, *Natvres Overthrow, and Deaths Trivmph,* in *Five Sermons Preached upon Severall Occasions* (London, 1637), pp. 164–5.

[2] William Fiston, *The Schoole of good Manners: or, a new Schoole of Vertue* (London, 1609), sig. A. 4.

[3] Maurice De Wulf, *Philosophy and Civilization in the Middle Ages* (Princeton, 1922), p. 225.

validated merely by human recognition or consensus, were anchored in the rationally structured universe itself.

Many things good to the judgement of sense, are in the eye of right reason abhorred as evil, in which case the voice of reason is the voice of God.

The light of natural understanding, wit, and reason, is from God; he it is which thereby doth illuminate every man entering into the world ... He is the author of all that we think or do by virtue of that light, which himself hath given.[1]

Contained in these statements of Hooker is the crucial belief that human reason facilitated an encounter with the divine reason, revealing those objective principles which lent coherence to the universe.[2] The universe was saturated with reason because it incorporated the design of its rational creator, which writers expressed by saying that it was regulated according to an eternal law.[3] But while every created form was subject to this law, man alone might conform voluntarily with its requirements. Doing so, he made a conscious decision to connect with the divine reason. What else is the law of human nature, asked Fortescue, but 'the *Truth of Justice, which is capable of being by right reason revealed?*'[4]

This optimistic assessment of human capacities was mitigated, of course, by the doctrine of the Fall. Mankind had inherited the weakness of Adam and was incapable of rising again without

---

[1] Hooker, *Of the Laws of Ecclesiastical Polity*, V. App. I, p. 544, III. ix. 3.

[2] cf. Robert Hoopes, *Right Reason in the Renaissance* (Cambridge, Mass., 1962).

[3] Antony Fawkner, *Nicodemus for Christ, or the Religiovs Moote of an Honest Lawyer* (London, 1630), pp. 4–5: 'the God of Order would be the example of Order. Now as all is made, all must be sustained, lest Order should againe be swallowed up in confusion. So that as all was created in order, all must bee so created, that it may remaine in order. Wherefore God will at once be . . . a Creator and a Lawgiuer; and with the same *Fiat* rouze from confusion and command to obedience. Each creature is so like it selfe, that it cannot be ought saue it self. The wisedome of his bounty giues it a Beeing; the wisedom of his order giues it but one Beeing. . . . Thus the Decree of God checkes all Nature: his Word created by a secret power; his Wisedome goucrnes by an eternall Law.' Christopher St. German, *Doctor and Student: or Dialogues Between a Doctor of Divinity, and a Student in the Laws of England* (15th ed., London, 1751), p. 3; 'Therefore as the Reason of the Wisdom of God (inasmuch as Creatures be created by him) is the Reason and Foresight of all Crafts and Works that have been or shall be; so the Reason of the Wisdom of God, moving all Things by Wisdom make to a good End, obtaineth the Name and Reason of a Law, and that is called the *Law Eternal*.'

[4] Fortescue, *De Natura Legis Naturae*, Pt. I, ch. xxxi.

divine assistance. This was why the Word had become Flesh. Rendered frail by sin, man's faculties could not direct him to that ultimate goal of beatitude for which he yearned. Led astray by passion, without faith in the reconciling power of Christ, his hope of perfect happiness through union with God was but an clusory dream.

There was disagreement, however, as to whether reason had been partially or totally impaired by sin. For the tradition of Christian theology running through Augustine to the radical reformers of the sixteenth century, the Fall had been totally disastrous. Miserable and depraved, man's only recourse was to depend on the scripturally revealed edicts of God. But more traditional thinkers, while accepting that rational capacities were enfeebled, held that man still naturally desired his good and might take steps to attain it.[1] Hooker suggested that no human good was beyond comprehension 'if Reason were diligent to search it out'.[2] The trouble with postlapsarian man was that, tainted with sin, he was not always sufficiently diligent and permitted reason to shirk its duties, either by failing to inform the will as to the proper course of action or by inclining it to an immediate sensory good in preference to a higher goal which entailed greater effort. In this way a short circuit, as Spencer calls it, occurred.[3] Despite the perversity of much human behaviour, a capacity of determining and acting upon an objective good was retained so long as sufficient care was taken. Thus grace 'doth not abolish Nature, but perfect it',[4] enabling its possessor to become what he naturally desired to be. Indeed, the Scriptures presupposed natural knowledge, for reason confirmed them as the Word of God and interpreted their message. Reason and faith were complementary means to human perfection so that the former was not to be denigrated because 'among all Gifts that God gave to Man, this Gift of Reason is the most noblest, for thereby Man precelleth all Beasts, and is made like to the Dignity of Angels, discerning Truth from Falshood, and Evil from Good'.[5]

[1] cf. John F. H. New, *Anglican and Puritan: The Basis of Their Opposition 1558–1640* (London, 1964).
[2] Hooker, *Of the Laws of Ecclesiastical Polity*, I. vii. 7.
[3] Spencer, *Shakespeare and the Nature of Man*, p. 24.
[4] Sydenham, *The Athenian Babler*, in *Five Sermons Preached Upon Severall Occasions*, p. 30.
[5] St. German, *Doctor and Student*, p. 42.

On this view, politics was necessarily a moral enterprise. For the duplication of the rational order of the universe within society entailed making the objective principles of reason operative in a communal context. But left unsettled at this level of theoretical generality was the question of who was competent to undertake the task of mediating divine norms of justice to the community. And this is the basis of my claim that the traditional world picture was sufficiently flexible to accommodate divergent strains of political thought.

On the one hand was a tendency to assimilate the political structure to the pattern of order recurrent in the universe. If nature was stocked with what Forset termed 'exemplary patterns' for human benefit,[1] and if the natural world displayed a hierarchical organization, it was legitimate to suppose that only the head of the body politic might act in a political capacity. Thomas Floyd illustrated this line of argument in comparing political society with the microcosm which was the human body. Monarchy was to be preferred because

arte or handicraft is the more excellent, by how much more it doth imitate nature. But an vniuersall Common wealth, is nothing els sauing an imaginary, or artificiall perpohted bodie, seyng that in such a naturall body, we do coniecture and see one head and many members wherefore a Citie or Monarchie, if it be so gouerned, it farre exceedeth: because it more imitates and resembles nature.[2]

The argument could be reinforced by the inescapable fact of sin. Disintegration in the human community was felt to be a consequence of the anti-social manifestations of passion which made men discontented with their place in the intricate web of supportive relationships. So it might be considered desirable for there to be a public figure, elevated above the community and therefore able to ensure that its members minded their own business by exclusively devoting themselves to the duties of their particular station. In this way those too feeble to restrain their impulses might be prevented from disturbing the divine order of the universe.

On the other hand was a tendency to emphasize the unique

---

[1] Forset, *A Comparative Discovrse of the Bodies Natvral and Politiqve,* 'To the Reader'.

[2] Thomas Floyd, *The Picture of a perfit Common wealth* (London, 1600), pp. 26–7.

generic feature of humankind. Though there was an affinity between the natural pattern and human society, which underpinned the belief that the latter was a stratified structure where all were enjoined to seek the public benefit, there was also a significant difference. The human species was distinguished as a repository of reason, for only its members consciously participated in the divine reason. Only they could comprehend the prescriptions of the eternal law and apply them in their individual and corporate lives. The implication was that there was some sort of equality between men, each a moral agent striving for a good desired by all. On this view, political society appeared as a group of rational beings organized towards a common end and so actively co-operating with one another in the rational order of the universe. The political implications of the common possession of reason derived from the fact that political activity was envisaged as the pursuit of rationally ascertainable objectives. It was legitimate to suppose, therefore, that men other than the single head were equipped to engage in decision-making procedures, that the community itself might make political provision for the common good. Moreover. a politically mobilized community might prove an effective method of counteracting the socially harmful manifestations of sin. The rational faculty of everyone being impaired by sin, it might be inexpedient to entrust the general well-being to one who was removed from the community's control. For he, sharing in the affliction of all, was fallible and through erroneous judgement or selfish desire might fail to ensure that the requirements of the objective moral order were mediated to the community. Far safer to make a collective communal reason responsible for political affairs because it was a more reliable indication of moral rightness than the weak judgement of one individual. The substantive component of legislative enactments could be secured by making politics a co-operative activity.

These tendencies were embedded in the network of inherited assumptions and were to crystallize in the theories of absolute and limited monarchy. It follows that an adequate context of understanding must include reference to the factors which persuaded writers to exploit the theoretical possibilities contained in the traditional *Weltanschauung*. I have already indicated the methodological inadequacy of an approach which implies that each text was occasioned by basic assumptions and therefore constitutes a miniature reproduction of a world picture. Lurking somewhere in this perspective is the supposition that particular ideas are a reflection of the Idea as it reveals itself in a particular epoch. But thinking, of course, is a social activity which derives from the practical concerns of the thinker.

The main trend of political thinking in the period was towards the elevation of monarchy and the consequent erection of an hiatus between the two functions of rulership and obedience. It was articulated in the main by members of a social group that had grown to prominence in the hundred and fifty years prior to the Reformation, was consolidated by its effects, and for almost a century longer was to focus on the crown as the source of economic prosperity and political stability. This group was the landed gentry, recruited in the fifteenth century from more prosperous tenant farmers, lawyers and merchants, and already politically significant as a counter weight against a greedy nobility. It was on this group that Henry VIII and his successors depended to lend practical and theoretical weight to the claim of the crown to be temporal and spiritual head of the English nation. In the effort to construct a viable political system the privileges of its established members were reinforced, and its ranks swollen by the extension of royal patronage to learned men of humanistic bent who could be expected to publicize the progressive features of the break with Rome. Many rallied willingly to the defence of the new regime. As the beneficiaries of an unprecedented market in land, they had good reason for doing so. For in order to overcome its financial difficulties, especially those incurred by war, by 1550 the crown had sold most of the monastic property seized at the Reformation. For the next hundred years the gentry flourished, its members expanding at a disproportionately higher rate than the general rise in population and its net income increasing as much as fourfold.

Not that all were motivated by the prospect of land-grabbing. Some genuinely believed that the monarch was the leaven in the lump of the body politic who would rectify abuses and so promote the 'commonweal'. Thomas Starkey, a humane and cosmopolitan scholar whose usefulness in the ideological campaign waged against the Bishop of Rome did not pass unnoticed by Thomas Cromwell, greeted the suppression of the monasteries with acclamation. In 1536 he took it upon himself to address his sovereign, expressing the fear that the newly acquired property would be leased on the basis of to him that hath shalt be given. He advised the king that such a policy of lining the pockets of the nobility and wealthy gentry 'schal much deface & gretly dymynysch the profyt of your acte & publyke vtylyte'. He hoped, rather, that monastic lands would be subdivided and leased on low rents to younger sons of the gentry, deprived of property by the practice of primogeniture, 'and to them wych be of lowar state and degre'.[1] In this way the idle rich would be encouraged to take up an honest occupation, an uncultivated and depopulated countryside made abundant, and the revenues from rents used to promote learning throughout the nation. Starkey was politically innocent but his sentiments did echo those of a significant section of the economically privileged who saw in the events of the 1530s possibilities other than the acquisition of larger estates.

So throughout the sixteenth century landed interests were the mainstay of strong monarchy. It was never a completely harmonious arrangement and there were underlying tensions which eventually exploded in civil war.[2] By the 1620s royal intransigence and paternalism, especially in the granting of monopolies and the high-handed treatment of parliament, were being felt as a hindrance to a thriving economy. Landed interests, many of whom were now engaged in commercial activities, along with professional groups, were becoming more self-confident and independent of the crown. What characterized the decades prior to the outbreak of war was a growing polarization between a plethora of local élites throughout the country and an increasingly isolated court with its strange mixture of gay abandon and High Anglican ritual. In these years the task of propounding a theory of absolute monarchy fell largely to a bunch of clerics. Fighting a rearguard action in their distance from other social groups, they engaged in a last ditch fling in the wildly inflated claims they made on behalf of God's vice-regent on earth. Inheriting a theory ready made, they elaborated it into a remarkable affirmation of the sanctity of regal authority. For many of the landed classes, whose forebears had helped to expound a doctrine that was now expanded by a spectacular

[1] *Starkey's Life and Letters in England in the reign of King Henry the Eighth*, ed. Sidney J. Herrtage, E.E.T.S., extra series, XXXII (London, 1878), p. lviii.
[2] These conflicts are cogently described by Lawrence Stone, *The causes of the English Revolution 1529–1642* (London, 1972).

display of theological gymnastics, the credibility gap between the supposedly visible representation of the deity and the actuality of monarchy must have seemed wide indeed. Yet there were sound reasons why, for most of the period, the crown was the focus of a surging nationalism for the bulk of the privileged members of the community.

Accepting as they did that a stable society emanated from strong government, writers managed to contain their social and economic analyses within the medieval theory of estates[1]—the picture of society as a plurality of functions organized towards a common goal by the co-ordinating activities of the head. It was not that they were operating with an outmoded set of concepts, as is sometimes suggested. Rather, the role they attributed to monarchy, that of maintaining stability by curbing socially divisive appetites, accommodated nicely with the old ideal of a disciplined social hierarchy. Of course, the inherited conception of a rigidly stratified structure was amended to take account of the upward social mobility of those new men of learning who were the recipients of royal patronage. In 1536 Sir Richard Morison condemned the 'worser sort' of people for not resting content with their lot. This did not prevent him commending his sovereign who

bothe by his owne great studye, to atteyne lernynge, wysdome, and other princely qualities, and also in giving offyces, dignities, & honour, well testified, that he woll all his subjects to contende, who may obteyne mooste qualities, moost wytee, most vertue; and this onely to by way to promotion, and here nobilitie to consyste. In all other thynges it lyttel avayleth whose sonne a man be.[2]

Undoubtedly, too, analyses were marked by a more concrete understanding of socio-economic forces than had previously been the case.[3] Occasionally, even, we catch a glimpse of an alternative set of social relations, as in Sir Thomas Smith's remark that 'profit

[1] cf. Ruth Mohl, *The Three Estates in Medieval and Renaissance Literature* (New York, 1962).

[2] Sir Richard Morison, *A Remedy for Sedition*, ed. E. M. Cox (London, 1933), pp. 16–17. On the Tudor humanists, see Fritz Caspari, *Humanism and the Social Order in Tudor England* (Chicago, 1954), and Paul N. Siegel, 'English Humanism and the New Tudor Aristocracy', *Journal of the History of Ideas*, XIII (1952), pp. 450–68.

[3] cf. A. B. Ferguson, 'The Tudor Commonweal and the Sense of Change', *Journal of British Studies*, III (1963–4), pp. 11–35, and *The Articulate Citizen and the English Renaissance* (Durham, N.C., 1965).

or advancement nourishes every faculty' and his belief that government regulation of market forces should operate on the basis that 'every man naturally will follow that wherein he sees profit'.[1]

But the bulk of Tudor commentators reiterated the medieval view of property as a trust to be used for the common benefit,[2] and accepted as incontrovertible that, in Starkey's words, 'overmuch regard of private weal, pleasure and profit is the manifest destruction of all good, public and just common policy'.[3] There was no place here for the belief that, in some mysterious fashion, private vices were transmuted into public benefits, that unlimited acquisition was a legitimate ambition because society possessed some internal mechanism for turning human appetite to public good. There was ample room for a paternalist theory of government in which the monarch was enjoined to apply fairly extensive remedies to the ills of the body politic. Amongst other measures, Starkey advocated State control of rents and house building, stringent regulation of imports and exports, and the appointment of town officers who would ensure that citizens engaged in socially productive work and that children received an appropriate education for some useful occupational role. Sir William Forrest, too, was convinced that the monarch should be super-active in economic and social matters by initiating wide-scale welfare legislation. He advised him to mitigate the effects of enclosure, fix rents and prices, administer a system of free education for children aged four and upwards, encourage the establishment of clothing factories in every village and town in order to curtail the profits made on the export of raw wool and its importation as a finished product, and generally protect the poor so that 'Pryuate Commodye withe Commone wealthe to scorse',[4]

Social commentators looked for a cohesive community forged by the firm and benevolent directives of the political centre. They were fortified in their desire by recurrent reminders of the essential fragility of the political structure. Papal bulls of excommunication

---

[1] *A Discourse of the Commonweal of This Realm of England,* ed. Mary Dewar (Charlottesville, Virg., 1969), pp. 58, 60.

[2] cf. A. J. Carlyle, 'The Theory of Property in Mediaeval Theology,' in Charles Gore (ed.), *Property : its Duties and Rights* (London, 1913), pp. 119–32.

[3] Thomas Starkey, *A Dialogue between Reginald Pole and Thomas Lupset,* ed. Kathleen M. Burton (London, 1948), p. 70.

[4] Sir William Forrest, *Pleasaunt Poesye of Princelie Practise,* ed. Sidney J. Herrtage, E.E.T.S., extra series, XXXII (London, 1878), p. xcvii. 'Scorse' meant to exchange.

and threats of holy war to recover the lost sheep dominated the horizon for a great deal of the period and created a persistent undercurrent of uneasiness. The fear was accentuated by the internal unrest contingent upon the split with Rome. From the start many watched unhappily as their country strayed from the fold of the universal church, and some expressed their opposition vehemently.[1] At first, of course, the more radical reformers were delighted, expecting the monarch eventually to purge the Church of all papal remnants and lending support by disseminating the Lutheran doctrine of his absolute supremacy within the national community. William Tyndale succinctly stated it in 1528.

God hath made the king in every realm judge over all, and over him is there no judge. He that judgeth the king judgeth God; and he that layeth hands on the king layeth hand on God; and he that resisteth the king resisteth God, and damneth God's law and ordinance. If the king sin, he must be reserved unto the judgment, wrath, and vengeance of God.[2]

The influx of such ideas into the traditional conception of monarchy was to outlive the brief alliance of their exponents with the crown. Mary's flirtation with the old faith led to a rush of exiles to Europe and from its Protestant presses issued a flood of denunciatory literature which adjusted the theory of obedience to take account of the new situation, thereby fostering a siege mentality in those who remained at home. From the safety of Geneva, Christopher Goodman informed his countrymen that it was impious to obey rulers who raised 'them selues aboue God and aboue their brethern, to drawe them to idolatrie, and to oppresse them, and their contrie'.[3] From Strasbourg John Ponet, former bishop of Winchester, asserted a communal right to depose an ungodly ruler, for 'as a sowe comyng in to a faire gardin, roteth up all the faire and swet flowres and holsome simples, leauing nothing behinde,

---

[1] Numerous examples are given in G. R. Elton, *Policy and Police : The Enforcement of the Reformation in the Age of Thomas Cromwell* (Cambridge, 1972), ch. 1. J. J. Scarisbrick, *Henry VIII* (London, 1968), p. 339; 'The Reformation did not bring a new unity to England; on the contrary, it created a new and long-lived disunity, inside a new sense of nationhood . . . Rarely, one imagines, had more sedition been spoken by so many, so suddenly.'

[2] William Tyndale, *The Obedience of a Christian Man,* in *Doctrinal Treatises,* ed. H. Walter (Cambridge, 1848), p. 177. For an account of the ideas and fortunes of the radical reformers during the Reformation, see William A. Clebsch, *England's Earliest Protestants, 1520–1535* (New Haven, 1964).

[3] Christopher Goodman, *How Superior Powers Ought to be Obeyed* (1558) repr. Facsimile Text Society (New York, 1931), p. 59.

but her owne filthye dirte: so dothe an euil gouernour subuerte the lawes and ordres'.[1] There was no doubt who was being cast in the role of a sow and provocation enough for her supporters to paint an equally dramatic picture of monarchical attributes.

Elizabeth was more successful in containing dissent to her religious policies, though from 1570 there was a campaign to shift the Anglican Church from its midway position of Reformed Catholicism to a purer form of Protestantism.[2] It began as a condemnation of clerical vestments, and was extended to an attack on episcopacy. Most so-called Puritans had no desire to establish their own presbytery, seeking rather to simplify Anglican worship so as to make the scripturally revealed Word of God more accessible to His people. Yet, as Richard Hooker recognized, embodied in the apparently innocent demands regarding church rites and ceremonies were the seeds of an ideology radically at odds with a traditional respect for established institutions; an ideology of subversion that located the standard of public rightness in the unaided judgement of the private individual. For the time being, it did not blossom into a doctrine of insurrection. From the other side, however, came statements of more overt opposition which again raised the prospects of foreign invasion. The Jesuit Robert Parsons said that monarchs exercised a communally delegated authority, 'so may the wealpublique cure or cutt of their heades, if they infest the rest, seeing that a body ciuill may have divers heades, by succession, and is not bound euer to one, as a body natural is'.[3] There was reason enough for loyalists to create a cult of obedience to the crown.

What more than anything shaped royalism was the groan of despair that arose from the mass at the bottom of the social pyramid, and which erupted again and again in concerted action. The medieval picture of a stable social hierarchy, in which everyone happily performed his particular duties, had always been a mixture of idealism, wishful thinking and ideological propaganda, reiterated so often because the actual world was so prone to disruption. Frequently, peasant frustrations were spear-headed in local

---

[1] John Ponet, *A Shorte Treatise of politike pouuer* (Strassbourg, 1556), p. 99; facsimile reprint in Winthrop S. Hudson, *John Ponet (1516?–1556) Advocate of Limited Monarchy* (Chicago, 1942).

[2] cf. Patrick Collinson, *The Elizabethan Puritan Movement* (London, 1967).

[3] [Robert Parsons], *A Conference Abovt the Next Svccession to the Crowne of Ingland* (1594), p. 38.

revolts against some specific grievance. A heavier tax, for instance, might provoke revulsion against disturbance of the traditional balance of relationships. Sometimes, as in the famous revolt of 1381, frustrations developed into mass movements which shook the fabric of society.[1] Then the more socially integrated peasantry would be joined by those on the fringe of society, the dispossessed who, sustained by preachers referring to the communitarian example of the early Christians and such apposite passages of the gospels as the twenty-fifth chapter of St. Matthew, would be inspired by the vision of an alternative society in which oppression and private property were abolished in one sweep when the poor inherited the fruits of the earth.[2] Seven years after the suppression of the 1381 rising, it was still apparent to Master Wimbledon 'that rich men eat the poore, as beastes done their lesous, holding them lowe'.[3] Periodic appeals such as this to a more primitive and human mode of communal distribution were inevitable because conflict and resentment were endemic to a system of social relations in which there were continual pressures to deprive the peasant even of subsistence.

Late medieval England saw the development of a *rentier* economy where, in response to higher costs and a deflated demand for food due to a declining population, large demesnes operating on the basis of labour services were divided into leaseholds with tenant-farming and wage-labour. Early modern England saw the emergence of a mass of landless peasants who became vagabonds and seasonal workers or gravitated to the towns in an often vain attempt to sell their labour power.[4] A population explosion—the population almost doubled between 1500 and 1620—generated unemployment and reduced real wages by a half. The situation was aggravated by the great transfer in land ownership concomitant with the appearance of monastic property on the open market, which led to rent increases and accelerated the trend towards enclosure. And the poor were now deprived of the charitable

---

[1] cf. Rodney Hilton, *Bond Men Made Free : Medieval Peasant Movements of the English Rising of 1381* (London, 1973).

[2] cf. Norman Cohn, *The Pursuit of the Millenium : Revolutionary millenarians and mystical anarchists of the Middle Ages* (London, 1970), esp. ch. 11.

[3] Cited in G. R. Owst, *Literature and Pulpit in Medieval England* (Cambridge, 1933), p. 305.

[4] cf. Alan Everitt, 'Social Mobility in Early Modern England', *Past and Present*, 33 (1966), pp. 56–73; Lawrence Stone, 'Social Mobility in England, 1500–1700', *Past and Present*, 33 (1966), pp. 16–55.

services formerly provided by the religious establishments; according to one commentator, they now got not 'one halpenny worth of almes'.[1] It was a time of marked relative deprivation, with the poor becoming poorer and landed and commercial groups benefiting from rising prices.

For many of the deprived, instructed by their empty stomachs that communal wealth was not available to all, rebellion seemed the only channel through which to articulate their misery. And they resorted to it frequently. Between 1536 and 1569 there were three major provincial uprisings and countless minor ones. For those with eyes to see the reason was simple and crystal clear, an inordinate degree of exploitation. Robert Crowley, a cleric who was a constant thorn in the flesh of the establishment, an intrepid trouble-maker who was deprived of several livings and eventually became one of the Marian exiles, put the issue plainly in *The Way to Wealth* (1550).

If I shuld demaunde of the pore man of the contrey what things he thinketh to be the cause of Sedition, I know his answere. He woulde tel me that the great fermares, the grasiers, the riche buchares, the men of law, the marchauntes, the gentlemen, the knightes, the lordes, and I can not tel who; men haue no name because they are doares in al thinges that ani gaine hangeth vpon. Men without conscience. Men vtterly voide of Goddes feare. Yea, men that liue as thoughe there were no God at all! Men that would haue all in their owne handes; men that would leaue nothyng fro others; men that would be alone on the earth; men that bee neuer satisfied. Cormerauntes, gredye gulles; yea, men that would eate vp menne, women, & chyldren, are the causes of Sedition! They take our houses ouer our headdes, they bye our growndes out of our handes, they reyse our rents, they leauie great (yea vnreasonable) fines, they enclose oure commens![2]

There seemed little alternative to sedition for the man whose children were raised, as someone said in 1548, merely to 'garnish gallow trees'.[3] A period of structural upheaval when relations between groups could not but be fraught with tension, it required the slightest provocation to bring conflicts roaring to the surface.

[1] *Henry Brinklow's Complaynt of Roderyck More* (1542), ed. J. M. Cowper, E.E.T.S. (London, 1874), p. 33.
[2] *The Select Works of Robert Crowley*, ed. J. M. Cowper, E.E.T.S., extra series, XV (London, 1872), pp. 132–3.
[3] Cited in Frances Rose-Troup, *The Western Rebellion of 1549* (London, 1913), p. 110.

And there were always those willing to harness the mass of discontent for their own purposes: local gentry disgruntled by
restraints imposed on the transfer of land by such measures of
central government as the Statute of Uses and who sought a
a revival of regionalism, clerics dismayed by the dissolution of the
monasteries who might convince the dispossessed that they were
embarking on a mission sanctioned by the Almighty.[1] Little
wonder that, peeping through the clamour of specific demands,
was a picture of an egalitarian communal organization in which all
would live abundantly. Archbishop Parker's secretary, Nevylle,
was not being unfair to the poor rebels when he tried to paraphrase
their sense of frustration and their aspirations.

The birds of the air, the fish of the sea, and all the fruits so unsparingly
brought forth by the earth, [the rich] look upon as their own, and conse-
consequently use them as such. Nature, with all her abundance and
variety, is unable to satisfy them . . . Since nature has made the same
provision for us as for them, and has given us also a soul and a body,
we should like to know whether this is all that we are to expect at her
hands. Look at them, and look at us: have we not all the same form?
are we not all born in the same way? Why, then, should their mode of
life, why should their lot, be so vastly different from ours?[2]

No wonder that the 'high and mighty folks', as Nevylle described
them, should have been scared out of their wits.

Not quite, for they retained sufficient wit to stage a massive
ideological campaign designed to quell the many-headed monster,[3]
each rebellion provoking a fresh crop of tracts, pamphlets and
sermons in which the virtues of obedience were extolled.[4] From
the start there were many who rushed to the theoretical defence of
the regime, actively encouraged by the patronage of Thomas
Cromwell and the availability of the government press.[5] In 1529

[1] For an analysis of patterns of leadership in one rebellion see M. E. James,
'Obedience and Dissent in Henrician England: The Lincolnshire Rebellion
1536', Past and Present, 48 (1970), pp. 3–78.
[2] Cited in F. W. Russell, Ket's Rebellion in Norfolk (London, 1859), p. 23.
[3] On the use of this phrase see 'The Many-Headed Monster in Late Tudor
and Early Stuart Political Thinking', in Christopher Hill, Change and Continuity in Seventeenth Century England (London, 1974), pp. 181–204.
[4] cf. James K. Lowers, Mirrors for Rebels: A Study of Polemical Literature
Relating to the Northern Rebellion 1569 (Berkeley and Los Angeles, 1953),
which ranges further than the title suggests.
[5] cf. Franklin le van Baumer, The Early Tudor Theory of Kingship (New York,
1966); W. G. Zeeveld, Foundations of Tudor Policy (Cambridge, Mass., 1948).

control of printing passed from the Church to the privy council, and censorship laws were made more rigorous and stringently enforced. A man like Richard Morison, recognizing that the crown smiled kindly on the new men of learning, was more than willing to become 'a professional writer of propaganda',[1] and penned some strong attacks on dissidence. At the time of Ket's Rebellion in 1549, Sir John Cheke launched into a vehement condemnation of sedition, 'the verie reading of' which, in Holinshed's somewhat optimistic assessment, 'is able to turne a rebellious mind to meekenesse'.[2] Hardly surprising that Cheke should have seen fit to compose *The hurt of sedition how greeuous it is to a commonwealth*, for he was tutor to the Prince Edward.

Even during the crucial Reformation years, however, by no means all the support received by government was directly sponsored by it.[3] Confronted with social dislocation at home and the prospect of destruction from without, large numbers of the 'high and mighty folks' responded by lending enthusiastic support to the one who was most likely to consolidate their position by maintaining the framework of a stable State. We have seen that the more enlightened among them, perhaps grasping that conflict about the distribution of communal wealth was embedded in the emergent pattern of social relations, looked to the crown to supply the initiative in applying remedial measures. Forrest said that the king should reform

> manye injuryes too the poore pliethe,
> done by the bygger without all Justice.[4]

But humanitarian sentiments like these, which tended to emerge whenever writers engaged in a serious analysis of social trends, were largely swamped by the imminent danger of popular revolt. While more sensitive observers were able to place rebellion in perspective, as the *cris de coeur* of men and women experiencing the harsh realities of a changing world, the main effect of social disorder was to close the ranks of the privileged sections of the community. From its members issued an onslaught of literature, the aim of which was to persuade, cajole, terrify potential dissidents

[1] G. R. Elton, *Reform and Renewal: Thomas Cromwell and the Common Weal* (Cambridge, 1973), p. 58.
[2] Holinshed, *Chronicles* (London, 1808), III, p. 987.
[3] The point is made by Elton, *Policy and Police*, ch. 4.
[4] Forrest, *Pleasaunt Poesye of Princelie Practise*, p. lxxxix.

into submission by flaunting before them the prospect of a fate too horrible to imagine.

And, of course, the campaign was reinforced in ballads and other forms of popular expression. In every natural disaster and personal misfortune could be detected an omen of national catastrophe and a warning from above of what would befall disruptive members of the body politic. For this was an age, says Keith Thomas, in which 'divine omnipotence was still believed to be reflected in daily happenings, and the world provided abundant testimony to the continuous manifestation of God's purpose'.[1] Poor Margaret Mere 'being vnmaryed, played the naughty packe', and bore a grossly deformed child. The misshapen limbs of the unfortunate creature were each made to represent some defect in the body politic. Thus:

> The leg so clyming to the head,
>   What meaneth it but this,
> That some do seeke not to be lead,
>   But for to leade amis?

> And as this makes it most monstrous
>   For foote to clyme to head,
> So those subjects be most vicious
>   That refuse to be lead.

> Wherefore to ech in England now,
>   Let this monster teach
> To men the monstrous life they show,
>   Least endles death them reach.[2]

Second-rate verse but indicative of popular sentiment, evidence that the nation was not neatly divided into two camps in which final destruction was averted only by a conspiracy of ideas contrived by those at the top of the social hierarchy.

Not that officialdom was slow in exploiting the upsurge of popular feeling in an effort to effect the hegemony of socially cohesive notions. The cult of the Virgin Empress who had emerged victorious over her internal enemies, stood courageously alone

[1] Keith Thomas, *Religion and the Decline of Magic, Studies in popular beliefs in sixteenth and seventeenth century England* (London, 1971), p. 78.

[2] 'The forme and shape of a monstrous Child, borne at Maydstone in Kent, the xxiiij. of October, 1568', in *A Collection of Seventy-Nine Black-Letter Ballads and Broadsides, Printed in the Reign of Queen Elizabeth, Between the Years 1559 and 1597*, ed. Joseph Lilly (London, 1870), pp. 194-7.

against the Antichrist at large, and was a pivot of expansionist policies, did much to create a sense of national identity in Elizabeth's reign. Celebrated by poets, the date of her accession to the throne turned into an annual festivity with much bell-ringing and fun-making interspersed with suitable laudatory sermons,[1] she was offered for popular consumption as something other than a merely virtuous lady. The process that was to culminate in the seventeenth century, in which royalists divested the monarch of human qualities by transmuting him into nothing less than a visible representation of the deity, was already well in hand in the sixteenth century. If the initial impetus to a cult of royal authority came from the threat of internal disintegration, it was sustained by a sense of national buoyancy and optimism in an age when some of the old fears had diminished.

With regard to rebellion, the attitude of dominant groups was summarized at the end of the sixteenth century in a remark of Thomas Floyd. 'Sedition is a hell to the minde, a horror to the conscience, supressing reason, and inciting hatred.'[2] It was this mixture of fear and disgust which provided the thrust to so much of the political thinking of the time, lending to it a simplicity and directness in which an outright condemnation of subversion was combined with a wholehearted affirmation of royal authority. Richard Vennard captured in one sentence the central message writers intended to convey to their audience: 'For surely hee cannot be a true seruitour of God, that is not a faithfull subiect to his Prince.'[3] More than anything it was the actuality of social disorder, and the threat of worse to come, which persuaded landed groups that their interests coincided with those of the crown, that the king was their sun in whose light they bathed and were nourished.[4]

Christopher Morris quite rightly says that 'the times were not

[1] cf. Roy C. Strong, 'The Popular Celebration of the Accession Day of Queen Elizabeth I', *Journal of the Warburg and Courtauld Institutes*, XXI (1958), pp. 86–103; Frances Yates, *Astrae: The Imperial Theme in the Sixteenth Century* (London, 1975).

[2] Floyd, *The Picture of a perfit Common wealth*, p. 297.

[3] Richard Vennard, *An Exhortacion to continew all Subiects in their dew obedience, together with the reward of a faithfull subject to his Prince*, in *The Right Way to Heauen: and the true testimonie of a faithfull and loyall subiect* (London, 1601), sig. G. iii.

[4] cf. Charles Merbury, *A Briefe Discovrse of Royall Monarchie, as of the Best Common Weale* (London, 1581), pp. 1–2; Henry Valentine, *God Save the King. A Sermon Preached in St. Paul's Church the 27th of March 1639* (London, 1639), p. 5.

propitious for the making of systematic treatises'.[1] Nevertheless, in
the process of informing people in the plainest possible terms of
the wickedness of any action that might precipitate the collapse of
an apparently precarious political order, writers did attain a level
of theoretical coherence.[2] They did so by arranging and confirming
those features of the medieval world picture which converged to
remove political activity from the competence of ordinary men.
The cards were stacked against an exploration of the possible
political implications of the common possession of reason, for the
image of man which impinged itself on the consciousness of those
with an interest in preserving the prevailing structure was that of
a sin-infected creature who had to be prevented from giving vent
to the socially disastrous proclivities of his corrupted nature. In
their eyes, rebellion testified to a massive upsurge of passion that
constituted a sinful departure from the divine scheme of things,
rather than to the inevitability of structural stresses emanating
from inter-group conflicts about the distribution of the communal
product. Hence they contrived a theory with a strong anti-intel-
lectualist flavour in its affirmation of the organizational identity of
political society and the universal pattern. They sought to illustrate that a configuration of carefully delineated subordinate and
superior social roles was natural and therefore inevitable. For this
was a means of sanctifying the one who was strategically placed to
maintain stability. Arguing that the monarch was endowed with a
monopoly of political acumen and authority, they pointed out the
logical and sinful absurdity of politically headless members of the
body politic seeking to determine the nation's destiny by meddling
in matters which did not concern them. In this way a theory was
constructed which was conveniently appropriated and developed
by writers in the late sixteenth and early seventeenth centuries
when factors besides the threat of popular revolt made a theoretical
defence of monarchy desirable.

If the bulk of writers felt impelled to proclaim the virtues of
practically unfettered monarchy, a smaller number affirmed the
desirability of communally limited monarchy. While most were

[1] Christopher Morris, *Political Thought in England, Tyndale to Hooker* (London, 1953), p. 4.
[2] Which is not to be gathered from the much too simple remark of J. W.
Allen, *A History of Political Thought in the Sixteenth Century* (London, 1960),
pp. 132–3; 'The Tudor theory of subjection was fundamentally utilitarian: it
has strict reference to immediate expediency and to time and place.'

busily asserting that God or His temporal deputy retained effective control of political affairs, they suggested that safeguards to the common good were to be discovered in a corporate wisdom, the mobilization of the members of the community by means of political institutions. The overall effect of their thinking was to demystify political activity by bringing it within the scope of a specifically human faculty common to all.

Yet their intention was certainly not that of advocating a form of representative democracy in which everyone retained ultimate control of government activities. Nor did they suggest that reason was distributed equally among the members of the community and, on this basis, claim that each should have the opportunity of gaining access to the decision-making procedures of the nation. They took it for granted that there were gradations of wisdom, that representative or mixed government meant something other than a process designed to mediate and secure the subjectively understood interests of each person. Far from defending it on the grounds that it was necessary to protect an individual right to acquisition, they argued in typically medieval fashion that mixed government was the most effective device for ensuring that human affairs were conducted according to objective moral standards.

Nor did the theory of limited monarchy originate in a desire to counter the arguments of royalists. Its exponents were usually intent on defending the actual system of government. Like the theory of absolute monarchy, it emanated from the trend towards political centralization and the dependence of landed groups on the crown. Intent on creating a viable system of national administration, the crown sought the co-operation of the gentry by strengthening its position in parliament. In this way, the theories of absolute and limited monarchy had their practical counterparts in divergent, though not opposed, tendencies: the growing importance of the crown as a bulwark against social dislocation, and the alliance which it initiated with landed interests as a means of fulfilling that function. Landed groups were not inclined to oppose centripetal political forces so that it was not until some time in the seventeenth century that the two theories were adapted to support competing claims for sovereignty. For the moment they harmonized, indicating the complementary needs of the political élite.[1]

[1] Historians have been puzzled by the fact that the statutes and pamphlets of the Reformation years embodied elements of both theories in an apparently

So it was that the literate members of the élite played a double role in their thinking about politics.[1] They produced, on the one hand, a theory that was rooted in the desire to protect their royal benefactor against the machinations of certain of his subjects and, on the other, one which took due account of the developments by means of which the crown was assisted in the task of forging national unity. What can be said about the respective theories is that, if the former sprang from immediate and urgent concerns, the other was inspired by a rather more cosmopolitan and reflective approach to political matters. It is no coincidence that the theory of limited monarchy was usually penned by those who tended towards a serious analysis of social and economic factors generally. In highlighting some of the progressive developments stimulated, though not originated, by the Reformation, it revealed a somewhat broader perspective than was usually evident in the theory of absolutism.

The transformation of the monarch's counsel of magnates into a parliament, in which matters touching the general welfare were dealt with by the joint activity of crown, lords and commons, was more or less complete by the fifteenth century. In the process, the lower chamber became relatively more significant, and the influence of the gentry extended. Their predominance secured in the shires by a forty-shilling freehold franchise and a £100 freehold qualification for representatives, the landed interests also encroached upon borough seats. This trend was reinforced by Tudor patronage so that by the close of the sixteenth century only about one-fifth of borough seats were represented by authentic burgesses, that is, merchants and members of guilds.

But it was during the Reformation that parliament became a vital political force because every measure whereby the crown assumed the jurisdictional powers of the papacy was confirmed by

[1] The only commentator to have fully appreciated the dual role of the political élite is Joel Hurstfield, 'Was there a Tudor despotism after all?' in *Freedom, Corruption and Government in Elizabethan England* (London, 1973), pp. 23–49.

contradictory manner. Scarisbrick, for instance, tentatively suggests a 'tussle' between them, polarized in Henry's addiction to a descending theory in which regal power was a direct gift from God, and Cromwell's attraction to an ascending theory in which power inhered in the community: see his remarks in *Henry VIII*, pp. 392–8. But what Scarisbrick terms 'the ideological ambiguity in the core of Henricianism' was due less either to confusion or latent theoretical disagreement between the chief architects of nationhood than to the fact that both theories, if carefully manipulated, could be rendered ideologically serviceable.

parliamentary statute.[1] There was, apart from the need to supply a novel situation with an aura of legitimacy, a very practical reason for involving parliament in these dramatic events, for it was necessary to enforce what had been done by means of legal sanctions.[2] During these climactic years parliament availed itself of the opportunity provided by frequent sessions to indulge in an outburst of legislative activity spreading far beyond merely ecclesiastical concerns. Parliament, in fact, was 'concerned with reform in virtually every area of English government and society'.[3] Thus, through its role in the febrile political activity surrounding the split with Rome, parliament established a claim to be the proper place for dealing with national affairs, an instrument by which representatives of the community might determine common requirements in conjunction with the crown.

Yet in spite of the acknowledgement of the supremacy of parliamentary statute and the extension of its sphere of competence to include every aspect of national life, which gives rise to the claim that these years were revolutionary,[4] parliament had not sufficiently detached itself from its medieval origins, as an assembly summoned by the monarch to assent to taxation in periods of emergency, to be assured of an undisputed and unbroken existence. The preambles to the Reformation statutes in no way referred to the utility of a national assembly in restraining kingship, the emphasis being on the divine origin of regal authority in the bestowal of which the community had no part. When Henry VIII admitted that 'we at no time stand so highly in our estate royal as in the time of Parliament, wherein we as head and you as members are conjoined and knit together into one body politic',[5] he was acknowledging an expansion, not an erosion, of regal authority, made

---

[1] A writer of the following century put it this way: throughout the succession of momentous events constituting the Reformation, 'the Law kept still upon the top, nor did the King enter into any Competition therewith, or lead the way thereunto, other then by especiall allowance of Parliament'. Nathaniel Bacon, *An Historicall Discourse of the Uniformity of the Government of England* (London, 1647–51), p. 223.

[2] cf. G. R. Elton, *England under the Tudors* (London, 1959), ch. 7, and *The Tudor Constitution: Documents and Commentary* (Cambridge, 1960), ch. 8.

[3] S. E. Lehmberg, *The Reformation Parliament, 1529–1536* (Cambridge, 1970), p. 253.

[4] cf. the debate between Penry Williams and G. L. Harriss, 'A Revolution in Tudor History?', *Past and Present*, 25 (1963), pp. 3–58, and G. R. Elton, 'The Tudor Revolution: A Reply', *Past and Present*, 29 (1964), pp. 26–49.

[5] Elton, *The Tudor Constitution*, p. 270.

possible by the enhancement of parliament. A partnership of sorts had emerged, but one largely manufactured by the crown and in which the latter was predominant. It suited Henry's purpose to describe a parliament in which he was present as the embodiment of the common well-being and the nucleus of the political system. In this way the trend towards political centralization could be represented as an act of national unity.

While that co-operation persisted the theory of limited monarchy, in which the king was obliged to exercise his legislative authority in parliament, flourished. It is significant that between 1565, when Sir Thomas Smith composed his *De Repvblica Anglorvm*, and the outbreak of civil war, the theory of mixed government practically sank into oblivion. After this date even ardent parliamentarians restricted themselves to reminding the monarch that he was bound to observe common law, rather than affirming that his legislative capacity was located in a representative assembly of the nation.[1] For, while parliament met in all but six of the years between 1529 and 1559, Elizabeth and James managed to govern without it for longer periods. As the Lord Keeper said in 1593, 'Her maiestie hath euermore been most loth to call for the assemblie of her people in parliament, and hath done the same but rarely.'[2] In fact, parliament met in Elizabeth's reign for an average of only three weeks in each year.[3] Dr. Hinton speaks of a decline in both the practice and the idea of parliamentary government from the middle of the sixteenth century.[4] When it did assemble parliament clarified and strengthened some of its procedures and was more vocal in oppos-

---

[1] J. W. Gough, *Fundamental Law in English History* (Oxford, 1955), p. 48, confuses the issue when he takes the absence of a full blown doctrine of sovereignty, an accurate observation, as sufficient evidence that a theory of mixed monarchy was generally accepted: 'Nobody conceived of sovereignty in the modern sense in the early seventeenth century. Nobody doubted that the English monarchy was a "mixed monarchy", and not autocratic – a *dominium politicum et regale*, as Fortescue had said. The king had prerogatives (and there might be disputes as to what they were), but nobody, not even James himself, believed that they amounted to sovereignty, making him a despotic ruler, "Turk-like".' But plainly, to deny the legitimacy of arbitrary monarchy does not amount to a recognition that the king was required to exercise certain important governing powers in a common assembly, as Fortescue and others understood he was.

[2] Cited in J. S. Roskell, 'Perspectives in English Parliamentary History', *Bulletin of the John Rylands Library*, 46 (1963–4), p. 456.

[3] J. E. Neale, *The Elizabethan House of Commons* (London, 1949), pp. 381, 433.

[4] R. W. K. Hinton, 'The Decline of Parliamentary Government under Elizabeth I and the Early Stuarts', *Cambridge Historical Journal*, XIII (1957), pp. 116–32.

ing the crown on specific issues, which explains why the latter treated it as one of several expedients to be employed in the business of government. Parliament was increasingly by-passed and government matters dealt with by means of proclamations and private petitions to the privy council. 'It was government of, for and by the people, under a scheme of which the apex and directing head was the king out of parliament.'[1]

Parliament's role in the political process was necessarily precarious while it remained in some sense an assembly occasionally summoned to aid the monarch in the task of ruling. Even the social commentator William Harrison who, by leaning heavily on Smith's account, was able to attribute a central political role to parliament, could not but notice that it 'is not summoned, but vpon vrgent occasion when the prince dooth see his time'.[2] The Stuarts certainly saw it in this light even though when parliament was reluctantly summoned it did not meekly do the crown's bidding by uncritically agreeing to replenish its depleted resources.

On these grounds it is suggested that the 'great divide' in parliamentary history did not come until the seventeenth century when it won the undisputed right to meet regularly.[3] Yet, according to the theory of limited monarchy, there was nothing abnormal about the assembling of parliament. Its authors affirmed that certain crucial public matters, such as the making and amending of laws, were dealt with on a regular and co-operative basis. They were not so naïve as to suggest that an adequate guarantee of good government lay in the fact that the king might find in parliament an occasional expedient for raising taxation and swelling the royal exchequer.

So the theory of limited monarchy was expressed at a time when the expansion of the royal prerogative was achieved by involving a significant social group in the process of legislation. An alliance instigated and overshadowed by the crown, it propagated the conviction that the nation was equipped with the institutional prerequisites for dispensing justice in every sphere of national life. The theory, therefore, did not stand as a challenge to the crown. Indeed, it was sometimes conceived as a defence of the monarch

---

[1] R. W. K. Hinton, 'Government and Liberty Under James I', *Cambridge Historical Journal*, XI (1953), p. 53.

[2] William Harrison, *The Description of England*, in Holinshed, *Chronicles* (London, 1807), I, p. 302.

[3] Roskell, 'Perspectives in English Parliamentary History', pp. 473–5.

in the face of opposition. John Aylmer, for instance, propounded a theory of mixed government in refutation of the charge of certain of the Marian exiles that the obligation of obedience was overridden in England because female rule was unscriptural and unnatural.[1] Himself an exile, Aylmer wrote his work in an effort to placate his sovereign shortly before he returned home, later to become bishop of London. He took the view that the gender of the monarch was of minor significance compared with the need of ensuring that government promoted the common good. Adopting the Aristotelian classification of the various types of government, Aylmer sought to demonstrate that this condition was secured in England where government was a balanced mixture of the three forms:

The regiment of Englande is not a mere Monarchie . . . nor a meere Oligarchie, nor Democratie, but a rule mixte of all these, wherein ech one of these haue or should haue like authoritie. Thimage whereof, and not the image, but the thinge in dede, is to be sene in the parliament hous, wherein you shal find these. 3 estats. The King or Quene, which representeth the Monarche. The noble men, which be the Aristocratie, And the Burgesses and Knights the Democratie.[2]

His point was that the English monarch could not govern in an arbitrary fashion because he or she was hedged about with communally beneficial restrictions. So long as parliament was vigilant in using its privileges, the monarch could do nothing of national importance without its assent. The monarch was required to govern in accordance with laws enacted there and to make executive judgements with the advice of counsel. What he or she was permitted to do singly—pardon an offender, for instance—did not constitute a threat to the public welfare. England possessing 'a mixte ruler' rather than 'a mere monarck', the consequence was sound government irrespective of the personality or sex of the particular occupant of the throne. The implication was that the common good was furthered because politics was a matter of joint effort that involved the representatives of the entire community in parliament.

The theory also proved a useful polemical device during the turbulent years of Reformation, and was expressed as such by

---

[1] e.g. John Knox, *The First Blast of the Trumpet against the monstrvos regiment of women* (Geneva, 1558).

[2] Aylmer, *An Harborowe for Faithfull and Trewe Svbiectes*, sigs. H. 2–3.

those whose imagination had been fired by the welter of legislative activity that was provoked. 'There is a tide in the affairs of men,' proclaims Shakespeare's Brutus, 'which, taken at the flood, leads on to fortune.' We have seen that for enlightened Englishmen the Reformation was a flood that gave unprecedented opportunity for wide-ranging social and economic reforms. Simultaneously, they urged the crown to seize the opportunity and erected a theoretical justification for what had been immediately accomplished. From the pen of Christopher St. German, a venerable jurist and in no way a government lackey, came a number of works in which he argued that the king's assumption of the spiritual powers of the papacy did not constitute a national danger because he was obliged to exercise his legislative functions in conjunction with parliament. The crown rightly saw an indispensable ally in an intelligent man like St. German, and *Doctor and Student*, his most substantial treatise which was first printed in 1523, went through four editions in 1531.

This fusion of reformist aspirations and actual events helps to explain the apparently ambiguous role which individual writers sometimes played. For some of them extolled the virtues of mixed government and also expressed views which, at the hands of other writers, became major ingredients of the theory of absolutism. Thomas Starkey's *Dialogue between Reginald Pole and Thomas Lupset* was replete with enlightened suggestions for national reform, and his plans for an improved polity went much further in the direction of limited monarchy than the crown could possibly have found acceptable. His *An exhortation to the people instructynge theym to vnitie and obedience*, in contrast, was a powerful argument to the effect that ecclesiastical rites and ceremonies, as well as the question of papal supremacy, were matters indifferent, neither commanded nor forbidden by Scripture 'but lefte to worldly polycie, wherof they take their ful authoritie, by the which as tyme and place requireth, they are sometimes good, and somtymes yll'.[1] It was an equally powerful justification of the obligation of obedience to the temporal prince in whom inhered the authority to amend and abrogate such practices. The government saw to it that the work was published under the auspices of its own press.

Seen in this perspective, the belief that the king in parliament

---

[1] Thomas Starkey, *An exhortation to the people instructynge theym to vnitie and obedience* (London, 1534), p. 6.

was the animating nucleus of the body politic from which all good things would flow, it is not difficult to appreciate why writers managed to accommodate the theory of limited monarchy in an essentially medieval framework. In no sense did the theory entail an undermining of traditional assumptions and it is too facile to suggest that its proponents were advocates of the middle class, as though latent within it is the spirit of individualism.[1] They were not advancing claims against the crown but reflecting a felt need for political direction from a centre which included them, but of which the crown was indubitably the apex. Nor was their theory couched in the language of men urging a political guaranteee of some natural, individual right to property. Far from hinting that society was composed of a series of exchange relations between independent proprietors, they generally confirmed that it was a functionally stratified structure with a corporate identity that radiated from the co-ordinating activities of the centre. For this conception was validated by their experience.

There was an ancient strain of thought, expressed by Aristotle and reinforced by the Thomist clarification of natural law as the repository of an absolute justice accessible to rational agents, which held that the king could hardly fail to govern for the common benefit if he was surrounded by the wisdom of the community. In Christian terminology, sin could be communally combated through combined effort. Making politics a co-operative activity was a means of averting the danger of the single ruler perverting justice through a predominance of passion. And this is what the English monarch had apparently done. He had obtained assistance in the dispensation of justice by seeking the co-operation of important social groups at the level of national politics. If recognition of the inescapable fact of sin prompted most writers to exalt monarchy in order to curb socially destructive passions, it also lent credibility to a line of thinking in which a primary function of government, lawmaking, was held to be a joint task of the king and

---

[1] e.g. Richard Schlatter's remark about Fortescue, an early exponent of the theory, in *Private Property; The History of an Idea* (London, 1951), p. 7: 'Fortescue was the fifteenth-century advocate of the middle class, the class whose rise to power is the essential ingredient in the transition from feudal to capitalist society. He defended that class and the property on which its power was based against magnates, royal despots, peasant radicals, and Lollard socialists. In doing so he combined the various medieval theories of property in the very fashion in which they were going to serve the purposes of bourgeois apologists for the next three or four hundred years.'

community gathered in parliament. There was nothing strikingly new in this, more an exploration of tendencies contained in the medieval world picture and a revitalization of a strand of political thought which had been periodically spelt out since at least the thirteenth century.

The theory hinged on the respectable adage that kingship was communally beneficial when it was supported by the reason of many. Many did not mean all, but rather the wisest members of the community. And a sign of wisdom was social station, for there was an analogy between the gradations of the social structure and those of the universal pattern. Thus, by adapting the Aristotelian proposition that wisdom was not found in equal measure throughout the community, writers were able to justify communal participation in political affairs without deriving radical conclusions from their acknowledgement of the political relevance of the common possession of reason. In other words, they developed a theory that corresponded to the heightened political significance of landed interests. There was nothing inconsistent in the claim of Starkey, the most radical advocate of communally restrained monarchy, that 'the people in euery comon weale be rude and ignorant, hauyng of them selfe smalle lyght of iudgement, but euer in simplicitie, as shepe folowe the herde, so folowe they their masters, euer treadynge in their steppes, whether so euer they go indifferently'.[1] Limited government did not entail doing the bidding of the intemperate masses. Nor was there anything inconsistent in Sir Thomas Smith immediately preceding his claim that the consent of every member of the realm was embodied in parliamentary enactment with a tacit admission that the electorate was restricted to less than half the adult male population.

. . . day labourers, poore husbandmen, yea marchantes or retailers which haue no free lande, copiholders, and all artificers, as Taylers, Shoomakers, Carpenters, Brickemakers, Bricklayers, Mason, &c . . . haue no voice nor authoritie in our common wealth, and no account is made of them but onelie to be ruled, and not to rule other.[2]

For everyone was supposedly represented in that the existence of parliament enabled the wisdom dispersed in the community to be channelled in the direction of sound government for all. Objective

---

[1] Starkey, *An exhortation*, p. 34.
[2] Sir Thomas Smith, *De Repvblica Anglorvm*, facsimile reprint (Menston, 1970), p. 33.

reason and not will, not the subjectively defined interests of each
frail and fallible private individual, supplied the standard of moral
rightness in politics.[1]

Cynics, of course, might well retort that a collection of men with
substantial interests to safeguard was hardly a promising formula
for securing the general well-being. Robert Crowley prepared a
petition for parliament in the reign of Edward VI, *An Informacion
and Peticion agaynst the oppressours of the pore Comons of this Realme*,
in which he enumerated the grievances of the poor and requested
remedies. Trenchant as always, his heart moved by compassion for
the victims of social injustice, he told parliamentary members that
he expected them to scoff at him, 'knoweynge that it is not the vse
of them that bee assembled to the intent to establish such thynges
as shall be for the welth of a whole realme, to condescende and
agree to those thynges whych shall be disprofitable vnto the chiefe
membres of the same'.[2] And Henry Brinklow saw in parliament
little else than a conspiracy of the rich, a sort of epiphenomenal
confirmation of class interests, for,

be he neuer so very a fole, dronkerd, extorcyoner, adouterer, neuer so
couetos and crafty a parson, yet if he be rych, beare any offyce, if he be a
ioly cracker and bragger in the contry, he must be a burges of the
parlament! Alas, how can any such study or geue any godly councel
for the commonwealth? But and if any man put forth anything against
Christes religyon, or agaynst the comon wealth, so that it make for the
profyght of Antichristes Knyghtes and temporal rulers of the reame,
thei shal be redy to geue their consent with the first.[3]

Brinklow considered parliament little improvement on papal
supremacy and flatly denied the claim of its defenders 'that what
so euer the parlament doth, must nedys be well done, and the
parlament, or any proclamacyon ow of the parlament tyme, cannot
erre'.[4] How far men like Crowley and Brinklow reflected popular

---

[1] So the notion of consent implied something very different from the connotation it was to assume during the Civil War when individual interests were elevated into a standard of political rightness. From now on, the concept was to
be used to justify the direct access of each to the political process as a means of
guaranteeing individual interests. For some enlightening comments on the sixteenth century, see Hurstfield, *Freedom, Corruption and Government in Elizabethan England*, pp. 40–2, 53–6.

[2] *The Select Works of Robert Crowley*, p. 167.

[3] *Henry Brinklow's Complaynt of Roderyck More*, p. 13.

[4] Ibid. p. 35.

sentiment is a matter for speculation. What is certain is that the doctrine of parliamentary infallibility, the myth of which Brinklow was seeking to expose, was held in good faith by writers who saw in the co-operation between the king and his influential subjects a guarantee that legislation would be framed according to the dictates of right reason, that the well-being of everyone would be protected through an institution geared to mediating divine justice to each regardless of station.

While the theory of limited monarchy corresponded to certain political developments, it remained in some sense the exploration of a potential and not simply a validation of the actual. For the co-operation achieved in parliament was a rather fragile creation that depended largely on the goodwill and current needs of the crown. From the latter's viewpoint, parliament was a convenient, but possibly dispensable device, for raising revenue and imparting its decisions to the nation. I think this explains why, compared with the theory of absolutism, that of limited monarchy did not feature prominently in political writings. For the crown it was a useful piece of propaganda, a means of illustrating that England was equipped with political institutions at least as viable as those of the papacy. Yet it contained implications which might be exploited in a manner not congenial to the crown. The overriding need was to represent the monarch as the symbol of national unity and the focus of national aspirations, not to pursue a line of thinking that set out to determine how monarchy might be restricted to good effect.

Marsilius of Padua had gone further than any other medievalist in locating legislative authority in a secular assembly. The government grasped the usefulness of his arguments in countering the claims of Rome and in 1535 authorized a translation of the *Defensor Pacis*. Yet Marsilius had also made the temporal ruler a mere executive agent of the community, a conclusion the crown had no wish to accept. Though a useful ally, the theory of limited monarchy was a potentially dangerous beast which the crown was careful not to let loose on a rampage. Starkey's *Dialogue*, written in Padua 1532–3, was largely shaped by the thoughts of Marsilius who, said Starkey, 'though he were in style rude, yet to be of grete iugement'.[1] While his treatise on obedience was officially sponsored,

---

[1] *Starkey's Life and Letters,* p. xxv.

the *Dialogue* did not find a printer and Elton's qualified suggestion that its 'radical tenor' of thought closely corresponded to government policy is surely a little exaggerated.[1]

Even when the theory appeared in less radical guise than Starkey's proposals for reform, it did not easily accommodate with the dominant ideological need of the age, that of rallying to the defence of the crown. It was not that the theory revealed a grasp of political realities which outran traditional concepts,[2] but that it usually evoked a more detached, less immediately propagandist perspective than was evident in the theory of absolute monarchy which sometimes verged on hysteria. Even those proponents of limited monarchy who were fully convinced of the singular excellence of the English constitution made a sober and scrupulous effort to identify the peculiar features which made it so laudable. They did so by way of an excursion into comparative politics. Sir John Fortescue, Chancellor to Henry VI and an early exponent of the theory, composed two of his most substantial treatises, *De Natura Legis Naturae* and *De Laudibus*, while exiled with the Lancastrians in France. His intention was to school the Prince Edward in the principles of kingship, and he was evidently impressed by the differences between the French and English systems of government. Approaching the subject steeped in Thomist philosophy and with the shrewd mind of the lawyer, Fortescue tried to explain why the English method of dealing with political affairs was so much better than that adopted by its neighbour.

Smith, too, was struck by the various forms of government. A clever man of the world, 'he looked at the throne and was neither dazzled by Gloriana nor bewitched by Eliza'.[3] Also writing in France, where he was English ambassador and so cushioned from the immediacy of English affairs, he engaged in a comparative analysis in order to discern the unique political characteristics of his native land. At the end of *De Repvblica Anglorvm*, Smith informed his readers that he had

---

[1] G. R. Elton, 'Reform by Statute: Thomas Starkey's Dialogue and Thomas Cromwell's Policy', *Procs. of the British Academy*, LIV (1968), pp. 165–88.

[2] As is suggested in regard to Fortescue by A. B. Ferguson, 'Fortescue and the Renaissance: a Study in Transition', *Studies in the Renaissance*, VI (1959), pp. 175–94.

[3] Mary Dewar, *Sir Thomas Smith: a Tudor Intellectual in Office* (London, 1964), p. 7.

declared summarily as it were in a chart or mappe . . . the forme and
manner of the gouernement of Englande, and the policie thereof, and
sette before your eies the principall pointes, wherein it doth differ
from the policie or gouernment at this time vsed in Fraunce, Italie,
Spaine, Germanie and all other countries, which doe followe the ciuill
lawe of the Romanes compiled by *Justinian* into his pandects and code:
not in that sort as Plato made his common wealth, or *Zenophon* his
kingdome of Persia, nor as *Syr Thomas More* his Utopia being feigned
common phantasies of Philosophers to occupie the time and to exercise
their wittes: but so as Englande standeth and is gouerned at this day the
xxviij of March *Anno* 1565.[1]

Smith noted that his purpose was to describe the English political
system so that his readers might themselves decide which nation
'hath taken the righter, truer, and more commodious way
to gouerne the people aswell in warre as in peace'. But there
is no doubt that he believed that, in devising a form of limited
monarchy, his own country had selected the more commodious
method.

This awareness of national variations, coupled with the patriotic
conviction that Englishmen inhabited the best of existing worlds,
was the single most important factor prompting writers to outline
the desirability of communally limited monarchy. In the main these
writers were not radicals, but they were progressives by virtue of
their defence of a political construction which might well prove
ephemeral. For, though the possibilities implied by the co-operation of the estates of the realm had been more than glimpsed in the
sixteenth century, the place of parliament in the political spectrum
was far from entrenched. So it is no surprise to find that their
thought gravitated to a higher and more systematic level of analysis
than was achieved by the theorists of absolutism. Nor is it any
surprise to find that, in quantitative terms at least, the former
theory remained very much the poor relation.

I have tried to sketch an adequate context for understanding the
two theories. The next chapter will explore their medieval ante-
cedents, and this will be followed by a fuller description of each
one. Though the theory of limited monarchy all but disappeared
in the middle of the sixteenth century, it will be shown that its
central ingredient, the belief that the nation gained direction from
the combined wisdom of its members, was revived in the theory of

[1] Smith, *De Repvblica Anglorvm*, pp. 118–19.

common law. There will then be an attempt to describe how elements of both theories were raised by Richard Hooker to a high level of philosophical coherence and how, finally, they were affected by the influx of individualist assumptions during the Civil War.

II

THE MEDIEVAL INHERITANCE

IN THIS chapter my concern is to trace the intellectual sources of the theories of absolute and limited monarchy. Both had a respectable ancestry in medieval theory, though the predominant trend of English political thinking from the thirteenth century was towards a theory of limited monarchy. The theory of absolute monarchy emerged from a convergence of Neoplatonic, Biblical, Aristotelian and juristic notions, threaded together so as to convey the impression that the community had no means of acting politically except through its single head. The theory of limited monarchy originated in a blending of Aristotelian ideas with a legal theory regarding the nature of corporate groups, issuing in the belief that the collective reason of the community should be harnessed for dealing with political affairs.

The first strain of medieval political thought was expressed in patristic writings in which the dominant image of man was that of a sinner who, lacking the capacity to control his behaviour by means of reason, was enjoined to submerge the remnants of his fallen nature in a community of the faithful. When linked with the Neoplatonic idea of a hierarchical universe, this image lent itself to the idea of a ruler whose unique political competence was created by an infusion of divine grace. The theory was originally articulated by Augustine who made it plain that Christian theology had no room for the classical view of political society as a community of men seeking a rationally apprehended and temporally attainable goal.[1] What replaced the classical conception was a vision of a coercive system that was designed to offset the destructive manifestations of sinful behaviour. An indispensable remedial device in a world echoing from the strife of sinful men, political organization was a means of introducing a measure of order, of injecting an element of security, into a situation constantly verging

[1] Augustine was originally sympathetic to the classical conception but it was submerged in his later works. The transition is described in R. A. Markus, *Saeculum: History and Society in the Theology of St. Augustine* (Cambridge, 1967), pp. 72–104.

on the chaotic. A bulwark against the endemic squabbling of men whom sin had made selfish, avaricious and desirous of power, political activity achieved a partial restoration of human affairs to that ideal of order which was evident throughout the natural world prior to man's transgression; a pattern which Augustine described in Neoplatonic terms as the harmonious interdependence of several parts in a functionally integrated and hierarchically diversified structure.[1]

While a restored political order approximated to the universal design, it was not a natural ordering of men because a product of divine grace. The political order was God's device for checking the worst excesses of a corrupted humanity; rulership was His means of counteracting the socially disruptive consequences of sin.[2] The effect was to exalt rulership and, correlatively, to place political activity beyond the scope of common men. Appointed by God and part of His inscrutable scheme for a fallen mankind, the ruler was not to be judged by rational criteria, standards which ordinary mortals with their proclivity to evil could not operate in any case. Even a tyrant, himself a wicked human being who shared in the ambitions of a corrupted humanity, was a divine remedy for sin, thus worthy of obedience. Not only was he an instrument for punishing wickedness and preventing perversity, he was sent to test the patience and fidelity of those who through baptism were already resident in the *civitas Dei*. In any case, the inconveniences of transient earthly existence were of minor significance compared with the future life of blessedness where mutual love would flourish and the coercive apparatus of political society be rendered superfluous.[3]

The heritage which Augustine and others bequeathed to the

---

[1] e.g. *The City of God,* ed. R. V. G. Tasker in 2 vols. (London, 1967), Bk. XIX, ch. xiii: 'Peace of man and man is a mutual concord; peace of a family an orderly rule and subjection amongst the parts thereof; peace of a city an orderly command and obedience amongst the citizens: peace of God's city a most orderly coherence in God and fruition of God; peace of all things is a well-disposed order. For order is a good disposition of discrepant parts, each in the fittest place'.

[2] A. J. Carlyle, 'St. Augustine and the City of God', in F. J. C. Hearnshaw (ed.), *The Social and Political Ideas of Some Great Mediaeval Thinkers* (London, 1932), pp. 42–52, emphasizes that, though originating in sin, political institutions themselves were not considered sinful, rather a divine remedy for sin.

[3] *The City of God,* Bk. V, ch. xvii: 'For what doth it matter in respect of this short and transitory life, under whose dominion a mortal man doth live, as long as he be not compelled to acts of impiety or injustice.'

Middle Ages led, naturally enough, to a descending theory of government. Biblical and Neoplatonic ideas were integrated into a picture of society differentiated into unequal social roles where the capacity for political action was wholly absorbed by the head of the social hierarchy.[1] The gathering of these ideas into a coherent theory was mainly the work of hierocratic writers,[2] though those wishing to press the claims of secular monarchs were not slow in appropriating the premises of papal thinking. As the recipient of the divine favour, the pope was the terrestrial representative of God and so wielded a *plenitudo potestatis* which provided him with an authority that was humanly unlimited. Situated on a pedestal beyond the control of his people, he could legitimately expect to be reverenced, loved, feared and, of greatest importance, unhesitantly obeyed.

A major factor in the growth of the theory which, by lending a juristic flavour to liturgical attributes of rulership, encouraged its adoption by secular theorists, were certain terminological changes in the concept of *corpus mysticum*, the mystical body of Christ.[3] Ever since Saint Paul had described the community of believers as a body of members united by the spiritual headship of Christ,[4] writers had made extensive use of the analogy of the Church with the human organism.[5] In the ninth century the term *corpus mysticum*

---

[1] The way Neoplatonic ideas were to be used was anticipated by Gregory the Great: 'The dispensation of divine providence established diverse ranks and distinct orders for this purpose: that while the less should show reverence for the more powerful and the more powerful should impose their will upon the less, one fabric of concord would be made from diversity and the administration of individual offices would be rightly performed. For a whole could in no way exist unless a great order of difference of this sort should preserve it. And the example of the celestial hosts shows that in truth created beings cannot be governed nor live in one and the same equality, because, since there are angels and archangels, it is clear that they are not equal, but one differs from the other in power and order, even as we do.' Cited in Ewart Lewis, *Medieval Political Ideas* (London, 1954), Vol. 1 p. 143, n. 12.

[2] cf. M. J. Wilks, *The Problem of Sovereignty in the Later Middle Ages* (Cambridge, 1963); for a relatively late expression of hierocratic ideas see Antony Black, *Monarchy and Community: Political Ideas in the Later Conciliar Controversy, 1430–1450* (Cambridge, 1970), pp. 53–84.

[3] These changes are described in Wilks, *The Problem of Sovereignty in the Later Middle Ages*, p. 23, and E. H. Kantorowicz, *The King's Two Bodies: A Study in Mediaeval Political Theology* (Princeton, N.J., 1957), pp. 194 ff.

[4] Romans 12, 5: 'So we, being many, are one body in Christ, and every one members of one another.' Also I Corinthians 12, 14 ff.

[5] e.g. in c. A.D. 96 Clement used the analogy in order to condemn dissension in the Church at Corinth. 'Why do we divide and tear asunder the members of

was used to identify the Eucharist, the sacramental element by which the Church mystically cohered. But as a result of the controversy about transubstantiation in the twelfth century, the Eucharist became known as the real body of Christ—*corpus Christi verum*—and the phrase *corpus mysticum* was applied to the *Ecclesia* as such, the society of the faithful considered administratively and politically, as well as spiritually. This politicization of the concept stimulated papal theorists to compare the body politic which was the Church with other ordered wholes, particularly the bodily organism. As the human body was a single unit consisting of many members unified by functional integration and overall guidance from the head so, it was said, was the Church a diversified structure united by a common allegiance to the pope as its earthly head. It, too, demanded a governing head who monopolized the political authority needed to maintain unity.

Another influence working to release the ruler from the control of the community was the idea, expressed with the aid of Roman legal concepts, that he occupied the office of intermediary between divine norms and positive law. Originally articulated in terms of the belief that the ruler was a unique source of human law because of a bestowal of divine grace, the idea received legal clarification in the doctrine that he was an image of a transcendent justice, a living law—*lex animata*—whose task was to transform objective principles into concrete rules appropriate to the community in which they were to operate. Eliciting support from a passage in Justinian's *Institutes* (I.ii.6) in which it was stated that the Roman people had conferred the sum total of legislative authority on the emperor by means of the *lex regia*, writers argued that the ruler was bound by no man-made law or human institution. Though morally enjoined not to abrogate divine standards, he was *legibus solutus* in the sense that he was their sole interpreter and could not be legally com-

---

Christ, and raise up strife against our own body, and reach such a pitch of madness as to forget that we are members one of another?' 'Let us take the body; the head is nothing without the feet, likewise the feet are nothing without the head; the smallest members of our body are necessary and valuable to the whole body, but all work together and are united in a common subjection to preserve the whole body. Let, therefore, our whole body be preserved in Christ Jesus, and let each be subject to his neighbour, according to the position granted to him.' 'The First Epistle of Clement to the Corinthians', in *The Apostolic Fathers*, trans. Kirsopp Lake in 2 vols. (London and New York, 1912), I, pp. 89, 73.

pelled to observe them.[1] By postulating the ruler as the sole holder of public power, the net effect was again to make it illegitimate for the community to interfere with him. For practical purposes, what pleased the prince had the force of law.

At this point it will be useful to survey the thought of the English writer, John of Salisbury, partly because it threads together some of the factors mentioned so far, but also because it tackles a problem that faced all those who removed the ruler from communal control, the possibility of evil government, in a manner which anticipated the sixteenth-century solution. Written in 1159, *Policraticus* anticipated the many attempts to compare the political order with the natural pattern of the universe which were to accompany the rediscovery of Aristotle in the thirteenth century.[2] For John suggested that the pattern of order obtained in political society coincided with the divine design that was reproduced throughout the natural world. Cicero and Plato, said John, 'laid down the same formula for the existing or projected body politic, namely that its life should imitate nature, which we have so often called the best guide of life... What Nature's design is, is disclosed even by creatures which are devoid of reason.'[3] In particular, its structure was identical with that of the human organism. John related in detail the correspondences existing between the two bodies. The priesthood, for example, resembled the soul in the human body, officials and soldiers the hands, husbandmen the feet, and cohesion in each depended on all parts performing their proper functions in a graded hierarchy of subordinate and superior ranks.[4]

In addition to the mutual support of its members, the coherence

---

[1] These ideas are elaborated in Kantorowicz, *The King's Two Bodies*, pp. 87–143.

[2] cf. Gaines Post, *Studies in Medieval Legal Thought : Public Law and the State, 1100–1322* (Princeton, N.J., 1964), pp. 515–19; Hans Liebeschutz, *Medieval Humanism in the Life and Writings of John of Salisbury* (London, 1950): and Beryl Smalley, *The Becket Conflict and the Schools : A Study of Intellectuals in Politics* (Oxford, 1973), pp. 87–108.

[3] *The Statesman's Book of John of Salisbury*, trans. John Dickinson (New York, 1963), Bk. VI, ch. xxi.

[4] Ibid., Bk. VI, ch. xx: 'Then and only then will the health of the commonwealth be sound and flourishing when the higher members shield the lower, and the lower respond faithfully and fully in like measure to the just demands of their superiors, so that each and all are as it were members one of another by a sort of reciprocity, and each regards his own interest as best served by that which he knows to be most advantageous for the others.'

of each structure demanded a common subjection to the head wherein was concentrated both the wisdom and power for co-ordinating the activities of the other parts into a single whole. Situated by God 'at the apex of the commonwealth',[1] the political head bore

the burdens of the whole community. Wherefore deservedly is conferred on him, and gathered together in his hands, the power of all his subjects, to the end that he may be sufficient unto himself in seeking and bringing about the advantage of each individually, and of all . . . Wherein we indeed but follow nature, the best guide of life; for nature has gathered together all the senses of her microcosm or little world, which is man, into the head, and has subjected all the members in obedience to it in such wise that they will all function properly so long as they follow the guidance of the head, and the head remains sane.[2]

In this way, John left no doubt that the well-being of the community demanded that each politically headless member devote himself to a correct performance of his duties and refrain from political activity. It was for the ruler singly to direct the community as a whole. Describing the responsibilities of his office, John resorted to the familiar idea that he was an image of justice who mediated to the community the precepts of a higher law. As 'the minister of the common interest and the bond-servant of equity',[3] he was called upon to translate objective norms into practical social rules.

Having elevated the ruler to the position of the single public personage, John had to face the fact of a specific ruler's insanity, that is, the possibility of a ruler degenerating into a tyrant by refusing to act in accordance with the norms of justice. Unwilling to concede any right of the community to act politically, he was unable to conceive of any institutional means of dealing with such a situation. True, he voiced the commonplace belief that the ruler had received his authority *via* the Church. But, having handed over the temporal sword, the priesthood was in no position to enforce his adherence to the standards of justice. The only recourse, therefore, was to the idea of divine intervention. Here John repeated the widely held conviction that 'tyrants are demanded, introduced, and raised to power by sin, and are excluded, blotted out, and

---

[1] Ibid., Bk. V, ch. vi.   [2] Ibid., Bk. IV, ch. i.
[3] Ibid., Bk. IV, ch. ii.

destroyed by repentance'.[1] A divine instrument for chastising a sinful people, the reign of a tyrant was terminated by patience and penitence, for, judging it expedient to remove him, God often chose to work through human agents, either by having him killed in battle or else authorizing one of his subjects to perform the task. So John upheld the view that political matters were beyond the comprehension of ordinary mortals, while devising an escape mechanism for the community where the common good was jeopardized by tyranny. His assertion that political matters were ultimately controlled from heaven, particularly the doctrine of tyrannicide, was essentially a safety device, the logical alternative to his denial of the right of a community to act in a collective capacity. It was a device to which thinkers were to resort often.[2]

The Aristotelian revival of the thirteenth century substituted for the Augustinian image of political society that of a group of rational agents, pursuing a good by partially natural means. No longer a mere remedy for human perversity, the political order was held to consist of moral agents able to regulate their actions in accordance with natural law. The seeds were sown, therefore, for a theory of communal involvement in political affairs.[3] In practice, however, many Aristotelians reiterated the essential tenets of the strand of thought emanating from Augustine. In this, they were influenced by two factors, the clarification of natural law accomplished by Thomas Aquinas and the assimilation of political society to other natural wholes.[4]

[1] Ibid., Bk. VIII, ch. xx.
[2] On John's doctrine see Richard and Mary Rouse, 'John of Salisbury and the Doctrine of Tyrannicide', *Speculum*, XLII (1967), pp. 693–709. For other attitudes to tyranny see Wilfrid Parsons, 'The Medieval Theory of the Tyrant', *Review of Politics*, 4 (1942), pp. 129–43.
[3] 'The fundamental conception is that of the dignity of the common element of human Reason, as it appears in every individual; and this conception, in turn, goes back to that of a 'common law', pervading all nature and the whole universe, and proceeding from a divine principle of Reason which expresses itself increasingly in the successive stages of created beings. The true nature of man is assumed to be the divine Reason operating in him, with its sovereignty over the senses and affections.' Ernst Troeltsch, 'The Ideas of Natural Law an Humanity in World Politics', in Otto Gierke, *Political Theories in the Middle Age*, trans. F. W. Maitland (Cambridge, 1900), App. I, p. 205.
[4] For this reason the thirteenth century was less of a watershed in political thinking than is often suggested. W. H. Ullmann, *The Individual and Society in the Middle Ages* (London, 1967) traces the process by which the idea of the citizen replaced that of the subject with no role to perform in creating the legal injunctions binding him. Ullmann takes the process to be a relatively chronological

As systematized by Aquinas, natural law appeared as a system of relatively flexible norms from which it was possible to derive rules of more detailed application.[1] Embracing all those moral imperatives which reason apprehended within the framework of the eternal law, natural law instructed men what to do in order to fulfil the potential naturally inherent in them. This meant that, besides the directive principle that good was to be done and evil shunned, it consisted of more specific precepts intended to guide humankind through the complexities of everyday life.[2] Unlike the speculative reason which derived conclusions from general propositions in a strictly logical fashion, the practical reason operated in a less strictly deductive manner because it was concerned with the contingent, concrete circumstances in which the moral life was embedded.[3]

This belief that natural law was relevant to the human striving for felicity in the contingencies of daily life was reflected in Aquinas' classification of human laws. While all shared the same substantive characteristic in that they were derived by way of right reason, human laws were nevertheless distinguished by the manner of their derivation. For while those laws common to every

[1] Prior to Aquinas the clarification of natural law was hindered by the fact that writers were uncertain as to its exact content. This was due largely to the ambiguities contained in the *Corpus Iuris Civilis*, the sixth-century compilation of Justinian (comprising the *Institutes, Digest* and *Codex*) through which Roman law was transmitted to the Middle Ages. Sometimes *ius naturale* was identified as that which all animals instinctively knew, sometimes as that which men discovered through reason, sometimes with universally accepted law (*ius gentium*). In addition, there was the problem of deciding whether natural law was identical with that which was known to men in the state of innocence, or with that which they had grasped as their rational faculties became more sophisticated. On the difficulties and Aquinas' achievement see A. P. d'Entrèves, *Natural Law : An Introduction to Legal Philosophy* (London, 1967), pp. 17–47.

[2] cf. R. A. Armstrong, *Primary and Secondary Precepts in Thomistic Natural Law Teaching* (The Hague, 1966).

[3] *Summa Theologica*, Ia 2ae, q. 94, a.4, concl., in *Selected Political Writings*, ed. A. P. d'Entrèves (Oxford, 1965).

development, the decisive factor being the revival of the classical image of man as a rational being. But Ullmann's scheme is too simplified, for both images of man continued to inform the consciousness through until at least the early modern period. Descending theories of government were not suddenly and neatly displaced by ascending conceptions. Jean Dunbabin's essay, 'Aristotle in the Schools', in Beryl Smalley (ed.), *Trends in Medieval Political Thought* (Oxford, 1965), pp. 65–85, is a suitable antidote against Whig historiography being extended way back to the thirteenth century through an automatic linking of Aristotelianism with a progressive constitutionalism.

nation (*ius gentium*) were deduced from general principles by a process similar to that of scientific reasoning, civil laws embodied the precepts of natural law in more specific forms, as an architect particularized the general idea of a house in designing a specific dwelling. In connection with this latter category, natural law was a repository of justice requiring translation into rules for the common benefit in a way which took due account of the needs of the particular community.[1] Human law, in this sense, was the lengthening out of natural law at precisely the point at which the requirements of the given community had to be taken into consideration.[2]

An immediate effect was to reinforce the case of those wishing to elevate the ruler beyond communal control. Aquinas had demonstrated the necessity of human decision in converting natural law into workable social practices, a legislative authority possessed of sufficient coercive power to endow the rationally derived rules with the status of legally enforceable commands.[3] Given the necessity of human discretion, it was argued that the ruler should not be hampered in his legislative capacity by the restrictions of already existing enacted law. Further, Aquinas admitted that, while subject to the directive force of law as a set of rational precepts, the ruler was *legibus solutus* in regard to its constraining power.[4] And Aegidius Romanus expressed the established opinion that, as a mediator between higher and written laws, the ruler occupied a unique position within the community. Freed from the restrictions of existing law, he might interpret the higher norms according to present social requirements.[5]

---

[1] Ibid., 1a 2ae, q.95, a.2 concl., and a.4. concl.

[2] cf. Ewart Lewis, 'Natural Law and Expediency in Medieval Political Theory' *Ethics*, L (1939–40), pp. 144–63.

[3] The emphasis placed on the need for a coercive power able to compel men to obey rational precepts was based on the belief that, as a creature infected with sin, man often used reason for evil purposes. *S.Th.* 1a 2ae, q.95, a.1 concl: 'And the Philosopher says (I *Politics*, 2): "Man, when he reaches the perfection of virtue is the best of animals: but if he goes his way without law and justice he becomes the worst of all brutes." For man, unlike other animals, has the weapon of reason with which to exploit his base desires and cruelty.'

[4] Ibid., 1a 2ae, q.96, a.5, ad 3um.

[5] Aegidius Romanus, *De Regimine Principum*, ed. Samuel P. Molenaer (New York, 1899), Bk. III, Pt. ii, ch. xxvii: 'nos dirons que li rois et chascuns prince est meeins entre le loy de nature et loi escrite; quer nul ne seignorist droitureument se il ne fet cen que droit en reson enseigne, por cen que reson doit estre rieule des eueves humaines. Dont li rois en governant son peuple est sougez

The ruler's elevation was also taken as a guarantee against a too literal interpretation of established law. Aristotle had recognized that written law could never be omnicompetent. 'For matters of detail about which men deliberate cannot be included in legislation.'[1] Here was the origin of the notion of equity which was to play an important role in medieval thinking. As a living law, the ruler might bring existing law into line with its initial intention by dispensing with it when occasion demanded, and by tempering its strict application with equity in particular cases. In this way, the Aristotelian renaissance encouraged many to accept that a ruler who was a set apart from the community by virtue of the discretionary and coercive power concentrated in his hands, was an effective means of transmitting the vital element of justice to public affairs.

In fully reintegrating the political order into the cosmic scheme, Aristotelian naturalism also stimulated its comparison with other natural wholes. A rightly organized community, on this view, was a particular manifestation 'of the order of divine providence, which disposes of all things in the most admirable manner'.[2] Reflecting the immutable universal pattern, political society appeared as a unity cohering through functional integration and the common subordination of all to the monarch.

Not that Aristotelians believed that the political order was identical in every respect to other segments of the natural world. For its members were conscious participants in the divine reason, each striving towards the natural goal of the common good. An association of rational agents did not exactly correspond, say, to a physiological organism in which the unconscious parts functioned solely in the interests of the whole. Pursuing a rationally discerned end on behalf of its members, the political order was not a substantial entity that totally absorbed the activities and transcended

[1] Aristotle, *Politics*, trans. Benjamin Jowett (Oxford, 1920), 1287b.
[2] Aquinas, *De Regimine Principum*, Bk. I, ch. iii, in d'Entrèves, *Selected Political Writings*.

a la loi de nature, quer en tant governe il bien son peuple que il ne forvoie mie de loy de nature, et est li rois de sus la loi que il a establie de s'auctorite . . . la noy ne puet determiner toutes les conditions particulieres d'aucun fet, por quoi il profit que cil seignorist seignourisse par droite reson et par loy nature le quele dieus a mis en nos pensees et en nos cuers, et adrecie la loy escrite et ne la gart mie la ou il ne la droit mie garder et la ou ele defaut.' This is a thirteenth-century translation, entitled *Les Livres du Governement des Rois*, of the Latin version.

the moral purposes of its individual components.[1] Consequently, the external unity obtained in political society by way of mutual co-operation and the co-ordinating effect of political activity towards the common good, differed from the intrinsic unity of a substance.[2]

Nevertheless, legitimate comparisons could be made between the political structure and the all embracing pattern of order. In this respect, humankind might glance beyond its immediate social environment in search of an adequate model for its temporal arrangements. And the first lesson to be adduced from the universally visible structure was the overriding necessity of unity. According to Dante,

'being' and 'oneness' and 'goodness' are related in steps of priority . . . Whence it comes about that 'being one' is seen to be the root of 'being good', and 'being many' the root of 'being bad' . . . It is clear, then, that

[1] This is central to the controversy sparked off by Gierke's contention that medieval thought was fundamentally inconsistent. Based on the assumption that social and political theorists must envisage society either as a substantial reality endowed with its own personality, or as a mental fiction that is finally reducible to its component members, Gierke argued that, while treating society as an organism, medievalists failed to apply to it the concept of a real personality. Failing to follow through their organic conception to its logical conclusion, they prepared the soil for the acceptance of modern natural law theories resting on atomistic and mechanistic premises. Some commentators have agreed with Gierke that medievalists adhered to an organic view of society: e.g. A-H. Chroust, 'The Corporate Idea and the Body Politic in the Middle Ages', *Review of Politics*, 9 (1947) pp. 423–52. Others disagree: e.g. I. T. Eschmann, 'Studies on the Notion of Society in St. Thomas Aquinas: I. St. Thomas and the Decretal of Innocent IV *Romana Ecclesia: Caterum*', *Mediaeval Studies*, VIII (1946), pp. 1–42, and 'Studies on the Notion of Society in St. Thomas Aquinas: II. Thomistic Social Philosophy and the Theology of Original Sin', *Mediaeval Studies*, IX (1947), pp. 19–55; Ewart Lewis, 'Organic Tendencies in Medieval Political Thought', *American Political Science Review*, XXXII (1938), pp. 849–76; Maurice De Wulf, *Philosophy and Civilization in the Middle Ages* ch. 10, and *Mediaeval Philosophy Illustrated from the System of Thomas Aquinas* (Harvard, 1922), ch. xv. They hold the view, valid at least as far as the Christian Aristotelians are concerned, that medieval political thought was not characterized by the antithesis described by Gierke. For these writers constructed a coherent theory by means of assumptions which led neither to an organic social image nor to the atomistic conception of individualism. Emphasizing the moral value of each person, yet believing that the good of each ultimately coincided, they represented political society as an organization of men united by common needs, shared purposes and functional diversity, and held together by the activities of government.

[2] Aquinas clearly distinguished between the political order and a substantial unity: e.g. *Commentary on the Nicomachean Ethics*, Bk. I, introd., in d'Entrèves, *Selected Political Writings*.

everything which is good, is good in virtue of consisting in unity. And that it consists in some unity, as in its proper root. Which root we shall discover if we consider the nature of meaning of concord. For concord is a uniform movement of more wills than one.[1]

Unity, then, was a prerequisite to the good life because disunity brought destruction to any whole, and a disintegrated community would attain none of the purposes which it existed to promote. Further, consolidation in the universe was achieved through hierarchical ranking and the principle of monarchy. The universe itself was subject to one God, monarchy was in evidence throughout the natural world, and the microcosm which was man was co-ordinated through the activities of the head or heart. Since art should imitate nature, it followed that monarchical government in human society was to be preferred, because several rulers might disagree, disagreement resulted in disunity and this posed a threat to the well-being of the entire community.[2]

So, while making all men potential rulers by recognizing that political activity fell within the scope of the common faculty of reason, Aristotelians generally identified the political reason of the community with its single head. Aquinas, for instance, made a clear distinction between individual reason and that appropriated by the head of the body politic.

Now in nature there is to be found both a universal and a particular form of government. The universal is that by which all things find their place under the direction of God, who, by His providence, governs the universe. The particular is very similar to this divine control, and is found within man himself; who, for this reason, is called a microcosm, because he provides an example of universal government. Just as the divine control is exercised over all created bodies and over all spiritual powers, so does the control of reason extend over the members of the body and other faculties of the soul: so, in a certain sense, reason is to man what God is to the universe. But because . . . man is by nature a social animal living in a community, this similarity with divine rule is found among men, not only in the sense that a man is directed by his reason, but also in the fact that a community is ruled by one man's intelligence.[3]

[1] Dante, *De Monarchia*, in *A Translation of the Latin Works of Dante Alighieri*, The Temple Classics (London, 1904), Bk. I, ch. xv.
[2] Aquinas, *De Regimine Principum*, Bk. I, ch. ii; Aegidius Romanus, *De Regimine Principum*, Bk. III, Pt. ii, ch. iii.
[3] *De Regimine Principum*, Bk. I, ch. xii.

In some ways, therefore, the thirteenth-century revolution in political thought was less of an epistemological disjuncture than is usually imagined, for it helped to revitalize the belief that the monarch alone was fitted for political activity, thereby ensuring its continuation through the late Middle Ages into the early modern period.[1]

The second strain of medieval political thought was rooted in the assumption that men beneath the king were sufficiently rational to engage in political activity and, aligned with this, that a collective reason was most likely to secure the general well-being. Even those generally favourable towards monarchy were encouraged by the rediscovery of Aristotle to consider the possibility of other forms of government, and thus to weigh the relative advantages or otherwise of alternative locations of political power. Originally developed in regard to specific groups such as cathedral chapters, the legal theory of corporations was subsequently applied to the whole Church and to secular political communities. Through it was filtered into political theory the idea that political authority was the possession of the collectivity of the members of the body politic who might themselves, therefore, dispose of political affairs in their corporate capacity.

As well as classifying the various types of government into monarchy, aristocracy and constitutional rule, and the perverted forms of tyranny, oligarchy and democracy corresponding to the just types, Aristotle considered whether it was desirable to be governed by one man's will or according to law. His answer was that justice was most likely to be transmitted to that community in which public matters were regulated by the rule of law, and where responsibility for legislation rested with a substantial number of people. For, while a law was a rational precept uncorrupted by passion, a ruler unrestrained by law might succumb to the influence of desire.[2] Also, his single mind was not sufficient to

---

[1] For a fourteenth-century illustration of these ideas, making use of the idea of the ruler as mediator and also of the Neoplatonic view of the universe, see W. H. Ullmann, *The Medieval Idea of Law as Represented by Lucas de Penna* (London, 1946).

[2] Aristotle, *Politics*, 1286a and 1287a: 'he is a better ruler who is free from passion and whereas the law is passionless, passion must ever sway the heart of man.' 'He who bids the law rule, may be deemed to bid God and Reason alone rule, but he who bids man rule adds an element of the beast; for desire is a wild beast, and passion perverts the minds of rulers, even when they are the best of men. The law is reason unaffected by desire.'

judge wisely in that area of legislation which entailed discretion. Here Aristotle posited communal participation in legislative matters as an effective means of securing the substantive quality of law. For,

the many are more uncorruptible than the few: they are like the greater quantity of water which is less easily corrupted than a little. The individual is liable to be overcome by anger or by some other passion, and then his judgement is necessarily perverted; but it is hardly to be supposed that a great number of persons would all get into a passion and go wrong at the same moment.[1]

And experience proved that the combined judgement of many was superior in rationality to that of any single individual, even should he excel in wisdom.

According to our present practice assemblies meet, sit in judgement, deliberate and decide, and their judgements all relate to individual cases. Now any member of the assembly, taken separately, is certainly inferior to the wise man. But the state is made up of many individuals. And as a feast to which all the guests contribute is better than a banquet by a single man, so a multitude is a better judge of many things than any individual.[2]

The fact that a collective reason gave a clearer perception of rightness than the judgement of one man was especially pertinent in view of the frequency with which particular laws had to be tempered in their application by equity. To argue that a single ruler should have exclusive responsibility for such cases was as absurd as supposing 'that a person should see better with two eyes, or hear better with two ears, or act better with two hands or feet, than many with many'.[3] Here was material for those medievalists who thought politics a much too important activity to be resigned into one man's hands.

The general effect of the Aristotelian revival was to cast an element of doubt on the supposition that a communally unrestrained monarch was an adequate guarantee of the public good. Even Aegidius Romanus, so convinced that rule by one was essential to preserve unity and mediate justice, was willing to concede the point that the many were less corruptible. And he accommodated it into his conception of kingship by advising the monarch to seek the advice of the wise in all matters.[4]

¹ Ibid., 1286a.   ² Ibid.   ³ Ibid., 1287b.
⁴ Aegidius Romanus, *De Regimine Principum*, Bk. III, Pt. ii, ch. iv.

Another manifestation of the Aristotelian influence was the distinction which writers began to draw between regal government, where the ruler possessed a plenitude of power and governed according to his own will or by laws which he himself had instituted, and political government in which he was obliged to govern according to laws enacted by the citizenry. As Aquinas put it in his *Commentary on Aristotle's Politics*:

Civitas autem duplici regimine regitur: scilicet politico et regali. *Regale* quidem est regimen, quando ille qui civitati praeest habet plenariam potestatem. *Politicum* autem regimen est quando ille qui praeest habet potestatem coarctatum secundum aliquas leges civitatis.[1]

This analytical distinction was only a tentative step towards asserting the necessity of communal involvement in political affairs, for as yet writers did not normally express a definite preference for either of the two forms. Nevertheless, some began to acknowledge that the ruler's removal from the control of the community left it devoid of safeguards to the common good.

For all his affirmation of the desirability of monarchy, Aquinas did attribute to the community the right to be politically active under certain circumstances. While political reason was normally concentrated in the head of the body politic, it did sometimes reside with its members. This was so when he acted contrary to the common good. The Roman people, for instance, had replaced their tyrants by aristocratic government, with publicly beneficial consequences.[2] So divine intervention was not the only means of destroying the tyrant, for 'the remedy against the evils of tyranny lies rather in the hands of public authority than in the private judgement of individuals'.[3] A community with authority to elect a

---

[1] Aquinas, *In Libros Politicorum Aristotelis Expositio*, ed. R. M. Spiazzi (Rome, 1951), Bk. I, Pt. i, ch. 1; also Johannes Parisiensis, *Tractatus de regia potestate et papali*, ed. Fritz Bleienstein (Stuttgart, 1969), ch. xvii: 'Dicere autem . . . quod papa tradit leges principibus et quod princeps non potest aliunde leges sumere nisi per papam fuerint approbatae, est omino destruere regimen regale et politicum et incidere in errorem Herodis putantis et tementis Christum regnum destruere terrenem, quia secundum Philosophum I Politicorum principatus tunc solum dicitur regalis quando aliquis praeest secundum leges quas ipse instituit; cum vero praeest non secundum arbitrium suum nec secundum leges quas ipse instituit sed quas cives instituerunt, dicitur principatus civilis vel politicus et non regalis.'

[2] Aquinas, *De Regimine Principum*, Bk. I, ch. iv.

[3] Ibid., Bk. I, ch. vi.

ruler could legitimately depose him; where the ruler had been appointed by a superior the community could make representation to him. Only a community which had failed to provide for the possibility of tyranny had no recourse apart from humble petition to God. Other remarks suggest that Aquinas conceived of community activity as something other than a sporadic intervention in the political realm during periods of tyranny. He said, for example, that a constitution combining the three types described by Aristotle was superior to any other form. A constitutionally limited monarchy, in which all the citizens participated in the election of a ruler who was assisted in his office by virtuous men, was the most effective precaution a community might take against the possibility of unjust government.[1]

In devising such alternatives to absolute monarchy medievalists were coupling the Aristotelian classification of governments with their conception of natural law as a repository of justice, and of man as a rational agent capable of directing his life according to its precepts.[2] In other words, they had begun to grasp the political relevance of the common possession of reason, indicating the direction in which political theory could move once humankind had been rescued from the oblivion into which it had been cast by Augustine. For it was no longer necessary to suppose that political reason was monopolized by the single head of the community.

Instrumental in transforming this belief in the community's political competence into a coherent theory was juristic reflection on the structure of corporations. Recognizing that groups like guilds, cathedral chapters and universities were required to act in a legal capacity, civilians and canonists borrowed Roman legal concepts in an effort to identify the legal character of each group, as well as the standing of those who represented it. The corporate

---

[1] S.Th., 1a 2ae, q. 105, a.l.

[2] C. J. Friedrich, *Transcendent Justice: The Religious Dimension of Constitutionalism* (Durham, N.C., 1964), pp. 43–4; 'Such constitutional government depends upon an abiding faith in human beings as rational and well-intentioned and therefore capable of effectively participating in the political order and in the making of its laws by electing those who speak for them. A transcendent faith in justice as a capacity of God mirrored in man is the font of this medieval constitutionalism. Thomas was only the greatest spokesman of this attempt at organizing society in operative "estates" which would have some prospect of success in the difficult task of making human laws reasonable, that is to say, worthy of that dignity of man which Christ had vindicated for all men.'

group was a *universitas*,[1] for legal purposes a fictitious person, distinguishable from its individual components and empowered to act as one unit. It might devise rules for regulating its members, elect officers, own property, appear in lawsuits, and generally do whatever was necessary for its preservation and well-being. Jurists defined the status of the corporation's head by adapting the Roman legal maxim, what touches all must be approved by all, arguing that he could do nothing which might jeopardize corporate rights and interests without the prior approval of its members. A prelate, for instance, might not alienate the property of his chapter without the consent of its canons. As principal, the corporation endowed its proctorial head with full power to appear in lawsuits on its behalf. In this way, notions of representation, accountability and consent began to seep into legal and political vocabulary. The corporation bestowed authority on its head for the purpose of safeguarding its common interests, which meant that he exercised a necessary measure of discretion in order to fulfil the function. But, as agent of the corporate group in which ultimate power was said to reside, he was answerable for the way in which he used his derivative authority.

The extension of corporation theory to the whole Church emanated from the terminological developments whereby *corpus mysticum* came to signify the society of the faithful considered administratively and politically. Envisaging the whole Church as a legal personage, conciliarists assimilated the position of the pope in regard to it to that of a prelate in relation to his chapter. John of Paris, for example, suggested that the papal authority of jurisdiction had been bestowed by the whole Church acting through the college of cardinals which might, therefore, correct or remove him should he act contrary to its general well-being. And subsequent writers, identifying the *universitas* which was the Church with its representatives gathered in a general council, argued that the papal office consisted in the execution of its sovereign enactments. Simultaneously, Nicolas of Cusa and others worked conciliarism into a constitutional theory applicable to both ecclesiastical and secular communities. In doing so, they illustrated how the novel

---

[1] cf. Gaines Post, 'Parisian Masters as a Corporation, 1200–1246', *Speculum*, IX (1934), pp. 423–4, '*Plena Potestas* and Consent in Medieval Assemblies', *Traditio*, I (1943), pp. 355–408, 'A Roman Legal Theory of Consent, *Quod Omnes Tangit*, in Medieval Representation', *Wisconsin Law Review* (1950), pp. 66–78, for the application of corporation concepts.

corporate conception of political activity could be blended with the traditional image of society as a hierarchical and stratified structure.[1]

Precisely how these various ideas merged into a theory of limited rulership is nicely illustrated in Marsilius of Padua's *Defensor Pacis* (1324) which, as we have noticed, was to exercise an influence in the sixteenth century. In addition to being suffused with the spirit of Aristotle, the work reveals a familarity with corporation theory which Marsilius gained as a native of Padua and as rector for a brief period at the University of Paris. More than any other medieval text, it expresses the conviction that a collective reason must be brought to bear on legislative matters in order to guarantee the substantive soundness of human law.

Like so many of his contemporaries, Marsilius deemed it appropriate to compare the political structure with other ordered wholes as a means of demonstrating that order issued from a functional integration of diverse parts. The direction of these various activities to the common good was the task of rulership, and here again Marsilius detected a parallel with the pattern of the natural world. Hence the fundamentally important principle of unity, described as tranquillity or peace, demanded that unity of action be preserved in the ruling part of the community.[2] But Marsilius did not interpret the necessity of unified governmental activity to imply

[1] cf. Brian Tierney, *Foundations of the Conciliar Theory: The Contribution of the Medieval Canonists from Gratian to the Great Schism* (Cambridge, 1955); Black, *Monarchy and Community*, pp. 1–52; Paul E. Sigmund, *Nicholas of Cusa and Medieval Political Thought* (Harvard, 1963).

[2] Marsilius of Padua, *The Defender of Peace*, trans. Alan Gewirth (New York, 1967), I. xvii. 9: 'Now since in the nature of things there is one primary ruler in number, not more, because "things do not wish to be ordered badly", as it is said in the twelfth book of the *First Philosophy*, therefore the primary government established according to the reason and art of men will also be only one in number.' Marsilius goes on to differentiate the unity of the political structure and that of a natural order in a way similar to Aquinas: 'This is a unity of order; it is not an absolute unity, but rather a plurality of men who are said to be some one thing in number because they are said to be related to one thing in number, namely the government, towards which and by which they are ordered and governed. For the city or state is not one through some one natural form, such as by composition or mixture, since its parts or offices, and the persons or parts of these parts, are many in actuality and formally separate from one another in number, since they are separate in place and in subject. Hence they are not one through some one thing inhering in them, or touching or containing them like a wall.' For an excellent account of Marsilius' thought which dispels many of the myths about this often misunderstood writer, see Ewart Lewis, 'The "Positivism" of Marsiglio of Padua', *Speculum*, XXXVIII (1963), pp. 541–82.

that most members of the community ought to be politically inactive. For only if the reason of the citizenry was mobilized against the misuse of power would the common welfare be secured.

Repeating the Aristotelian classification of the three forms of government and their corresponding perversions, Marsilius concerned himself mainly with a consideration of monarchy which, still with Aristotle, he thought should be limited in accordance with law. Rulership, he maintained, 'must be regulated by the law in judging, commanding, and executing matters of civil justice and benefit, for otherwise the ruler would not act towards his proper end, the conservation of the state'.[1] The function of the ruling part was to co-ordinate communal activities by a norm of justice of which properly constituted human law was an embodiment, for, properly considered, a law was a blending of coercive and normative elements. It was, in other words, an ordination regarding justice and the common benefit to which sanctions had been attached to give it the formal status of law.[2] But rulers unfettered by law were deflected by passion from the task of transmitting communal justice. 'For every soul sometimes has a vicious emotion.'[3] And their unaided judgement was less efficacious than laws that emerged from the careful consideration given to civil matters by a large number of people over a long period. A collective wisdom in its historical dimension, argued Marsilius relying on Aristotelian arguments and anticipating an important strain of thought in early modern England, was superior in rationality to the judgement of one man at a particular moment in time. For lawmaking was a complex, cumulative process that depended upon the prudence or practical reason of generations of men.[4] Hence, given that

---

[1] Ibid., I. xv. 7.

[2] Ibid., I. x. 3–4: 'In its fourth and most familiar sense, this term "law" means the science or doctrine or universal judgment of matters of civil justice and benefit, and of their opposites. Taken in this last sense, law may be considered in two ways. In one way it may be considered in itself, as it only shows what is just or unjust, beneficial or harmful; and as such it is called the science or doctrine of right (*juris*). In another way it may be considered according as with regard to its observance there is given a command coercive through punishment or reward to be distributed in the present world, or according as it is handed down by way of such a command; and considered in this way it most properly is called, and is, a law . . . Law, then . . . is an ordinance made by political prudence, concerning matters of justice and benefit and their opposites, and having "coercive force", that is, concerning whose observance there is given a command which one is compelled to observe.'

[3] Ibid., I. xi. 6.   [4] Ibid., I. xi. 3.

rulers were required to exercise discretion in making law operative and to temper its 'rigorous universality' with considerations of equity, their judgement could be presumed reliable, that is, in accordance with justice and the common good, only when informed by the wisdom of many as it was revealed in existing law.

Similar considerations regarding the effectiveness of a collective reason in securing the essential substantive features of law were operative in persuading Marsilius to identify the authority of enacting law with the whole citizen body. A group of wise men with expertise in such matters might conveniently be elected for the purpose of devising laws, but it was the assembled citizenry that endowed the ordinations of the wise with the status of legally enforceable commands. Here Marsilius drew upon the presumed rationality of men, as well as the concepts of the theory of corporations. Communal participation in the legislative process would most likely produce laws for the common utility because a corporate whole exceeded any of its parts in both quantity and virtue. Not only would the many have a clearer perception of the common good than the few, they would be less inclined to enact laws favouring the private advantage of a segment of the community. Moreover, it was a principle of corporations that matters 'which can affect the benefit and harm of all ought to be known and heard by all, in order that they may be able to attain the beneficial and to avoid the opposite'.[1] There was also the practical consideration that men were more willing to obey laws which they themselves had made.

Marsilius was assuming that the majority of men were sufficiently qualified to be politically active, and he made the assumption explicit in his refutation of the notion that common men were too ignorant and depraved to participate in legislative matters. Conceding the Aristotelian proposition that distinctions of virtue and wisdom existed naturally among men, which justified the discovery and formulation of laws being entrusted to those who excelled in prudence, he nevertheless held that ordinary mortals were intelligent enough to assess the proposed measures. 'For most of the citizens are neither vicious nor undiscerning most of the time; all or most of them are of sound mind and reason and have a right desire for the polity and for the things necessary for it to endure,

[1] Ibid., I. xii. 7.

like laws and other statutes or customs.'[1] Drawing an analogy with the creative arts, Marsilius held that, even though most men were insufficiently wise or inventive to devise law, they were not devoid of the capacity to judge its quality. 'For many things which a man would have been unable to initiate or discover by himself, he can comprehend and bring to completion after they have been explained to him by someone else.'[2] The whole community being wiser and more virtuous than any of its parts taken separately, it was for its assembled members to determine whether the proposals of the wise were adequate, and to stamp them with the seal of approval by which they were transformed into laws.

The citizenry being competent to make political provision for itself, the ruling part became the executive agent of the community in which final authority resided. It might be elected, corrected and removed by the community. In a revealing analogy with the human body, Marsilius likened the citizenry to the soul which appointed a part, corresponding to the heart, for the task of regulating the activities of the other members. In it the soul implanted a virtue, law, within the bounds of which the ruling part was to perform its task. But whereas the heart in the natural body was incapable of acting in a manner unnatural to it, rulers were human, creatures of intellect and appetite, thus subject to the frailties of human nature. Through ignorance or selfishness, they might fail to govern according to the norms of justice that were embodied in enacted law. It was necessary, therefore, for them to be held accountable to the community for the performance of their public duties.[3] Contingent upon their governing for the common advantage, their powers were revocable should they fail. By turning the traditional correspondence upside down and assimilating the directing part of the human body to the citizenry rather than the head of the body politic, Marsilius was effectively articulating the political implications of an image of the community as a group of rational beings organized for the pursuit of a rationally apprehended goal.

Two strains of medieval political thought have been distinguished, one asserting that the capacity for political activity inhered exclusively in the single head of the body politic, and the other suggesting that the community itself was entitled to make provision for the common good. What inclined the bulk of English

[1] Ibid., I. xiii. 3.   [2] Ibid., I. xiii. 7.
[3] Ibid., I. xv. 5–7; I. xviii. 2–3.

writers between the thirteenth and fifteen centuries to the latter doctrine were the institutional changes by which the crown was raised to national prominence with the co-operation of landed groups. The emergence of parliament freed the monarch from his position as one, albeit powerful, baron intricated in a plethora of local and particular rights and obligations, enabling him to levy taxation and create a system of national administration. But it also gave practical expression to 'one of the deepest principles of feudal hierarchy within the nobility, the duty of the vassal to provide not only *auxilium*, but *consilium* to his liege-lord: in other words, the right to give his solemn advice in matters of gravity affecting both parties'.[1] So the gradual expansion and qualitative transformation of the *curia regis*, the gathering of a coterie of magnates individually summoned to assist the king in matters vital to his office, into a more representative and procedurally regulated assembly, was seemingly an instance of the principle that public affairs ought to be dealt with by a collective wisdom. Addressing themselves to the question of who was competent to take care of the *status regni*, the general welfare of the realm, writers clarified the idea of the community as a *universitas* which might act in a corporate political capacity.

Perhaps because of the greater degree of geographical and political integration existing in England and its tradition of common law, English thinkers were slightly more suspicious of metaphysical abstractions than their continental counterparts. Preferring the concrete and tangible, they were never entirely happy with the proposition that, as mediator between the precepts of justice and actual law, the ruler was a *lex animata* limited only by his voluntary conformity to objective standards. He was, they argued in a more pragmatic vein, bound by the edicts of justice as found in existing law, in the English case the minutiae of customs by which social practices were regulated and which had attained the status of law through the approval of king and magnates and by extended usage. But this apparently simple idea, that the king was subject to existing law, raised a number of theoretical difficulties, for writers were hampered by the absence of effective institutions in trying to provide a precise definition of his prerogative.

This imprecision is reflected in Bracton's *On The Laws and Customs of England*, written in the later part of the thirteenth

---

[1] Anderson, *Lineages of the Absolutist State*, p. 46.

century.[1] By virtue of certain jurisdictional and coercive powers, bestowed for the purpose of dispensing justice, the ruler was God's vicar on earth without equal in the community. Wielding these powers, he could not be subjected to the coercive force of law. And yet, like Christ and Mary, he was morally bound to observe the concrete manifestations of justice, in the ruler's case the existing laws of the land, in so far as departure from them would constitute a negation of the purpose for which his office was ordained. Enhanced above the law in that he was granted special powers to promote the common good, he was yet under it in that refusal to conform to rules he had deemed necessary to dispense justice could only lead to the destruction of the general well-being. A ruler, therefore, who refused to bridle himself in accordance with laws he had established, who did precisely that which he considered necessary to restrain others from doing, ceased to be a minister of the deity and became a tyrant. Such a ruler, said Bracton, using the analogy of the head and members of the natural body, spread corruption throughout the realm.

Conceiving no procedure by which the community might enforce the king's adherence to existing law, Bracton was compelled to reiterate the duties of kingship. Like John of Salisbury before him, he was labouring under the burden of writing at a time when institutional alternatives to personal government were practically non-existent. Where Bracton differed from John, however, was in the belief that the monarch's conformity to the directive force of law was in some measure secured by his having to fulfil the functions of his office in the presence of his magnates. The initiative in legislative affairs might lie with him, but he was required to associate the barons with him in undertaking the task. For, in England, 'whatever has been rightly decided and approved with the counsel and consent of the magnates and the general agreement of the *res publica*, the authority of the king or prince having first been added thereto, has the force of law'.[2] The feudal obligation on the part of the suzerain to consult with the barons in devising, altering and nullifying laws, provided in Bracton's eyes an assurance that whatever proposals came to have the status of

[1] The imprecision is also reflected in the conflicting interpretations of Bracton. But see Brian Tierney, 'Bracton on Government', *Speculum*, XXXVIII (1963), pp. 295–317.

[2] Bracton, *On the Laws and Customs of England*, trans. S. E. Thorne (Cambridge, Mass., 1968), vol. 2, p. 19.

law were never 'anything rashly put forward of his own will'.[1] And this amounted to rather more than John of Salisbury's belief that his powers were in no way communally limited.

In affirming the responsibility of the monarch to legislate through the counsel of his magnates, Bracton was not simply describing the reciprocal obligations entailed by the contractual nature of feudal bonds. His argument implied that the magnates met with the king to consider matters concerning the welfare of the realm, in contrast with private matters of interest only to the individuals involved. And in this Bracton was articulating a general conviction, that the bridle placed upon the power of the king by influential men was of relevance to the realm. For by the thirteenth century the magnates were commonly referred to as a *universitas regni*, a corporate group called upon to assist the king in the government of the realm. In 1242 the monarch summoned the barons to 'treat' with him 'concerning arduous business of ours which specially touches the estate of us and of all our realm'.[2]

As well as recognizing that the king's prerogative extended beyond the sphere of personal rights to embrace the public welfare, such statements embodied the principle that he had to gain the approval of those who stood for the welfare of the realm whenever such rights were jeopardized. In wartime, for instance, necessity demanded that the king raise extraordinary taxation for the public safety, but he was required to win the assent of those affected by such measures. In effect, these developments were an application of the Roman legal maxim, what touches all must be approved by all. Edward III declared in 1330 that 'we wish all men to know that in future we will govern our people according to right and reason, as is fitting our royal dignity; and that matters which touch us and the estate of our realm are to be disposed of by the common counsel of the magnates of our realm and in no other manner'.[3] For the sake of the general welfare, the ruler possessed powers which transcended, and occasionally overrode, the agglomeration of private rights, yet these powers were to be exercised in such cases in conjunction with those whose rights were threatened, the magnates as a *universitas regni*.

[1] Ibid., vol. 2, p. 305.
[2] Cited in B. Wilkinson, *Constitutional History of Medieval England*, 1216–1399 (London, 1958), vol. III, p. 301.
[3] Cited in B. Wilkinson, 'The "Political Revolution" of the Thirteenth and Fourteenth Centuries in England', *Speculum*, XXIV (1949), p. 509, n. 23.

These developments were as yet but a small step towards the creation of a partnership between king and significant social groups and the consequent emergence of viable political institutions. The corporate body of magnates was still envisaged as an instrument of regal government and Robert Bruce was expressing the conventional wisdom when he said in 1291–2 that 'kings are established to govern the people, not to be governed by them'.[1] Nevertheless, the notion that matters of common concern ought to be commonly dealt with was beginning to implant itself. And this constituted an application of the Aristotelian supposition that rule by one man was not a sufficient guarantee of the common good. In his *Commentary on Aristotle's Politics* (c. 1340), Walter Burley wrote of the need for the ruler to surround himself with the wisdom of many by associating with him a number of co-rulers. The reason given was,

that many can inquire and judge better than one what is to be done and what not. Which is proved by examples in support. Just as it is improper to say that one man with two eyes and two ears perceives better than many men with many eyes and ears, and as it is improper to say that one man acts better with two hands and feet than many hands and feet, so it is improper to say that one man judges better by his own wisdom than many. And therefore we see that the rulers make for themselves many eyes and many feet and hands, because they make for themselves many co-rulers. These the ruler calls feet, hands and eyes, because through these he sees and acts.[2]

Perhaps it is not too fanciful to interpret this English statement of Aristotelianism as the philosophical justification of what in practice was occurring.

The story of the transformation of the king's counsel of magnates into a parliament of monarch, lords and commons has yet to be related in detail and historians are not agreed as to the significance of contributory factors.[3] But the major outlines are relatively clear. Financial pressures facilitated the summoning of representatives of landed groups other than the mighty barons before the royal

---

[1] Cited ibid., p. 508, n. 22.
[2] Cited in Wilkinson, *Constitutional History of Medieval England*, vol. III, p. 108.
[3] For a neat summary see G. R. Elton, *The Body of the Whole Realm : Parliament and Representation in Medieval and Tudor England* (Charlottesville, Virg., 1969), pp. 1–12; and Edward Miller, *The Origins of Parliament*, Historical Association Pamphlet (London, 1960).

council. By the end of the thirteenth century lower clergy, knights and burgesses were appearing before it endowed with full power to petition the rights of local communities. The phrase 'community of the realm' in the famous Statute of York of 1322 referred to these representatives, as well as to magnates and prelates.[1] Sometimes the commons were energetic in opposing regal demands for extraordinary taxation,[2] but it was not until the fifteenth century that they assumed prominence alongside the lords in framing legislation. In the intervening period, there were continual efforts to regulate the procedures of parliament.

What concerns us is the way in which writers sought to express the feeling that things held in common ought to be commonly dealt with. For their language began to reveal a readiness to acknowledge that the community could be corporately organized for the pursuit of shared objectives. Of course, there was no drastic change in the way in which political affairs were discussed, and writers never failed to affirm the importance of kingship. As the point was made in a political poem of the fifteenth century:

> God geueth his doom to alle kynges that be;
> As a god, in erthe a kyng hath mygt.[3]

The temptation to attribute thaumaturgical qualities to the monarch is evidence that he was recognized as the crucial public figure, an eminence achieved rather than eroded by the growth of parliament. Similarly, writers never tired of situating him at the top of the social pyramid. Likening him to the head of the natural body, a fifteenth-century poet described at some length the correspondences existing between the two bodies: the king's counsellors were analogous to the human brain, the priesthood to the breast, magnates to shoulders, yeomen to fingers, and the well-being of each was said to issue from mutual interdependence and a common subordination to the head.[4] And in 1468 Bishop Stillington repeated the familiar idea that justice accrued to that community in which each member

---

[1] On the significance of the Statute see Post, *Studies in Medieval Legal Thought*, pp. 310–22.

[2] cf. Alan Rogers, 'Henry IV, the Commons and Taxation', *Mediaeval Studies*, XXXI (1969), pp. 44–70.

[3] *Twenty-Six Political and Other Poems,* ed. J. Kail, E.E.T.S. (London, 1904), p. 53.

[4] Ibid., pp. 64–9.

performed the duties of his estate, and the king assumed overall responsibility for administering law and maintaining peace.[1]

But, alongside statements enhancing kingship, there was a tendency to separate the common good from the person of the monarch. Writers began to distinguish the crown from the particular occupant of the throne.

> What doth a kynges crowne signyfe,
> Whan stones and floures on sercle is bent?
> Lordis, comouns, and clergye
> To ben all at on assent.
> To kepe that crowne, take good tent,
>   In wode, in feld, in dale, and downe.
> The leste lynge-man, with body and rent,
>   He is a parcel of the crowne.[2]

It was to the crown, symbolizing the unity of the nation and its well-being, that head and members of the body politic owed allegiance. Other remarks also reflect a willingness to depart from the idea of personal monarchy, the rejection of the notion that the king alone in his capacity as head of the body politic might determine public requirements. Increasingly, it was taken for granted that parliament was the proper place for disposing of matters of public concern.

> Whanne all a kyngdom gadrid ysse
> In goodis lawe, by on assent,
> For to amende that was mysse
> Therfore is ordayned a parlement.[3]

Most indicative of the recognition given to the significance of communal political activity was the use writers made of the phrase *corpus mysticum* to describe the community. In 1373 Bishop Brinton described the realm of England as a mystical body which cohered through the functional diversity of its various parts.[4] And

---

[1] Cited in B. Wilkinson, *Constitutional History of England in the Fifteenth Century* (London, 1964), p. 315.

[2] *Twenty-Six Political and Other Poems*, p. 51.   [3] Ibid., p. 55.

[4] 'In this Mystical Body there are many members, because the heads are the kings, princes, and prelates: the eyes are wise judges and true councillors; the ears are religious; the tongue, good doctors: the right hand is the soldiers ready to defend; the left hand is the merchants and faithful mechanics; the heart is the citizens and burghers placed in the centre; the feet are the farmers and labourers supporting the whole body firmly.' *The Sermons of Thomas Brinton, Bishop of Rochester*, ed. Sister Mary Aquinas Devlin in 2 vols. for the Camden Society, 3rd Series, LXXXV–LXXXVI (1954), vol. I, p. xxiii.

in a sermon of 1483, Bishop Russell referred to England as a mystical body animated by a parliament in which the king together with other estates were present.[1] As 'the place of worldely policie', parliament was the life-giving nucleus of the nation. Analogous, interestingly enough, to the stomach in the natural body, it was by means of a strong parliament that the unity of the mystical body of the realm was conserved, and from it that the well-being of every member emanated.[2] The message Russell intended to convey is clear. It was that England was well provided for in that its stomach was sound because parliament, the vehicle through which representatives of various sections of the community became mobilized to deal with political matters in conjunction with the king, was responsible for maintaining national unity and promoting common purposes. A healthy parliament was at once the embodiment and assurance of the general well-being.

For all this, the institutional developments which brought politics within the scope of men other than the monarch had not proceeded sufficiently far by the close of the fifteenth century to inhibit thinkers from reverting to the idea of monarchical absolutism. The initiative in summoning parliament lay with the king still. Henry VII did without it for most of his reign, preferring to govern through a council of advisers. Professor Sayles is quite right in suggesting that parliament was probably saved from extinction by the exigencies of the Reformation, and not by some inexorable long-term process towards representative government.[3]

[1] S. B. Chrimes, *English Constitutional Ideas in the Fifteenth Century* (New York, 1966), p. 180: 'In thys politike body of Englonde there by iij. estates as principalle membres vndir oone hede, –thestate of the lordys spiritualle, thestate of the lordes temperalle, and thestate of the comminallete. The hede ys owre soouerayne lord the kynge here presente. What due proporcion and armonye ought to by yn thys body, amonges alle the membres grett and smalle, Synt Paule, takynge hys similitude from the naturalle body of man, declareth at large j. Cor. contendynge that, lyke as yn that body naturalle there ys no membre, be he ever so nobille, that may sey to the leste or to the vileest of them alle, I have no nede of the, but that eche hathe hys necessarie appropred operacion a parte, So ys hyt yn the mistik or politike body of the congregacion of the peuple, that every estate ys ordeigned (to support other, Vt non sit) scisma in corpore, to thentent, as the apostill seyth, that all maner scisme and division schuld be eschewed.'

[2] Ibid., p. 175: 'What ys the bely or where ys the wombe of thys grete publick body of Englonde but that and there where the kyng ys myn self, hys court and hys counselle?'

[3] G. O. Sayles, *The King's Parliament of England* (London, 1975), pp. 135–6: 'Must we believe, no matter the facts, that the English kings recognised some

The political co-operation achieved by widening the circle of those involved in the governmental process also entailed an extension of the royal prerogative. Even the notion of an impersonal crown, embracing all estates and standing for the public good, was not so radically dissociated from the person of the king that it would hinder future writers reuniting the two. We have seen that factors in the sixteenth century were to encourage many to supply the theoretical ratification of practically unfettered monarchy, providing a picture of kingship undiluted by any restraints which the community might wish to impose on its head. It is to these thinkers that we now turn.

---

constitutional imperative to summon parliament? . . . Parliament did not disappear . . . for a quite unpredictable turn came in the tide of events and Henry VIII, faced with other possibilities, deliberately selected parliament in 1529 as an instrument to his liking and set it upon a new career as a legislative assembly, with the commons as a pliant but necessary tool for his purposes. Common assent could thereby be obtained under conditions of the fullest publicity and binding upon the whole country . . . With so much dependent throughout the fifteenth century on accident and caprice, with so much power in the king to continue, interrupt, or break the sequence of parliaments, we must regard parliament as it was regarded then, as a device of government with an uncertain tenure of life, liable like any other such device to be out moded and superseded or, if circumstance and convenience determined, to be remodelled and revivified. But if parliaments are an administrative contrivance for which there is often an effective alternative in great councils, if political power rests perpetually in king and peerage, if the only gainer in the contests of the fifteenth century is the monarchy, why do we concentrate our gaze on the commons in parliament and fail to look at the history of the fourteenth century without illusion and the history of the fifteenth century without disillusion? For the medieval parliament ended in strong monarchical rule, not in constitutional democracy.'

III

POLITICS MYSTIFIED

WE HAVE considered the factors which dissuaded the bulk of English writers in the early modern period from making any concession to the idea of a community corporately organized for political activity. Confronted by social instability and the prospect of external invasion, they selected for emphasis those values of the inherited world picture which were in greatest danger of erosion. Thus, the primacy of order was asserted to the degree that other political values—the necessity, for instance, of ensuring that policies were rationally defensible—faded into relative insignificance. The effect was to elevate the crown as the sole source of the public good and, correlatively, to devalue the political relevance of the common possession of reason. The tone of the theory was set initially by the fear of unrest. But it was sustained in the Elizabethan period by a sense of national optimism prevalent among members of the dominant social groups. The Stuarts were less agile than their predecessors in satisfying the expectations of these groups, and the seventeenth-century supporters of the crown responded by elaborating the theory into an ever more positive affirmation of the sanctity of monarchy.

What emerged, then, was a theory of absolute monarchy; absolute in the sense that the prerogative of the king was held to be unrestricted by such communal institutions as a representative assembly of the nation. However, this did not amount to a full doctrine of sovereignty. None of the king's defenders sought to exclude him from the directive force of objective standards; none, that is, argued that his arbitrary enactments supplied adequate criteria of political legitimacy. Objective reason, not will, was the standard of political rightness. Their case, therefore, hinged on the assumption that regal authority was an adequate embodiment of reason, that his enactments were acceptable because they were the product of a will that had been informed by reason.

And here the theory underwent a significant development between the sixteenth and seventeenth centuries. Its early proponents argued their case from largely naturalistic assumptions. Assimilating the political structure to the pattern of order revealed in the natural world, they suggested that the king was normally a mediator of divine norms of justice. Like their medieval predecessors, however, they had to face the fact that a community unable to act politically was left unprotected against occasional manifestations of tyranny. Their solution was the idea that God sporadically intervened directly in the political process. He did so in order to remove a ruler whose evil activities threatened the general well-being.

By the seventeenth century, a more overtly supernaturalistic dimension had been added to the theory. The monarch was still envisaged as the apex of a naturally ordered social hierarchy. But inserted into the conception was the belief that he participated uniquely in the omnicompetency of the deity. A probable reason for this shift of emphasis was that the most fervent supporters of the crown by this time were a group of clerics whose Arminianism inclined them to worship God in the beauty of holiness. At any rate, their image of the monarch was that of a being who hallowed the nation by his possession of a mixture of aesthetic and spiritual attributes. In a sermon preached in 1639, Henry Valentine said that the community was beautified by the presence of the king, without whom it 'would be but . . . A masse of *confusion*, and ugly and deformed Monster'.[1] And John Rawlinson, a chaplain to the king, added a familial flavour to kingship by referring to 'an entercourse of *loue* and *duty* betweene the *King* & his *Subiects*'.[2] The general effect was to relegate the apparent problem of tyranny to the status of a pseudo-problem. For the impression conveyed was that the king was in no sense an ordinary mortal. Partaking of divine qualities, he was genetically incapable of behaving arbitrarily. He was, in short, infallible. Politics was not a realm of normal human activity because it demanded skills not encompassed by ordinary human reason.

The theory of absolute monarchy was grounded in the conception of a hierarchically arranged universe. Believing with medievalists that unity was 'the mother of order',[3] writers sought to demonstrate

---

[1] Valentine, *God Save the King*, p. 5.
[2] John Rawlinson, *Vivat Rex* (Oxford, 1619), p. 13.
[3] James I, *Basilkon Doron*, in *The Political Works of James I*, ed. C. H. McIlwain (New York, 1965), p. 23.

that a properly integrated society was but one instance of a universal pattern. It followed, therefore, that social stratification and inequality were inevitable. In Henry King's words:

There is nothing so much sets out the Vniuerse as *Order*, to see how subordinate causes depend of their Superiours, and this sublunary Globe of the Celestiall. Were not this method, what could hinder a second Chaos? For in the Worlds beginning all lay in one common wombe of darkenes, it was onely order and that Method Gods *fiat* brought a long, which gaue distinctions and visibility of things. A heauen aboue the earth, and light to separate day from night. Man as Lord to rule the Creatures, and God himselfe Lord ouer all. Should all haue been equall, what had mad beene better than the beasts, saue only his shape? . . . Vnisons yeeld no Musicke, for Harmony consists of variety in stops higher and lawer, and equality amongst men would breed nought but confusion . . . All were not borne to be rich, nor all to be wise, nor all to teach, nor all to rule, but some for *Disciples,* some for *Masters,* some for the *Throne,* some for the *Mill,* some for *Seruants,* some for *Lords.*[1]

The implication, then, was that the entire creation supplied a normative pattern from which humankind could in no way depart. William Fulbecke was not the least surprised that throughout history men had been aware of the imperative embodied in the universal pattern of inequality, 'for nature her selfe hath taught the nations her schollers this lesson'.[2] Much of this was no more than a restatement of an old theme, though the need for functional grading was asserted with particular vigour throughout the period. Along with the call for order in diversity went a concern that each member of the community should find complete satisfaction in performing the particular duties of his ascribed role. This familiar medieval idea was transmitted through such works as Edmund Dudley's *The Tree of Commonwealth* (1509). The root of social integration or concord lay, he said, in a 'good agreement and conformytie emongest the people or the inhabitauntes of a realme . . . and euery man to be contcnt to do his dewtie in the office, or condicion that he is sett in, And not to maling or disdaine any other'.[3] A willingness on the part of each member of the body

[1] Henry King, *A Sermon Preached at Pavls Crosse, The 25, Of November, 1621* (London, 1621), pp. 25–7.

[2] William Fulbecke, *The Pandectes of the Law of Nations* (London, 1602), p. 62.

[3] Edmund Dudley, *The Tree of Commonwealth*, ed. D. M. Brodie (Cambridge, 1948), p. 40.

politic to perform his ascribed functions in the social fabric was the foundation of a rightly organized community. For it was from selfless fulfilment of assigned tasks that the common good, that good in which all particulars were included and harmonized, issued.

Though there was nothing novel in the idea that social integration entailed functional differentiation, the point was made with a sense of urgency in the period. The result was that some writers went to extreme lengths by propounding an organic conception of the human community in which the individual was attributed little value apart from his contribution to the smooth operation of the whole. Here the distinction which medieval Aristotelians usually made between the external unity of political society, attained through functional diversity and the co-ordinating effects of political activity, and the intrinsic unity of a substance, tended to be blurred. Rather less emphasis was given to the fact that an ordered community permitted each individual to seek fulfilment than to the necessity of each behaving in a manner conducive to the preservation of stability.

The implication was that the well-being of each member of the body politic was somewhat less significant than the continuing existence of the larger whole into which he was absorbed. This emerged in the concept of sacrifice, the view that individuals might be legitimately disposed of should their activities threaten communal integration. In 1607, Nicholas Breton directed a pamphlet against those who complained about the occupants of authoritative offices. In music, said Breton, harmony emanated from a concord of different voices. In the body, health was preserved by the concurrence of the various component parts. The same principle was applicable to the human community, for discordance in any member adversely affected the whole. Unity being the prerequisite of the common good, 'it is better that a few murmurers perish with their murmuring, then a whole kingdome perish with their mallice; if they hand offend thee, cut it off: better to enter heauen with one hand, or one eye, then with both into hell'.[1] Like the malfunctioning part of the natural body, the disruptive member of the body politic was worthless in regard to the requirements of the whole. His existence, therefore, might be conveniently terminated.

[1] Nicholas Breton, *A Murmurer*, in *The Works*, ed. A. B. Grosart (New York, 1966), II p. 11.

The description of society as a system of rigidly graded ranks was intended to convey the necessity of political quiescence, for its effect was to remove from the individual competence to transcend his particular station in order to become politically active. Here, writers found argument by correspondence a particularly fertile device, especially the analogy between the natural body and the body politic. 'A comune welthe is lyke a body,' suggested Sir Richard Morison in his discourse on rebellion,

ans soo lyke, that it can be resembled to nothyng so conuenient, as unto that. Nowe, were it not by your fauthe, a madde herynge, if the fote shuld say, I wyl weare a cappe, with an ouche, as the heade dothe? If the knees shulde say, we woll carie the eyes, an other whyle: if the sholders shulde clayme eche of them an eare: if the heles wold nowe go before, and the toes behind? This were undoubted a mad heryng . . . But if it were so in dede, if the fote had a cap, the knees eies, the sholders eares, what a monstrous body shulde this be?[1]

It was as monstrous for members of a political community to assume functions for which they were ill equipped as it was for the parts of a natural body to perform tasks for which they were unqualified. The responsibility of the politically headless members of the body politic consisted in diligent performance of their ascribed tasks. Only in this way could they make a specific contribution to the general well-being. For them to participate in political affairs, the prerogative of the ruling head, was an absurdity.

So as to leave no doubt of the specifically political implications of this picture of society as a graded structure of unequal degrees, writers superimposed upon it the relationship of rulership and subjection. Using analogical argument in order to assimilate the monarch to some vital part of the human body, they erected an insurmountable barrier between the two functions. As Valentine said, identifying the public welfare with the person of the monarch, the king was 'a common good' who, like the soul in the natural body, 'inanimates and informes the whole collective body of the people, and every particular man of it'.[2] The analogy with the head was used more extensively, and just as effectively. The king, claimed Rawlinson, 'is the Head of the Politike body; being to it as

---

[1] Morison, *A Remedy for Sedition*, pp. 20–21. For a useful discussion of the use of analogical argument in the period, see J. E. Phillips, *The State in Shakespeare's Greek and Roman Plays* (New York, 1940), ch. iv.

[2] Valentine, *God Save the King*, p. 17.

is the head to the rest of the members, the fountaine both of sense, and motion'.[1] From the head sprang the direction and movement of the whole body, so that in the king inhered the responsibility of guiding every member towards the common good. As the reason which co ordinated the various members of the natural body resided in the head or soul, so, too was the political wisdom which conserved the public welfare deposited in its ruling part. In addition to the orderly coherence contingent upon functional diversity, it was through common subordination to the king that the common good was attained. Humphry Sydenham summarized the doctrine neatly. '*Command* and *obedience*,' according to him, 'are the *body* and *soule* of *humane societie*, the *head* and *foot* of an *establish't Empire*.'[2] Clearly, the well-being of king and commonwealth were inextricably intertwined, for he had the exclusive task of providing overall direction to the community.

This paternalist conception of government, based on the belief that the members of the body politic were utterly dependent on the king for political guidance, was expressed by means of similes other than those of the natural body. The monarch was likened, for example, to a shepherd and his people to a flock of sheep which would be dispersed without his continual care and direction.[3] Similarly, he was described as the father of an extended family. 'The child is bound to the priuat father,' wrote Sir John Cheke in his admonition to rebels in 1549, 'and be we not all bound to the commonwealths father?' This analogy, of course, was to be used extensively in the seventeenth century. The inference was that any subject who neglected the duty of obedience subverted the natural order itself.

For we see that the sheepe will obeie the shepheard, and the neat be ruled by the neathered, and the horsse will know his keeper, and the dog will be in aw of his maister, and euerie one of them feed there, and of that, as his keeper and ruler dooth appoint him, & goeth from thence, and that, as he is forbidden by his ruler.[4]

---

[1] Rawlinson, *Vivat Rex*, p. 9.
[2] Sydenham, *Moses and Aaron, or the affinity of Civill and Ecclesiasticke power*, in *Five Sermons Preached upon Severall Occasions*, p. 135.
[3] Valentine, *God Save the King*, p. 6.
[4] Sir John Cheke, *The hurt of sedition how greeous it is to a commonwealth*, in Holinshed, *Chronicles* (London, 1808), III, pp. 991, 993. James I, *The Trew Law of Free Monarchies*, in *The Political Works*, p. 55: 'By the Law of Nature the King becomes a naturall Father to all his Lieges at his Coronation.'

Amply supplied with examples of correct behaviour from the natural world, it was inconceivable why any man should wish to forsake his role of passively receiving the injunctions of his king. Devoid of the capacity to be politically active, he could not but respond with willing compliance to the commands of the one appointed to take care of such matters.

In seeking to exclude members of the body politic from sharing in the office of rulership, writers were not intending to imply that the king was entitled to do whatever he pleased. All agreed that he was enjoined to further the public welfare by enacting suitable legislation. John Carpenter likened him to an archer whose arrows were wise laws, framed in accordance with the common good.[1] For laws were intended to dispense communal justice which, as Richard Compton, citing Bracton, defined it, was 'a constant and perpetual will, to yeelde to euery one his right'.[2] No one sought to defend any abrogation of divine norms on the part of the king. He might be *legibus solutus* in regard to the constraining power of law, but he was subject to its directive force in so far as it consisted of rational precepts. He was not fully sovereign, for a king who made his rationally uninformed will to stand as law was indistinguishable from a tyrant.[3]

This conception of rulership as the pursuit of rational objectives led some writers to modify slightly their theory of communally unlimited monarchy. If the general welfare was so dependent on the ruler's continual execution of justice, it was vital that he should remain aloof from those corrupting influences of fallible human nature which might divert him from his purpose. As Thomas Floyd put it, comparing the king to the soul in the body, 'for as the minde of man in it selfe is more precious and excellent then all the other parts, as beyng voyde of indignitie and blemish: so ought the

[1] John Carpenter, *A Preparatiue to Contentation* (London, 1597), p. 139.

[2] Richard Crompton, *A short Declaration of the ende of Traytors* (London, 1587), sig. E. iii.

[3] Rawlinson, *Vivat Rex*, p. 7: 'A King then though he be free from *coaction* to keepe the law, yet must he voluntarily submit his will to the *direction* of the law: the difference betweene a *good King* and a *tyrant* being but this; that a *King* makes the law his will, because he will's, that which the law will's: But a *tyrant* makes his will a law, because what he will's, he will haue to be law.' Charles Merbury, *A Briefe Discovrse of Royall Monarchie, as of the Best Common Weale* (London, 1581), p. 44: The king 'is subiect vnto lawes both ciuill, and common, to customes, priuileges, couenantes, and all kinde of promises, So farre forth as they are agreable vnto the lawe of God: Otherwise we thinke that he is not bounde to obserue them.'

iudgement and sentence of a king be incorrupt and irreprehensible in all points.'[1] This persuaded some thinkers to encourage the monarch to seek the counsel of the wise in matters concerning his prerogative. Edward Forset admitted that, being subject to the infirmities of human nature, rulers might enact imperfect laws. The solution was for them to seek advice in the business of law-making, by assembling 'the noblest and choisest aduisours that the State affourdeth: thereby drawing supplies out of their politicall bodie, to make good what wanteth in their naturall'.[2] This was a concession on Forset's part, for his more typical view was that the ruler was not devoid of the political wisdom necessary to govern the community justly.

The idea that a collective wisdom provided a guarantee of the moral acceptability of human laws, used by some medievalists to explore the possibility of communal participation, was not exploited by Forset and most of his contemporaries. As with such medievalists as Aegidius Romanus, it was not a major ingredient in the theory of absolute monarchy. The general opinion was that communal restrictions to unadulterated monarchy were made irrelevant by the fact that God retained control of political matters, either by removing a tyrant when occasion demanded or by equipping the king with sufficient qualities to govern well.

In justifying the monarch's elevation above the community, writers used similar arguments to those which had led medieval Aristotelians to suggest that the provision of the public good ought to be the monopoly of one man. Occasional reference was made, for example, to the need for a public authority which, unhampered by existing law, was able to convert the precepts of natural law into more specific rules. Fawkner spoke of the indispensability of an enacting authority which might elicit 'from the common precepts of Nature (as particular and vnknowne conclusions are drawne from Command and apparent principles) . . . Canons for the more particular disposition of the community in order: which should deterre those from vice by feare of punishment, whome the instructions of Nature cannot persuade to be good by loue to vertue'.[3] Drawn out of the principles of natural law with regard to

---

[1] Floyd, *The Picture of a perfit Common wealth*, p. 31.
[2] Forset, *A Comparative Discovrse of the Bodies Natvral and Politiqve*, pp. 16–17.
[3] Fawkner, *Nicodemus for Christ*, p. 8.

the concrete requirements of the given community, these rules were subsumed under the category of 'indifferent', for they called for discretion on the part of the lawgiver from whom their binding force was derived. They were not directly enjoined by natural law, but received their obligatory force from the fact that the legislative authority deemed them expedient for the well-being of the community. As John Buckeridge explained, outlining the proper conditions for the making of laws:

First there must bee . . . a due matter, that is iust and lawfull, or else indifferent in it selfe: for in things simply good or euill, which are commanded or forbidden by God and Nature, No man hath power to crosse the will of God. And in these things mans power is declatory and exe-cutory, not soueraigne of it selfe; In things indifferent there is a power to command for circumstances of time, place, order, and the like, and there is a necessity of obedience, and that for conscience sake, else man hath no power to command any thing of himselfe; And yet it is the sinne of disobedience . . . not onely to do that which is euill, but that also which is forbidden.[1]

This awareness of the discretionary factor involved in legislation did not necessarily imply the political competence of a single individual. It merely highlighted the fact that a public authority was called for in order to particularize natural law into specific legal commands, an authority endowed with sufficient coercive power to ensure obedience to those commands. But, when connected with the comparison of the political order to other aspects of the world, it did buttress the case of those wishing to defend communally unlimited monarchy.

In fact, it was largely through argument by correspondence that the defence of monarchy was conducted. Sir Thomas Craig held that the natural world was replete with instances of the appropriate political form, for, 'tis most certain that Brutes even by Natures instinct tend to a Monarchy'.[2] Being no less a part of nature than the birds and the bees, there was no reason why man should attempt to depart from the universal pattern. God's government of the universe was also an instance of the desirability of monarchy,

[1] John Buckeridge, *A Sermon Preached at Hampton Court before the Kings Maiestie* (London, 1606), pp. 6–7.

[2] Sir Thomas Craig, *The Right of Succession to the Kingdom of England* (London, 1703), Bk. I, p. 12. The work was originally printed in Latin in 1693, a reply to the Jesuit Parson's attack on the English crown.

for it was proof of the principle that rule by one was the most effective means of preserving unity. Henry King held that no form of human government approximated closer to that operated by the deity, 'which is the Archetype, the first and best patterne of all others; as the Monarchicall, when a state is governed by a King as sole Commander over all. For in this singularity of power, that person who is . . . the lively Image of God, will some way represent the Unity of his Maker too.'[1] All the evidence pointed to the superiority of monarchy because God had not excepted human society when, on creating the world, He had intended His design to be everywhere reproduced.

It was through argument by correspondence, too, that writers were best able to demonstrate the lack of political wisdom amongst members of the body politic. Without actually denying that reason was the distinctive generic feature of humankind, they borrowed the Aristotelian idea of natural inequality to illustrate that reason was suffused through the community in markedly unequal measures. There was a natural basis to the social hierarchy in that its various grades corresponded to the unequal distribution of human intelligence. In other words, each member of the community had been divinely endowed with just the right amount of intelligence to permit him to perform his duties adequately. In his defence of monarchy, Sir Thomas Elyot went so far as to claim that more wisdom was deposited in the king than in the whole lump of the body politic.

For who can denie but that all thynge in heuen and erthe is gouerned by one god, by one perpetuall ordre, by one prouidence? One Sonne ruleth ouer the day, and one Moone ouer the nyghte; and to descende downe to erthe, in a littel beest, which of all other is moste to be maruayled at, I meane the Bee, is lefte to man by nature, as it seemeth, a perpetuall figure of a iuste gouernaunce or rule: who hath amonge them one principall Bee for theyr gouernor, who excelleth all other in greatness, yet he hath no pricke or stinge, but in hym is more knowledge than in the residue.[2]

---

[1] Henry King, *A Sermon Preached at St. Pavls March 27. 1640 : Being the Anniversary of His Maiesties Inauguration to His Crowne* (London, 1640), pp. 14–15. James I, *The Trew Law of Free Monarchies,* in *The Political Works,* p. 54: Monarchy, 'as resembling Diuinitie, approacheth nearest to perfection, as well the learned the wise from the beginning haue agreed vpon; Vnitie being the perfection of all things'.

[2] Sir Thomas Elyot, *The Boke named the Gouernour* (London, 1907), pp. 8–9.

Natural inequality prevented politics being a co-operative activity because the rational capacities of men beneath the king were insufficient to provide them with insight into communal requirements. From a political perspective, the members of the community were like the senses which required direction from the rational soul of the body.[1] Democracy, said Fulbecke, was a nonsensical notion: 'for the heele can not stand in place of the head, vnlesse the bodie be destroyed and the anatomie monstrous: it is against the nature of the people to beare rule: for they are as vnfitte for regiment, as a mad man to giue consaile'.[2] Thus, the unsuitability of men other than the single ruler to engage in political activity was a cardinal assumption of this strain of thought. These writers never for a moment contemplated the idea that political reason might be shared alike by head and members of the body politic, and, consequently, they had little or nothing to say about the desirability of safeguarding the public welfare by associating the members with the head in determining its legislative requirements. On the contrary, they envisaged normal men as beings who, so far from seeking to apprehend and follow the precepts of an objective moral order, were constantly yielding to irrational desires.

The dread with which they contemplated the perverse behaviour of sinful men emerged most clearly in the vehemence with which they condemned rebellion. Rebellion, it was said, had awful repercussions because it rapidly spread corruption through the realm, encompassing 'a whole hell of faults'.[3] The Church *Homily* of 1571, described as 'the epitome of all the literature of submission',[4] proclaimed 'all sins possible to be committed against God or man be contained in rebellion: which sins if a man list to name by the accoustomed names of the seven capital or deadly sins, as pride, envy, wrath, covetousness, sloth, gluttony and lechery, he shall find them all in rebellion'.[5] Basically, it was pride, the arro-

---

[1] King, *A Sermon Preached at St. Pavls March 27. 1640*, p. 19: 'if there be but one soule to informe the naturall body, why should there be more than one to rule the body of a State? In the predominance of the will or the phantasie, or the affections, or the passions, above reason which should be Soveraigne, we see what a distracted Man is made. Is it not the same in a State?'

[2] Fulbecke, *The Pandectes of the law of Nations,* pp. 28–9.

[3] Cheke, *The hurt of sedition,* in Holinshed, *Chronicles,* III, pp. 1,009–10.

[4] Helen C. White, *Social Criticism in Popular Religious Literature of the Sixteenth Century* (New York, 1965), pp. 168–9.

[5] 'An Homily Against Disobedience and wilful Rebellion,' in *Homilies Appointed to be Read in Churches* (Oxford, 1814), p. 488.

gance of ambitious men convinced that they were provided with special knowledge of communal needs, which was the cause of rebellion. 'There was never yet division, there was never any discord or dissension,' preached Bishop Jewel in a sermon extolling the Christian virtues of patience and humility, 'but pride was the first cause and author thereof.'[1] Rooted in the human proclivity to evil, rebellion was likely to occur whenever fallen men permitted their passions to go unchecked; whenever, that is, they refused to co-operate with their fellows in the rational order of the universe. Thus, even when writers referred to the distinctive feature of humankind, their intention was not to explore the political possibilities of harnessing the collective wisdom of the community in order to make divine standards operative within it. Their intention, rather, was to stress the especial inexcusability of men attempting to subvert the natural order of the world. James I suggested that, if even storks reverenced their parents, it was unforgivable that certain men, supposedly higher in the scale of creation by virtue of their reason, should not display similar respect to their political father.[2]

Given that so many were seemingly unwilling or unable to follow the example of the storks, a powerful ruler was needed to consolidate the natural order within human society. A strong king was the external agent who could subject to rational control the actions of men too corrupt and feeble to restrain themselves. As Rawlinson suggested, the king was analogous to the brain in the body which subdued the passions of the other members: 'If then there shalbe dissensions and heartburnings among the people, it's the braine and wisdome of the King that must compose them; like as *Aristotel* notes, that the cold moistnesse of the braine is it that cooles and qualifies the ouerboyling heat of the heart.'[3] There was an overwhelming feeling that, with the aid of an effective legal apparatus, the king stood as a bulwark between a fragile social order and the chaos which would engulf society should he relax his control over subjects.

Political theorists had always been impressed by the capacity of law to restrain men who might otherwise behave in a manner

[1] John Jewel, *The Works*, ed. John Ayre (Cambridge, 1845–50), II, p. 1,092.
[2] James I, *The Trew Law of Free Monarchies, in The Political Works*, p. 65.
[3] Rawlinson, *Vivat Rex*, p. 14.

detrimental to public order. Now that a note of disharmony had been injected into the divine scheme by the perversity of irrational men, prominence was attached to this function of law. Floyd said that, besides the promotion of justice, law had been invented 'to chastise the insolent and hauty behauiour of lewd persons'.[1] In a distinctly Augustinian vein, the *Homily* of 1571 claimed that laws had been instituted as a divine remedy for sin. As John Ferne made the point, 'to take away the force of lawes from amongst men, is to make a confusion of all things, and to dissolve the frame of humane life.'[2] A society without a ruler who, through the penalties attached to his commands, might compel men to virtuous behaviour, would simply dissolve into confusion. And this function of government, the maintenance of stability, was, it was implied, the most important responsibility devolving on the monarch.

What little writers had to say about the origins of political society is also indicative of the importance they attached to monarchy in preventing men from giving vent to the excesses of their corrupted nature. Believing that the political order was an integral aspect of the divine scheme, they had no difficulty accepting the Aristotelian proposition that the political relationships of command and obedience were more than mere expedients devised by God once man had departed from his state of innocence. Order called for arrangement into grades, and this principle applied to political society irrespective of the fact of human sin. John Buckeridge argued that, 'Sinne brought in tyrannie and slaverie . . . But order of superioritie and subiection is the instinct of purest nature; For in heauen there is order amongst the blessed Angels.'[3] Viewing the political order as something other than a divine remedy for sin, writers nevertheless worked into their account of its origins their conviction that rulership was an indispensable means of diminishing the effects of sinful behaviour. Setting out to prove that only hereditary monarchy was a legitimate form of government, Sir Thomas Craig reasoned that original societies consisted of families. Fearing the seizure of their possessions, each family joined forces with others and appointed a king to arbitrate between disputatious factions. As there existed no positive law at this time compelling men to accept monarchy, Craig concluded, 'twas only Nature, the

---

[1] Floyd, *The Picture of a perfit Common wealth*, p. 61.
[2] John Ferne, *The Blazon of Gentrie* (London, 1586), p. 41.
[3] Buckeridge, *A Sermon Preached at Hampton Court*, pp. 18–19.

Divina Particula Aura, which excited them to it'.[1] Monarchy was the original and most natural form of government, approximating most closely to the rule of a father in a nuclear family. Democracy and aristocracy had emerged later, in response to the tyrannical measures of certain kings. Thus, 'by the only Instinct of Nature, by meer Inclination and Choice of the mind, Men embrac'd Monarchy for their own safety, to oppose unjust Force, and to enjoy by mutual help the Common advantages and benefits, which arise from their being duly Incorporated into Bodies Politick'.[2] Having grounded monarchy in a natural instinct, Craig was equally firm that it 'was from the beginning, of Gods appointment, and brought in by Him, as the true expedient, for refraining the Ambition of some, preuenting or remouing strife and factions; and obliging His people to liue orderly.'[3]

In such ways, writers constructed an image of the political structure as a system enabling men to live together in peace and unity. Preoccupied with the problem of order, and perceiving all men to be potentially rebellious in view of their fallen nature, they searched for a means of introducing an element of stability into a community threatened by disintegration. A strong ruler and submissive subjects were, they believed, the basic ingredients of a well-ordered society. It was an Augustinian conception of politics contained within a picture of a rationally ordered universe that men through reason could comprehend; a picture which encouraged others to define the political relevance of the shared faculty of reason.

The arguments converged into one simple doctrine, that the king alone was fitted for political activity. The description of the community as a stratified hierarchy, the sharp distinction made between the office of rulership and the function of obedience, the numerous correspondence devised between the political order and other ordered wholes—especially the comparison of the king with the directing part of the body and the subjects with the senses— were all designed to establish the political incompetence of the members of the body politic.

This tendency to mystify political activity was exhibited most clearly in the logical devices inserted into the theory as a safeguard against the arbitrary activities of a tyrant. We have seen that a clear

---

[1] Craig, *The Right of Succession,* Bk. I, p. 15.
[2] Ibid., Bk. I, p. 16.   [3] Ibid., Bk. I, p. 10.

distinction was drawn between a good ruler and a tyrant. 'The one embraceth equitie, and iustice, the other treadeth both Gods lawe, and mans lawe vnder his feet. The one hath his minde, and all his care vpon the health, and wealth of his subiectes: th'other esteemeth his owne pleasure more then their profit, his owne wealth, more then their good willes.'[1] With such a vital role to perform, it was essential that the ruler should remain faithful to those divine norms which made his government communally just and beneficial. The alternative to removing from the community a right to limit kingship was to assume the existence of some other agency, able to protect a community which fell foul of tyranny. And this could be none but God. In this way, the problem of erroneous and perverse regal judgements received theoretical solution in the idea that political affairs were disposed of in heaven by a benign deity.

As was suggested at the outset of the chapter, this idea was developed at two levels. The first level of argument hinged on the assumption that the authority of the king emanated directly from God, that he had been 'placed in the steede of God himselfe among us'.[2] This implied that kings were answerable only to their appointee, 'to whom onely they must make their accompt'.[3] Now God in His great wisdom sometimes judged it expedient to appoint a harsh ruler to chastise a sinful people. No less than a generous ruler was he an instrument of divine goodness, for his appointment was intended to discourage people from the paths of wickedness. The idea was expressed by Bishop Gardiner in a work published in 1535, generally regarded 'as the ablest vindication of the royal supremacy then written'.[4] Gardiner was a formidable adversary, and detested by radicals. He was, consequently, a source of malicious gossip and Henry Brinklow, for instance, spread the rumour that Gardiner sought the attention of other men's wives. God, suggested Gardiner somewhat quaintly, 'committeth the people vnto the princes charge, som time naughtie people to a naughty prince . . . sometime good people to a good prince'.[5] If a

---

[1] Merbury, *A Briefe Discovrse of Royall Monarchie*, p. 13. cf. W. A. Armstrong 'The Elizabethan Conception of the Tyrant', *Review of English Studies*, XXII (1946), pp. 161–81.

[2] Richard Crakanthorpe, *A Sermon at the Solemnizing of the Happie Inauguration of . . . King Iames* (London, 1609), sig. G. 3.

[3] Buckeridge, *A Sermon Preached at Hampton Court*, p. 12.

[4] J. A. Muller, *Stephen Gardiner and the Tudor Reaction* (London, 1926), p. 65.

[5] Stephen Gardiner, *De Vera Obedientia* (Leeds, 1966), fols. xv–xvi.

naughty prince was a divine instrument for chastising a recalci-
trant people, it followed that his subjects could not legitimately
resist his commands. 'For whosouer maketh warre agaynste hys
prince,' wrote John Christopherson, 'he maketh warre agaynst
God, forasmuch as the prince is appoynted by God.'[1] Subjects
had no part in the making and unmaking of kings, for this properly
was God's preserve. He ensured that a nation received a government worthy of it. Anyone who pretended that it was his business
to interfere with a tyrant was doing no less than setting himself up
as a better judge than God of the community's needs. No matter
how evil a ruler might appear, said Richard Crompton, a subject
was never justified in rebelling

against his Prince, whom God hath placed in y throne of gouernment,
either for the comfort of good people, or for the punishment of the bad,
if ought be to be reformed touching gouernment in the king, it dooth not
belong to the subiect to redresse the same, but he must refer the matter
to God onely, who hath the hartes of Kinges in his order, and disposeth
them as it seemeth best to hys godlie wisedome. The duety of the Subiect is always to be obedient, as S. Paule saith, *Submitte your selues
vnto higher powers, for there is no power but of God, & all powers that be,
are ordeyned of God, who that resisteth powers, resisteth the ordenaunce of
God, and procureth vnto himselfe damnation.*[2]

Nothing could be clearer than that.

All this did not leave the community helpless in the face of
tyranny. Appointed as a scourge for sin, the tyrant's reign would
be terminated abruptly once his subjects had manifested their
repentance. Being part of God's plan for the ultimate good of
mankind, the tyrant would be removed whenever subjects restrained their pride by submitting meekly to his commands. For
'patience, earnest prayers to God, and amendment of their liues
are the onely lawful means to moue God to relieue them of that
heauie curse'.[3] Tyranny was a burden to be borne as a punishment
for sin, and just government the reward of virtue. Obedience was
the only legitimate response of subjects to good and bad rulers
alike.

In case anyone should fail to be deterred by arguments which

---

[1] John Christopherson, *An Exhortation to all menne to take hede and beware of
rebellion* (London, 1554), sig. J. vi.

[2] Crompton, *A short Declaration of the ende of Traytours,* sig. D. 4.

[3] James I, *The Trew Law of Free Monarchies,* in *The Political Works,* p. 67.

sought to establish the moral indefensibility of rebellion, it was made quite clear that God would not brook any transgression of the moral law. Rebels would certainly meet a bad end, because God could not but support His appointee. The popular *Mirror for Magistrates* provided numerous instances of God's intervention to prevent rebellion succeeding. We are told that the downfall of the infamous Jack Cade was inevitable.

> Full litell we knowe we wretches what we do.
> > Whan we presume our princes to resist.
> We war with God, against his glory to,
> > That placeth in his office whom he list,
> Therefore was never traytour yet but mist,
> > The marke he shot, and came to shamefulle end
> Nor never shall til God be forst to bend.

Cade's monstrous behaviour was doomed to failure, 'For God can not but maintain his deputie.'[1]

At this level, it was not argued that rulers never acted perversely and irrationally, nor that their subjects were unable to distinguish between just and unjust acts of government. It was simply maintained that the appointment of kings was the exclusive prerogative of the deity. As the crux of the matter was expressed in a political poem of 1565:

> Though kinges forget to gouerne as they ought,
> Yet subiects must obey as they are bounde.[2]

Even at this level, however, something more was intimated than was immediately apparent from the premises of the argument. The fact that a ruler was controlled from above suggested that subjects were not fully competent to judge the rightness of his commands. To suppose otherwise was to imagine that they could penetrate the operations of the deity. Gardiner said that it was the mark of a rebellious spirit to question the doings of a superior.

We are commaunded doutles to obey: in that consisteth our office, which if we minde to accomplish with the fauour of god & man, we must nedes shew humbleness of hart in obeieng autorite, how greuous

---

[1] Lily B. Campbell (ed.), *The Mirror for Magistrates* (New York, 1938), pp. 176, 178.

[2] Thomas Sackville and Thomas Norton, *Gorboduc* (Menston, 1968), sig. G. ii.

so euer it be, for gods sake, not questioning, nor inquiring, what the king, what the master, what the husband, ought or mai commaund other to do: but if thei take vpon them (either of their own head, or when it is offered them) more than right & reason is, they haue a Lorde, vnto whom they either stand or fall, and that shal one day sit in iudgement euen of them.[1]

In another sense, too, this first level of argument pointed beyond itself. Having been specifically selected by God to rule, it could not be imagined that the king had been left devoid of the qualities needed to govern. Having raised the monarch above other men, it was reasonable to suppose that God had endowed him with sufficient acumen to fulfil the task. According to Gardiner, God had appointed 'princes, who as representours of his image vnto men, he wold haue to be reputed in the suprem & most hie roume, & to excell among all other humane creatures'.[2] The implication was that the ruler became a being qualitatively different from other men by virtue of the divine favour bestowed upon him. It was here that the second level of argument emerged, and was developed most explicitly in the first part of the seventeenth century.

At this level, the total mystification of politics was achieved. On the one hand, it was argued that ordinary men could not assess the king's actions because they lacked his special gifts. On the other, it was said that the recipient of these gifts was released from those ordinary afflictions of human nature which might prevent him from governing justly. James I told his parliament in 1609 that, 'Kings are not onely GODS Lieutenants vpon earth, and sit vpon GODS throne, but euen by GOD himselfe they are called Gods.'[3] Endowed with super-human qualities, the king, said Valentine, was 'the bright *Image* of God, and the most magnificient and conspicuous representation of the Divine Majesty'. He was the community's great benefactor, for 'when he comes, all good things whatsoever come together with him'.[4] Even his physical attributes bore witness to his uniqueness among men. 'For there is,' said Rawlinson, 'an impression or character of dreadfull Maiestie stampt in the very visage of a King.'[5] From the community's viewpoint,

---

[1] Gardiner, *De Vera Obedientia,* fol. xxii.
[2] Ibid., fols. xv–xvi.
[3] James I, *A Speach to the Lords and Commons of the Parliament at White-Hall,* in *The Political Works,* p. 307.
[4] Valentine, *God save the King,* pp. 5, 7.
[5] Rawlinson, *Vivat Rex,* p. 9.

he was love incarnate, a fount of unfathomable goodness and prosperity. This, at any rate, was the opinion of Roger Maynwaring whose sermons constitued one of the grandest eulogies to monarchy.

The poorest creature, which lyeth by the wall, or goes by the high-way-side, is not without sundry and sensible tokens of that *sweat* and *Royall care*, and *prouidence*; which extendeth itself to the lowest of his *Subiects*. The way, they passe by, is the *Kings* high-way. The *Lawes*, which make prouision for their reliefe, take their binding force from the *Supreame* will of their *Liege-Lord*. The bread, that feedes their hungry soules, the poor ragges, which hide their nakedness, al are fruit and superfluity of that happie plenty and abundance caused by *wise* and peaceable gouernement.[1]

There are traces here of the early Tudor theory of kingship, which itself was an extension of the medieval doctrine of estates, the belief that the king was the co-ordinating pivot from which all communal benefits radiated. But the theory had been raised to an altogether more esoteric plane. The power of the king was not merely human, but super-human, a participation in the omni-competency of the deity which had been communicated directly to God's vice-regent on earth. Ordinary mortals could never fully appreciate the significance of the authority, they could simply marvel at its effects.

It was Forest who developed the implications of the argument most systematically. The king was analogous to the human soul which transformed the body from 'a confused lump' into a vital entity.[2] As the soul participated to a greater degree than the other members in the wisdom and goodness of God, so was the king that degree more pre-eminent than the members of the body politic. Now it was inconceivable that the soul should behave in an unnatural manner by harming the body. As the repository of reason, it was an unceasing source of bodily care and sustenance. Analogically it was no more imaginable that the king would seek to destroy the well-being of the community.

Let me proceed a little farther in the discerning of the wisdome and goodness of the Creator, in the ordeining and enduring with propertie of these principall receptacles of the soule, the head, and the heart: we doe

---

[1] Roger Maynwaring, *Religion and Allegiance : in two sermons preached before the Kings Maiestie* (London, 1627), p. 9.
[2] Forset, *A Comparative Discovrse of the Bodies Natvral and Politiqve*, p. 23.

not find that either of them is naturally enabled to offer any wrong by any meanes vnto the body, or once to encline by any so much as imagination of mischiefe thereunto . . . If the application hereof to our states soule: How comfortable may we conceiue, & euen glory in our happinesse, that stand vndubitably assured of our Soueraigne goodnesse . . . that this politicall soule . . . will be so farre from depriuing and impayring of our necessarie nutriments, as that he will rather draine his own heart bloud drie, than the wealth of the land should either be wastfully exhausted, or not suffisingly maintained.[1]

It followed from this attribution of infallibility to the ruler that any apparent evil on his part could be explained as a misconception by his subjects, an erroneous judgement arising from the fact that they lacked the unique wisdom of the king. Political matters could be safely entrusted to him, for he was incapable of acting in a communally harmful fashion.

Nature hath so prouided, that no sences of the bodie doeth penetrate into the essence or inwardnesse of the soule; they be espials for him, not spyers into him . . . Then in the same sort . . . let mee set it downe for a positiue trueth, that euen herein also our manners and dutie should contemplate and imitate nature, as with a modest reuerence to forbeare to intormit our animaduerting curiositie into the bosome of sacred and vnsearchable Maiestie: which who so doth with an humbled spirit find it to be so great an Arcanum in polcie, as the soule can bee in nature'.[2]

So, by assimilating the political order to the natural world, Forset was able to deny subjects any role in political affairs while, simultaneously, creating the presumption that this in no way jeopardized the public good.

The monarch was infallible, not sovereign. It could be presumed that he acted from a will which was constantly rational, which was rather different from saying that the standard of public rightness

---

[1] Ibid., pp. 34–5; p. 8: 'In that the soule is authour of action and motion in the body passiue, himselfe being neuer idle, it sheweth by similitude, that the soueraigne both vncessantly care and labour for the publike good.' p. 5: 'It is worthie the noting, that albeit the bodie doeth vnthankfully rebell against the soule, yet the soule euer loueth the body, still seeking to reduce it to the better, euen as a workeman mendeth his tooles, or a Musician his Instruments . . . The welfare and prosperitie of the bodie giueth to the soule sweet contentment, as secured thereby from the cares, perplexities, and griefes which want occasioneth: so the plentifull and abundant estate of the subiects, is by a good Soueraigne both maintayned and reioyced at, sith it siueth to him assurance of supply and comfort in all necessities.'

[2] Ibid., pp. 99–100.

was defined in accordance with what he actually willed. His enactments were just by virtue of the fact that they embodied objective
rational precepts, not merely because he determined them in his
public capacity. But if his will was always rational, there was
correspondingly less need to affirm that he must always seek to
abide by objective moral principles. In this way, a theoretical
climate receptive to a full doctrine of sovereignty was created. For
some writers during the Civil War suggested that the actual content of laws was of no great significance, so long as they were
geared to preserving the stability of the nation. Using essentially
Hobbesian arguments, they effectively asserted that whatever
pleased the prince had the force of law.

IV

IN PRAISE OF THE
ENGLISH CONSTITUTION

WHILE MOST writers were busy constructing a radical gap between the singular exercise of political power and the mass function of obedience, there emerged, with less belligerency, another image of political activity that featured co-operation in government matters by members of the community. If the main trend of thought was towards the elevation of monarchy and the consequent mystique of political affairs, the absorption of dominant social groups into the power structure of sixteenth-century England provided some writers with sufficient motive to concentrate their search for infallibility in politics on the mobilization of a communal wisdom through parliament.

Each in his specific manner, these writers developed the political implications of the Thomist clarification of natural law as the repository of a divine justice that was accessible to rational agents. Their argument was that a politically active community was an adequate preventive measure against the abuse of political power. It was a patriotic rather than partisan theory, testifying to the conviction that the coronation oath, *sub Deo et sub lege*, was not empty rhetoric in England where there existed an effective method for eliminating selfish partiality from public affairs. Manifestly present within the English nation, in the form of parliament, was a device which facilitated co-operation between crown and community in a way that denied to sectional interests the opportunity of asserting themselves in the guise of the common good. In particular, that co-operation was a means of incapacitating any monarch who might seek to promote his private advantage by disregarding the imperatives of communal justice.

Like the theorists of absolute monarchy, these writers accepted that monarchy was the form of government most conducive to social integration, and they therefore attributed to the crown a prominent position in the political spectrum. Where they differed from them was in recognizing a qualitative difference between the political structure and the universal pattern of order. Able to grasp those norms which provided the standard of legitimacy for all forms of human activity, the members of the political order were conscious participants in the divine reason. And, reason being diffused through the community, men besides the king could not be thought to lack the requisite qualities for engaging in political activity, which was the pursuit of rational objectives. In addition, it was inexpedient to entrust political matters to a single ruler, for he, like all humankind, was subject to selfishness and error. There had to be devised some method of restraining his passionate excesses. At an individual level, a man might achieve a partial victory over the promptings of his lower nature so long as he was diligent in allowing reason adequate scope to do its work. At the communal level, the effects of sin could be mitigated through combined effort. While no individual was unscathed by sin, the pooled reason of the community was a more reliable guide to rightness than the impaired faculty of the unassisted ruler. Politically organized through its representatives, a community was equipped with the institutional prerequisites for combating the detrimental effects of a fallen human nature.

Thus, the monarch might be dissuaded from acting contrary to the common welfare if he was enjoined to associate with the members of the body politic as he sought to dispense justice to the community. In particular, that process by which natural law was converted into specific rules convenient to the community ought to be a combined affair, for communal matters were dealt with largely by means of statute. A community in which king and community joined in making law was assured of beneficial government because the product of many minds was as objectively sound as any human determination could be. So convinced were writers that the English parliament was a guarantee of just policy, they declined to consider whether its enactments could ever be communally harmful. It was inconceivable that a collective wisdom might jeopardize the public well-being. Parliament, in short, was attributed with infallibility.[1]

Infallibility but not sovereignty, not if the latter is taken in the

---

[1] The doctrine of parliamentary infallibility has been noticed by Baumer, *The Early Tudor Theory of Kingship*, p. 76; and in the excellent article by R. W. K. Hinton, 'English Constitutional Theories from Sir John Fortescue to Sir John Eliot', *English Historical Review*, LXXV (1960), p. 418, n. 2.

usual sense to indicate a voluntarist conception of law. All that was being claimed was that the existence of mixed government, in which the king could not do certain things singly, was sufficient to counteract the socially damaging affects of human appetite. Parliament was a sort of filter that enabled objective standards to be incorporated into human enactments untarnished by human perversity and imperfection. It was certainly a doctrine of parliamentary omnicompetency but grounded on the assumption that the monarch in parliament was the communal embodiment of an objective reason. It did not imply that the validity of statute hinged solely on the fact that it had emerged from accepted institutional procedures and represented, therefore, the collective will of the nation. The theory was firmly in the traditional mould, adapting familiar medieval arguments in defence of limited monarchy to an English context by identifying the wisdom of the community with its assembled representatives.

Sir Roger Twysden revealed the premise on which the theory depended when, evoking the authority of Aquinas and Fortescue, he said of English statutory laws that, they 'are made with that circumspection and care they may bee well held "rationis ordinatio", and to be framed "ad bonum commune", so many beeing to concur before it can bee binding'.[1] Twysden's description of English government was out of date when he set to work on his treatise, probably in 1640. Clearly, whatever powers might be attributed to parliament were rendered inoperative if that assembly was rarely summoned by the crown. Twysden was a moderate who sought to revive the theory of limited monarchy because he countenanced with dread the likely outcome of the collision course embarked upon by crown and parliament.[2] He gave a picture of how things should be, an ideal account that would have been more appropriate a century earlier. But, as a reactionary work, *Certaine Considerations upon the Government of England* conveys the thought processes embodied in the theory of limited monarchy before 1570 when there was no felt need to challenge the medieval conception of society as a corporate entity infused with a common purpose from a political centre; and, therefore, no felt imperative to enunciate a doctrine of sovereignty.

[1] Sir Roger Twysden, *Certaine Considerations upon the Government of England*, ed. J. M. Kemble for the Camden Society (1849), p. 90.
[2] cf. Frank W. Jessup, *Sir Roger Twysden 1597–1672* (London, 1965).

In so far as the flowering of parliament during the Reformation was something of a triumph for landed groups, as well as the king, a relatively effective means of harmonizing the claims of dominant élites, it remained possible to think in terms of an integrated community that was nourished by an institutionalized collective wisdom. Only during the Civil War, when competing groups were asserting themselves in the name of the common good, did a complete doctrine of sovereignty emerge. With the collapse of political structures, and in the manifest absence of social integration, it became apparent to some that the common interest had to be superimposed through an agency that was endowed with full authority to deal with conflicting claims in whatever way was deemed necessary to obtain security. In the sixteenth century, however, there was no need to raise questions of sovereignty. There was a need to justify the co-operation of the crown with influential groups in parliament. And this could be accomplished quite adequately within a medieval framework.

The argument was that Englishmen had discovered in parliament institutional procedures for co-operating with one another in the rational order of the universe. Parliament was evidence of the fact that men were capable of taking deliberate measures to bring their activities into conformity with divine injunctions. Writers were highlighting this distinctive characteristic of humankind when they sometimes said that men were subject to the law of reason, rather than the law of nature, and it is simply mistaken to interpret this terminological innovation as an indication that belief in objective norms was beginning to fade.[1] Christopher St. German, a proponent of the theory of limited monarchy, put it very plainly: 'when the Law Eternal . . . is known to his Creatures reasonable by the light of natural Understanding . . . that is called the Law of Reason'. The language is Thomist and there is nothing in this to warrant the suggestion that a doctrine of sovereignty was beginning to unfold, nothing to indicate that the acceptance of a higher law was being eroded by a belief in the absolute validity of human law.

Parliament, then, was infallible rather than sovereign. Nothing

[1] Mosse, *The Struggle for Sovereignty in England*, p. 9: 'The sixteenth century witnessed the gradual disintegration of the medieval concept of the state, for it was during the Tudor period that the sovereignty of the "King in Parliament" emerged, while the law of reason challenged the law of nature as the higher law.'

it did could be imagined to infringe objective moral standards, which was subtly but significantly different from denying the final authority of such standards. Nevertheless, the absence of a complete doctrine of parliamentary sovereignty did not preclude a conception of man-*made* law. There is a widespread assumption, propagated in the writings of Professor McIlwain, that parliament in the early modern period was envisaged as a High Court which merely declared fundamental law.[1] This adequately characterizes seventeenth-century opinion when the supposed immutability of common law provided little scope to the idea of legislative initiative. Statutes contrary to custom were said to be null and void. In regard to the sixteenth century, however, it is inaccurate. Again we can permit the reactionary Twysden to be our guide to the late medieval world. He described parliament as a High Court precisely because it could make and unmake law, and justified its legislative capacity by reference to its presumed infallibility.

The power of parlyaments is with us so transcendent, as King James doth remember a saying of my Lord treasurer Burghley, that hee knewe not what an act of parliament could not doe in England. And, indeede, how can it bee otherwise? for that court, beeing so high as it makes law that which is not, and that which is it abolisheth, and man having found to guide his actions by but law, how can there bee any thing of greater auctority than what, upon mature and sound advise, passeth from it?[2]

For the sixteenth-century advocates of limited monarchy, statutes had to conform to the precepts of natural law rather than to custom. But we have seen that these precepts were believed by medievalists to be sufficiently flexible to allow for the derivation of more particular rules. These latter were framed according to the exigencies of everyday life and the requirements of the particular community, with its unique traditions and social practices. Natural law could be drawn out in a way that took into account the specificity of each cultural manifestation, which made the legislative organ of each community rather more than a mere executive agency

---

[1] Though English scholars have been generally more reluctant than their American counterparts to accept McIlwain's thesis. Questioning it in 1912, W. S. Holdsworth wrote: 'In the sixteenth century . . . it is clear that the supremacy of an unchangeable law, taught by Bracton and the Year Books, has come to mean, not the supremacy of an unchangeable law, but the supremacy of a law which Parliament can change. The supremacy of the law is coming to mean the supremacy of Parliament.' *Essays in Law and History*, eds. A. L. Goodhart and H. G. Hanbury (Oxford, 1946), p. 68.

[2] Twysden, *Certaine Considerations*, p. 173.

of objective standards. Government did not simply rubber-stamp general rational precepts. Its function was to shape them into communally relevant commands. Had the medieval inheritance contained a more rigid conception of natural law, writers might have been compelled to enunciate a doctrine of parliamentary sovereignty somewhat earlier than the mid-seventeenth century. As it was, they were able to suggest that parliament was a perfectly competent formula for devising a workable set of laws convenient to the English community, while adhering to the traditional idea that this legal system was but one example of a divine justice operative in the world.

As the theory of limited monarchy was elaborated by relatively few thinkers, each of its main exponents will receive separate consideration. At the end of the chapter we shall see that, though the theory of limited monarchy declined in the later part of the sixteenth century, the attributes with which parliament had been endowed were transferred more or less intact to custom in the early part of the seventeenth century.

Chronologically, a discussion of Sir John Fortescue's ideas ought to have been contained in the chapter on the medievalists, for he wrote towards the close of the fifteenth century. It is included here because, collectively, his writings vividly illustrate how the theory of limited monarchy was situated very firmly within the context of a rationally ordered universe. In addition, they are an explicit adaptation to the English scene of certain medieval political ideas. Fortescue drew upon the belief that a communal wisdom was efficacious, used the medieval idea of equity, and reworked Aquinas' distinction between regal and political government, in order to justify the English system of government as he understood it. It was largely through him that the theory of limited monarchy was given a specifically English connotation and transmitted to the early modern period.[1] Fortescue composed three works of note. *De Natura Legis Naturae*, which is usually ignored by commentators, supplies the philosophical backdrop against which the more overtly political arguments of *De Laudibus Angliae* and *The Governance of England* may be adequately comprehended.

[1] Though *De Laudibus* was the only work printed before 1714, his ideas were very influential in the early modern period. cf. Caroline A. J. Skeel, 'The influence of the Writings of Sir John Fortescue,' *Transactions of the Royal Historical Society*, 3rd Series, X (1916), pp. 77–114.

These two books have been described as 'the first treatises on the English constitution, as distinct from the more purely legal expositions of Glanvil and Bracton'.[1] In fact, they were an application to the English political context of a Thomist philosophical perspective, most fully articulated in *De Natura*.

Fortescue confirmed the traditional belief that the universe had been created by a fecund deity who manifested his rationality through an eternal law. In its regulation of the natural world, it was referred to as natural law and 'begins from the beginning of the rational creation, and varies not by time, but abides immutable'.[2] Man was subject to it throughout his temporal existence, and Fortescue cited Aquinas to the effect that his adherence was the participation of a rational being in the divine reason. Natural law being 'the truth of justice, such as human reason is capable of unfolding',[3] it was through right reason that men were enabled to direct their actions towards the attainment of felicity. All men naturally desired happiness, defined by Aristotle as '"the perfect exercise of virtues."'.[4] And the precepts of natural law taught humankind what virtuous behaviour entailed. Fortescue did not commit the pagan heresy of supposing that temporal fulfilment was the ultimate goal of mankind, which required a supernatural aid for its attainment. But, grace completing and not destroying nature, natural law was relevant to the postlapsarian condition, the difference being that men were liable to err in regard to its prescriptions. Nevertheless, they were incapable of desiring anything 'unless under expectation of good',[5] and were able to act virtuously so long as they permitted reason to function properly.

So natural law was relevant to every detail of temporal existence. In the form of a natural impulse, it had persuaded men to seek human companionship by associating in a political society governed by a monarch. By it they learned that such government was necessary to co-ordinate their diverse activities to the common good, for no community could sustain itself unless unified. In this sense,

---

[1] Max A. Shepard, 'The Political and Constitutional Theory of Sir John Fortescue', in *Essays in History and Political Theory in Honor of Charles Howard McIlwain* (Cambridge, Mass., 1936), p. 290.

[2] Fortescue, *De Natura Legis Naturae*, Pt. I, ch. v.

[3] Ibid., Pt. I, ch. xxxvii.

[4] Sir John Fortescue, *De Laudibus Legum Angliae,* trans. S. B. Chrimes (Cambridge, 1949), ch. iv.

[5] Ibid., ch. v.

argued Fortescue in typically Thomist language, the political
order duplicated the natural pattern, for, 'since art, as the Philosopher says, imitates nature so far as it can, nations have
constituted rulers for the multitude of their societies, just as nature
in everything made up from the unions of divers things, constitutes something to rule'.[1] Political activity was also natural in the
Aristotelian sense that those who excelled in wisdom and virtue
were superior to those endowed with physical strength. Relationships of superiority and inferiority were of the essence of political
life, for, 'if there were not inequality in human society, there
would be no order in that society, because the name of order imports inequality'.[2] Societies having been formed and political rule
established under the impetus of natural law, the latter continued
to define the legitimate areas of government activity. A ruler might
never contravene natural law because 'all the power of a king ought
to be applied to the good of his realm',[3] which good was encompassed within the law of nature. All man-made laws, whether
customs or statutes, had to be derived from it because they were
'instruments whereby the Divine law developes its virtues in
human actions'.[4] As rules for the dispensation of communal justice, they deserved the nomenclature of law only if they were
designed to attain that moral purpose which was their *raison
d'être*.[5]

All this was conventional, though clearly expressed. Where
Fortescue came into his own was in adapting Aquinas' distinction
between regal and political government. In addition to these two
forms, in which what pleased the prince had the status of law or
in which the king governed by laws authorized by his subjects,
Fortescue admitted the possibility of a third form that incorporated
the essential features of the other two.[6] Whether, as Fortescue
claimed, Aquinas had actually referred to a *dominium regale et
politicum* is disputable, though it is suggested that the term was
culled from the twentieth chapter of *De regimine principium*, where

---

[1] *De Natura*, Pt. I, ch. xviii.   [2] Ibid., Pt. I, ch. xxxiv.
[3] *De Laudibus*, ch. xxxvii.
[4] *De Natura*, Pt. I, ch. xliii. J. G. A. Pocock uses Fortescue to illustrate some
of the difficulties entailed by the view that customs and statutes were the embodiment of universal principles of justice: cf. *The Machiavellian Moment:
Florentine Political Thought and the Atlantic Republican Tradition* (Princeton
and London, 1975), pp. 9 ff. I regret that Pocock's work appeared too late to give
textual consideration to its many fruitful ideas.
[5] Ibid., Pt. I, ch. x.   [6] Ibid., Pt. I, ch. xvi.

Aquinas considered imperial government.[1] A more probable explanation is that the phrase represents Fortescue's own idiosyncratic refinement of the Thomist classification as a means of conceptualizing the English form of government.

What is clear is that the phrase was used in *De Natura* to refer to any form of government which, being neither purely regal nor political, combined characteristics of both in one of a variety of possible permutations. The Roman Empire had been one instance of this third type; regal because law was made by the Emperor, but political because he had governed in the common interest and his rule was not hereditary. Similarly, the government of the Jews had been a mixture: 'political, because the Judges under whom they were ruled administered everything for their common advantage . . . and their government was a royal one, because the King of all kings had ruled it as His peculiar kingdom'. Finally, contemporary England did not conform to either of the pure types. Its government was regal because laws required the authority of the king who ruled by hereditary succession, yet political because 'the kings make not laws, nor impose subsidies on their subjects, without the consent of the Three Estates of the Realm'. In *De Natura*, then, Fortescue used the concept of a *dominium regale et politicum* in a somewhat slipshod fashion. It denoted any form of government that was a hybrid, in so far as it did not conform exactly to either of the basic forms. His classification was more of a conceptual tool, used to delineate the essential features of alternative forms of government, than a device employed to advocate any particular form.

---

[1] cf. Felix Gilbert, 'Sir John Fortescue's "Dominium Regale et Politicum"', *Mediaevalia et Humanistica*, II (1943), pp. 88–97. Donald W. Hanson, *From Kingdom to Commonwealth: The Development of Civic Consciousness in English Political Thought* (Cambridge, Mass., 1970), pp. 217–252, somewhat labours the point that Fortescue found in Aquinas the seeds of a doctrine of double majesty – rather than mixed government – which could be shaped to suit the English scene. Hanson's exercise seems to be motivated by the desire to discover in Fortescue an unresolved ambiguity which was to erupt in the conflicts of the seventeenth century. The main point, surely, is that Fortescue was seeking for a convenient way of expressing a conviction shared by the other writers considered in this chapter, namely, that England was assured of sound government because the pooled wisdom of the community was brought to bear on public matters. Hypersensitivity about the precise terminology employed betrays a retrospective inclination to locate Fortescue in the spectrum of an unfolding doctrine, rather than the proper intention of conveying the main thrust and significance of his thought in the context in which it was expressed.

Even here, however, Fortescue's preference for the hybrid was barely concealed. Of importance, he suggested, was not whether a king governed regally or politically, but that he should rule justly, that is, in accordance with the precepts of natural law.[1] And *dominium regale et politicum* was to be preferred because it was most likely to have this result. Why this should be so emerged in the advice which Fortescue gave to kings ruling either regally or politically. From the advice given to political kings, it is evident that he believed that the ruler, as the most vital public figure, ought to be in possession of a prerogative that was absolute in certain circumstances. A political king could not avoid acting regally during periods of domestic or foreign war, for example, 'where time will not allow to do everything which the necessity of resisting and repelling attack requires in due form, and by process of the laws which prevail in the kingdom in the time of peace.'[2] Emergencies sometimes necessitated the king acting beyond the scope of existing law. In normal conditions, too, it was occasionally imperative for him to act outside the boundaries established by custom and statute. He was required to exercise discretion in mitigating punishments. He had, that is, to temper established law with equity, 'lest the strictness of the words of the law, confounding its intent, should hurt the common good . . . Equity, as saith Aegidius Romanus, is indulgence above what is just, for human nature always begs for pardon.'[3] Following Aegidius Romanus, and making use of an idea which formed a major ingredient of the theory of absolute monarchy, Fortescue likened the king to a 'living Law' that gave vitality to the strict letter of existing law. For human law could never be framed in a manner which took due account of all possible cases. Clearly, Fortescue perceived the advantage to the community of a king who, in a strictly defined sense, was elevated above it.

But he was acutely conscious of the dangers of unlimited rulership. Aquinas, he said, had apparently favoured a form of government in which the king had to govern by means of laws to which his subjects had assented. Such a ruler was no less powerful than a regal king, for power was the capacity to do good and a ruler who acted tyrannically was really exhibiting his impotence.[4] Here the suggestion was that a king was more likely to dispense

---

[1] *De Natura*, Pt. I, ch. xxv.
[2] Ibid., Pt. I, ch. xxv.
[3] Ibid., Pt. I, ch. xxiv.
[4] Ibid., Pt. I, ch. xxvi.

communal justice if he was obliged to associate the members of the body politic with him in the normal business of making laws. For a collective reason was able to counteract the selfishness and weakness of one man. This was the familiar Aristotelian notion that the many were qualitatively superior to a single individual: 'He who is taught by the wisdom of many, is strong in their prudence, but he who depends upon his own wit hath evidently only the wisdom of one.'[1]

Even in the relatively abstract considerations of *De Natura*, then, Fortescue indicated that the disadvantages of the two basic forms of government might be overcome in a combination which preserved the laudable characteristics of each. This third type would permit the ruler sufficient discretion to promote justice, while ensuring that he could not harm the general welfare by virtue of the fact that he was required to legislate through a communal wisdom.

It was in *De Laudibus* and *The Governance of England* that the concept of a regal and political government assumed a more precise and recommendatory meaning.

Ther bith ij kyndes off kyngdomes, of the wich that on is a lordship callid in laten *dominium regale*, and that other is callid *domminium politicum et regale*. And thai diuersen in that the first kynge mey rule his peple bi suche lawes as he makyth hym self. And therfore he mey sett vppon thain tayles and other imposicions, such as he wol hym self, with owt their assent. The secounde kynge may not rule his people bi other lawes than such as thai assenten vnto. And therefore he mey sett vpon thain non imposicions with owt thair owne assent.[2]

Equipped with this dichotomous classification, and having explained that Aquinas had preferred the latter on the grounds that it was less likely to degenerate into tyranny, Fortescue illustrated why the inhabitants of England were so much more fortunate than their French neighbours. The French king was a harsh ruler who oppressed his subjects with unreasonable laws and iniquitous impositions such as the salt tax.[3] The reason was that he governed regally, according to the Roman legal maxim that what pleased the prince had the force of law.[4] In England, in contrast, the people

[1] Ibid., Pt. I, ch. xxiii.
[2] Sir John Fortescue, *The Governance of England*, ed. Charles Plummer (London, 1926), ch. i.
[3] Ibid., ch. iv, and *De Laudibus*, ch. xxxv.
[4] *De Laudibus*, ch. ix.

could limit rulership to good effect because their king was regal and political. He could, therefore, neither make nor alter laws, nor burden the people with taxes, without obtaining the 'assent of his whole realm expressed in his parliament'.[1]

Trying to explain the difference between the two countries, Fortescue offered an account of the origins of their respective governments. Regal government had originated in conquest, the French people ultimately accepting the patrimony of the aggressor as the lesser of two evils. But political government emanated from a conscious decision by a number of people to form themselves into a political society. The transition to this state of affairs entailed the appointment of a governor, for a politically headless society was as absurd a notion as an acephalous natural body. Using argument by correspondence, Fortescue held that the emergence of political society was analogous to the birth of the natural body from the embryo. From the intention of the people to provide for their common well-being there issued 'a body mystical, governed by one man as head'. Corresponding to the heart from which all life sprang, the will of the people was the animating nucleus of the mystical body politic, communicating to head and members alike its intention that government should be conducted in accordance with just laws.

The law, indeed, by which a group of men is made into a people, resembles the nerves of the body physical, for, just as the body is held together by the nerves, so this body mystical is bound together and united into one by the law . . . and the members and bones of this body which signify the solid basis of truth by which the community is sustained, preserve their rights through the law, as the body natural does through the nerves. And just as the head of the body physical is unable to change its nerves, or to deny its members proper strength and due nourishment of blood, so a king who is head of the body politic is unable to change the laws of that body, or to deprive that same people of their own sustenance uninvited or against their wills . . . a king of this sort is obliged to protect the law, the subjects, and their bodies and goods, and he has power to this end issuing from the people, so that it is not permissible for him to rule his people with any other power'.[2]

The kingdom of England having 'blossomed forth' in this way, the rights and properties of its people received adequate protection. For the monarch might not enact law nor abrogate old law

[1] Ibid., ch. xxxvi.   [2] Ibid., ch. xiii.

without winning the approval of the people in parliament. In a passage explaining the substantive soundness of English statutory law, Fortescue expressed most clearly the doctrine of parliamentary infallibility, the belief that a combined wisdom could never devise rules that were deficient in respect of the common good. In a regal kingdom, corrupt laws were enacted frequently, sometimes because the ruler was selfish and sometimes because he did not give sufficient thought to their formulation.

But the statutes of England cannot so arise, since they are made not only by the prince's will, but also by the assent of the whole realm, so they cannot be injurious to the people nor fail to secure their advantage. Furthermore, it must be supposed that they are necessarily replete with prudence and wisdom, since they are promulgated by the prudence not of one counsellor nor of a hundred only, but of more than three hundred chosen men—of such a number as once the Senate of the Romans was ruled by . . . And if statutes ordained with such solemnity and care happen not to give full effect to the intention of the makers, they can speedily be revised, and yet not without the assent of the commons and nobles of the realm, in the manner in which they first originated.[1]

Laws that were the product of co-operative effort were necessarily shaped by right reason to the common good. While the French king could do in practice whatever he pleased because his subjects were without institutional devices for holding him within the prescriptions of natural law, the English king was obliged to associate with the members of the community in legislative matters. Political reason being shared by head and members of the English body politic through the legislative process, just and communally beneficial government was the ineluctable consequence.

Like Fortescue, whose *De Laudibus* he acknowledged as having read,[2] Christopher St. German was a lawyer by profession. He never set out to construct a systematic political theory. Yet he did express, albeit in a somewhat disparate fashion, the essential tenets of the theory of limited monarchy. More than any of his contemporaries, St. German elaborated the capacity of human reason to devise appropriate communal rules,[3] and it is against this

---

[1] Ibid., ch. xviii.
[2] St. German, *Doctor and Student*, p. 276.
[3] cf. Paul Vinogradoff, 'Reason and Conscience in Sixteenth-Century Jurisprudence', *Law Quarterly Review*, XXIV (1908), pp. 373–84.

background that his assertion of parliamentary competency must be read. For, spanning the Reformation period, the idea was used to justify the monarch's assumption of the spiritual powers of the papacy.

Doctor and Student was originally published in 1523, and its intention was to set forth the grounds of English law. At the outset, St. German sought to illustrate how all valid law derived from the eternal law, known as the law of reason in its application to humankind. St. German admitted that the rational faculty was often 'culpable . . . either because she is deceived with an Error that might be overcome, or else through her pride or Slothfulness she enquireth not for Knowledge of the Truth that ought to be enquired'.[1] Nevertheless, reason was an indispensable guide to right behaviour. Implanted in each individual was a natural facility of the soul, known as *sinderis*, which inclined him to harness reason in search of the good. Through it, he learned that evil was to be abhorred, truth sought, and justice done. In addition, from these general precepts reason could derive more particular determinations 'which be as necessary Conclusions derived of the first. As of that Commandment, that Good is to be beloved; it followeth, that a man should love his Benefactor.'[2] This was the usual Thomist view that reason was competent to direct men to virtuous behaviour in the detailed circumstances of daily life.

St. German wove this conviction that reason was applicable to the contingencies of existence into his discussion of human law. He believed, for example, that it could formulate laws relevant to the needs of the given community. Thus, a requisite property of a law was that it be 'convenient for the Place and Time'.[3] And he classified laws operative in England according to whether they were universally valid or peculiar to this one country. To illustrate the second type, which he included under the rubric of the law of reason secondary, St. German gave as an instance a situation in which a man had impounded an animal belonging to one of his tenants who had failed to pay his rent. The animal subsequently died from lack of food, and the question arose as to who was responsible for its death. According to English custom, the owner of the beast was at fault in refusing to pay his dues. And this custom, indicated St. German, was rationally defensible.

---

[1] *Doctor and Student*, p. 43.
[2] Ibid., p. 7.   [3] Ibid., p. 12.

In another sense, too, he outlined the ability of reason to apply law to particular cases. Equity was called for when a strict adherence to the letter of the law would thwart its original intention. 'Wherefore in some Cases it is necessary to leave the Words of the Law, and to follow that Reason and Justice requireth, and to that Intent Equity is ordained; that is to say, to temper and mitigate the Rigor of the Law.'[1] Thus, though English law prohibited anyone from entering freehold property without the owners' permission, reason made an exception should cattle stray into a field of corn. The law could be legitimately ignored on this occasion to prevent the crop being destroyed.

St. German was evidently convinced that reason was able to devise even the most detailed rules for promoting the general welfare. And it is within this context that his affirmation of the efficacy of a collective reason in statutory matters may be understood.

There is no Statute made in this Realme but by the Assent of the Lords Spiritual and Temporal, and of all the Commons, that is to say, by the Knights of the Shire, Citizens and Burgesses, that be chosen by Assent of the Commons, which in the Parliament represent the Estate of the whole Commons: And every Statute there made is of as strong Effect in the Law, as if all the Commons were there present personally at the making thereof.[2]

The fact that English statutory law was made by a representative assembly of the nation provided a safeguard against the possibility of unjust enactments. For it was unimaginable that such a body of men would 'recite a thing against the truth'.

In his later works, this idea of parliamentary infallibility was exploited in order to dispel the alarm of those who objected to the king being made Supreme Head of the English Church. In *An answere to a letter*, for example, he adopted Fortescue's classification to establish the superiority of the English form of government.

And here it is to be noted/that there be two maner of powers that kynges and princes haue ouer theire subiectes: The one is called/Jus regale/that is to saye a kyngely gouernaunce: And he that hathe that power maye with his counsell make lawes to bynde his subiectes/and also make declaration of Scrypture for the good order of his subiected/ as nede shall requyre/for appeasyng of varyance. The other is called/

---

[1] Ibid., p. 48.   [2] Ibid., p. 272.

Jus regale politicum/that is to saye a kyngle and a polytyke gouernaunce. And that is the most noble power that any prince hath ouer his subiectes/ and he that ruleth by that power/maye makes no Lawe to bynde his subiectes without their assent/but by their assent he maye so that the lawes that he maketh be nat agaynste the lawe of God/nor the lawe of reason: And this power hathe the kynges of grace in this Realme: where he by assente of his lordes spirytuall and temperall: and of his common gathered togyther by his commaundement in his parlyamente maye make lawes to bynde the people And of those law/there neeeth no pclomation/bicause they be made by all the people/for the pliament so gathered togyther/representeth the estate of al the people within this realme/that is to say of the whole catholyque churche therof.[1]

There was no justification in curtailing the power of the English monarch to purely temporal matters because he was required to exercise his legislative prerogative in conjunction with the whole community gathered in parliament. For, 'why shuld nat the parlyament than whiche representeth the whole catholyke churche of Englande expoiunde scrypture rather than the conuocacyon which representeth onely the state of the clergy'. The implication was that the essential substantive characteristic of all English statutory law was secured by the fact that it was the responsibility of a representative assembly of the entire realm. It was illogical, therefore, to object to the extension of the prerogative of the crown to matters of spiritual legislation.

We have already seen that Thomas Starkey was a radical, using the turbulence of Reformation to advocate an extensive programme of social, economic and political reforms. This surely explains why his *Dialogue between Reginald Pole and Thomas Lupset* was not published until the nineteenth century. Influenced by the thought of Marsilius of Padua,[2] Starkey felt that England still had some way to go in the direction of communally limited rulership. But he shared with Fortescue and others the basic assumption that the community must be in possession of institutional devices to ensure that politics remained the pursuit of rational objectives.

The dignity of man as a rational agent was a constant theme of the *Dialogue*. God had singled out man to be a special object of His creative wisdom, making him an 'earthly god' by endowing him with a rational faculty. Starkey admitted that men were fre-

---

[1] Christopher St. German, *An answere to a letter* (London, 1535?), ch. vii.
[2] cf. Franklin le van Baumer, 'Thomas Starkey and Marsilius of Padua', *Politica*, 2 (1936–7), pp. 188–205.

quently moved by passion, but he expressed the optimistic conviction that,

none there is so rude and beastly, but, with care and diligence, by that same sparkle of reason given of God, they may subdue their affections and follow the life to the which they be institute and ordained of God; the which order when man with reason followeth, he is then governed by the providence of God; like as, contrary, when he be negligence suffer this reason to be overcome with vicious effects, then he, so blinded, liveth contrary to the ordinance of God and falleth utterly out of His providence, and is led by his own ignorance.[1]

It was reason, operating in conjunction with a natural impulse, that persuaded men to gather into societies and to establish government. For, while naturally inclined to a life which facilitated the cultivation of virtue and the exchange of knowledge, it was reason which enabled them to advance from a rudimentary form of woodland existence to their present condition. Starkey laid special emphasis on this 'diligence of man' in bringing to completion the natural desire for perfection when he explained why human laws were necessary. For reason had a truly creative function in drawing conclusions known as civil laws out of the general precepts of natural law. 'Devised by the politic wit of man', such laws were an example of how effective reason was in dealing with the detailed requirements of social life.[2]

When he described the ideal society, Starkey resorted to argument by correspondence in order to emphasize the necessity of mutual co-operation for obtaining that good which all men sought. The diversified and unified structure contingent upon such mutual assistance was comparable to the natural body, for strength in both depended upon the various parts performing their assigned duties. Detailing the correspondences existing between the two bodies, he likened the heart to the ruler, the head to other officers, the hands to craftsmen and soldiers, the feet to agricultural workers

---

[1] Starkey, *A Dialogue between Reginald Pole and Thomas Lupset*, p. 153.
[2] Ibid., p. 32: 'This law taketh effect of the opinion of man; it resteth wholly in his consent, and varieth according to the place and time, insomuch that in diverse time and place contrary laws are both good and both convenient to the political life . . . [The law of nature] is the ground and end of the other, to the which it must ever be referred, none otherwise than the conclusions of arts mathematical are ever referred to their principles . . . For all good civil laws spring and issue out of the law of nature, as brooks and rivers out of fountains and wells.'

and so on.[1] Starkey went on to characterize the ills of the body politic in terms of diseases which afflicted the natural body. A society in which craftsmen and ploughmen were slow in performing their allotted tasks, for instance, was like a body in which the hands and feet were smitten with gout.

Starkey did not, however, use analogical argument in a way which precluded members of the body politic from being politically active. Here his conception of politics as the pursuit of rationally discernible objectives was prominent. It was by means of wise laws, which Starkey likened to the soul that transmitted life to the body, that justice was mediated to the community. And, as a man governed by passion could never attain perfection, so, too, could a community never obtain justice unless its affairs were disposed of rationally.[2] Tyranny was rooted in the frailties of human nature, those temptations which all men had to allow their bestial aspects to predominate. This was why it was inexpedient to remove a ruler from the control of those who were subject to him. Sharing in the dualism of all mankind, the king was liable to succumb to the influence of passion, with disastrous consequences. 'For what is more repugnant to nature, than a whole nation to be governed by the will of a prince, which ever followeth his frail fantasy and unruled affects? What is more contrary to reason than all the whole people to be ruled by him which commonly lacketh all reason?'[3] It was because of this possibility that the community ought not to be politically passive. Political activity was not excluded from the principle that God required man's active co-operation in the government of the universe. Starkey explicitly denied the belief that political matters were properly disposed of in heaven.

to say, as many men do, that the providence of God ordaineth tyrans for the punishment of the people, this agreeth nothing with philosophy nor reason; no, nor yet to the doctrine of Christ and good religion. For by the same mean . . . you might say that it is the providence of God that

---

[1] Ibid., p. 153: 'Even as every particular man, when he followeth reason, is governed by God, and, contrary, blinded with ignorance by his own vain opinion so whole nations, when they live togidder in civil order institute and governed by reasonable policy, are then governed by the providence of God, and be under His tuition; as, contrary, when they are without good order and politic rule, they are ruled by the violence of tyranny—they are not governed by His providence nor celestial ordinance, but as a man governed by affects, so they be tormented infinite ways by the reason of such tyrannical power.'

[2] Ibid., p. 104.   [3] Ibid., p. 57.

every particular man followeth his affects, blinded with ignorance and folly, and so it would follow, the folly and vice cometh out of the providence of God, which is no way to be admitted but only this: that the providence of God hath ordained, of His goodness, such a creature to be, which may by his own folly follow his own affects. But when he doth so, this is sure: he followeth not the ordinance of God, but overcome by pleasure and blinded with ignorance flieth from it and slippeth from his own dignity. Therefore never attribute tyranny (of all ill the greatest) to the providence of God . . . But . . . attribute this tyranny partly to the malice of man, who by nature is ambitious and of all pleasure most desirous, and partly to negligence of the people, which suffer themselves to be oppressed therewith.[1]

So it was communal inactivity which encouraged tyranny to flourish.

Starkey argued that rulers might be legitimately controlled on the grounds that they were agents of the community in which ultimate authority resided, a Marsilian assumption. It was for the community, therefore, to determine an appropriate form of government. It might choose to be governed by an individual, a counsel of the wise, or by a larger number. What mattered was that government should seek the common good, which was why rulers ought to be hedged in with restrictions. An elected ruler was to be preferred because he was easier to control or remove should he degenerate into a tyrant. For, 'this is in man's power: to elect and choose him that is both wise and just, and make him a prince; and him that is a tyran, so to depose'.[2] The members of the community had only themselves to blame if they provided ineffective limitations to rulership.

In outlining his proposals for the reform of English government, Starkey claimed that the country had been insufficiently diligent in holding its rulers to account. Whereas Fortescue thought that England possessed the paradigm of a well-balanced constitution, Starkey evidently believed that the balance had been allowed to swing in favour of the monarch. Consequently, England had been governed by princes 'which by their regal power and princely authority have judged all things pertaining to the state of our ream to hang only upon their will and fantasy . . . It is thought that all wholly hangeth upon his only arbitrament.'[3] Even the existence of parliament provided no guarantee against the abuse of power

[1] Ibid., p. 154.   [2] Ibid., p. 153.   [3] Ibid., p. 99.

because it had been through statutes that the royal prerogative had been extended to the extent that the king was able to abrogate laws at his pleasure.

Recognizing that English government was parliamentary in character, Starkey's plans for reform centred on that assembly. He thought it expedient, for instance, to replace hereditary by elected monarchy, the ruler being chosen by parliament. But he was willing to modify his proposals to suit English conditions in that antagonistic factions, each supporting their own candidate for the office, might bring the nation to the verge of civil war.

If election was unacceptable, there was greater need to invent devices that would prevent arbitary government. Here Starkey drew upon the basic assumption of this strain of thought, that a combined wisdom was more reliable than that of one man. 'For this is sure: the wit of one commonly cannot compass so much as the wit of many, in matter of policy; for it is commonly said: "Many eyes see better than one".'[1] To permit the monarch singly to deal with public matters was openly to invite tyranny. Parliament, therefore, ought to reassert its privileges in order to prevent the king from overriding laws which it had wisely enacted. In addition, it ought to appoint a counsel of wise men, composed of lords, judges, citizens, and headed by the Constable of England, which, endowed with authority to act on behalf of parliament when it was not in session, might ensure that the king and his counsel proper governed in accordance with existing law. Responsible for matters like the making of war and peace, it was to have the power to recall parliament whenever the general welfare was in jeopardy. Starkey also suggested that the king's counsel proper should be chosen more carefully in order that his actions and judgements might always be tempered with the advice of the wise.

If England adopted these expedients, it would approximate closer to the ideal of a 'mixed state' in which no member was so powerful that he could harm the public good. 'For when any one part hath full authority, if that part chance to be corrupt with affects . . . the rest shall suffer the tyranny thereof and be put in great misery.'[2] It was, in short, by enclosing the ruler within the wisdom of the community that the common good would be protected. The community could safeguard itself against the abuse

[1] Ibid., p. 101.   [2] Ibid., p. 165.

of political power only if it was prepared to mobilize itself for political activity.

Sir Thomas Smith was English ambassador to France when he wrote *De Repvblica Anglorvm* in 1565. He 'was not a philosopher. He was a man of affairs, a jurist, a scholar, a man of the world of practical politics.'[1] His non-philosophical outlook probably explains why he conducted his enquiry into the English system of government without alluding to a system of objective precepts that was accessible to man as a rational being. There are no grounds for assuming that this omission is an indication of the fact that natural law no longer played a significant role in contemporary thinking.[2] There is nothing in Smith's book to suggest that he was so radically out of step with the conventional wisdom as to find the conception of a rationally ordered universe unacceptable; nothing to signify that he was an isolated harbinger of a novel world view. His discussion of politics certainly had a traditional flavour, in that he used Aristotelian and other established notions. It is reasonable to suppose, therefore, that his work exhibits the growing confidence of some in parliament as an institution geared to securing the common good. It would appear that Smith was so sure that a representative body of the nation could not enact unjust laws that he felt no imperative to spell out the fact that its determinations were subject to a higher standard. This was simply assumed. If this assessment is accurate, his readiness to discuss parliament without reference to natural law indicates that he took the doctrine of parliamentary infallibility to be incontrovertible.

Smith concurred with Aristotle's judgement that man was naturally inclined to associate with his fellows, so that only a beast or a god could dispense with political society. Still with Aristotle, he held that government originated in the household because nations emerged when families expanded in size and number and formed themselves into larger groups. Using the Aristotelian classification of governments, he suggested that all three types were acceptable, so long as they were suited to the character of the people and were directed to their general well-being and peaceful coexistence. He believed, in fact, that long-established societies had experienced all three forms, including their perverted analogical

---

[1] Allen, *A History of Political Thought in the Sixteenth Century,* p. 263.

[2] cf. Mosse, *The Struggle for Sovereignty in England,* ch. i, and 'Change and Continuity in the Tudor Constitution', *Speculum,* XXII (1947), pp. 18–28.

types, at some stage in their history. The reason was that, like the natural body, the body politic was subject to mutability.[1] Recognition of the impermanence of political arrangements, due partly to the fact that men were for ever striving to improve their earthly lot,[2] probably explains why Smith thought that government in pure form was to be found but rarely. In nature, the four elements and humours of man were invariably mixed in varying proportions. And governments, too, were usually a mixture of the three types, their description deriving from the element which was predominant.

His remarks about absolute monarchy, which he practically identified with tyranny, reveal that he recognized the advantages of a form of mixed government. The term tyranny, he observed, was originally a neutral concept that was used to denote absolute power in which the ruler was unrestrained by law. The term eventually assumed an odious connotation because, generally speaking, absolute rulers had been evil, each seeking 'to satisfie his vicious and cruell appetite, without respect of God, of right or of the law'.[3] Apart from wartime, when exceptional circumstances demanded that existing laws be overridden, absolute power was inherently dangerous because of 'the frailtie of mans nature, which (as Plato saith) cannot abide or beare long that absolute and uncontrowled authoritie, without swelling into too much pride and insolencie'.[4] This was the familiar idea that unlimited monarchy was harmful to the community because of the sinful aspects of human nature which tempted the holder of political office to pursue his private advantage. The alternative was to erect barriers against tyranny from within the community. And this entailed the community being organized for legislative matters. Smith thought communal participation in lawmaking to be such an essential feature of good government that he incorporated its absence into his definition of tyranny.

Where one person beareth the rule they define that to be the estate of a king, who by succession or election commeth with the good will of the people to that gouernement, and doth administer the common wealth by the lawes of the same and by equitie, and doth seeke the profit of the people as much as his owne. A tyraunt they name him, who by force commeth to the Monarchy against the will of the people, breaketh

---

[1] Smith, *De Repvblica Anglorvm*, p. 4.
[2] Ibid., p. 22.   [3] Ibid., p. 9.   [4] Ibid., p. 8.

lawes alreadie made at his pleasure, maketh other without the aduise and consent of the people, and regardeth not the wealth of his communes but the aduancement of him selfe, his faction, & kindred. These definitions do containe three differences: the obtaining of the authoritie, the maner of adminiotration thereof, & the butte or marke whereunto it doth tend and shotte.[1]

The implication was that the consent of 'the whole bodie and the three estates of the common wealth' to the ruler's activities was an effective device for securing the public good. Smith mentioned France, where the monarch made and unmade laws, and imposed taxes, at his pleasure, as a contemporary instance of tyranny — at least, he said that it was judged to be so by some, without deferring from their opinion.

It is within this context, the assumption that communal participation in political affairs provided a safeguard to the common good, that his analysis of the English system of government may be understood. English government, he held, had been parliamentary in character for several centuries, because King John's action in resigning the crown to the papacy had been invalidated by its failure to be 'established by act of parliament'.[2] At the centre of the English system stood the king, 'the life, the head, and the authoritie of all thinges that be doone in the realme of England'.[3] He was absolute in time of war and his prerogative was extensive in other matters. He had discretionary powers in regard to coinage, he could temper the letter of the law with equity in pardoning offenders, and it was his function to appoint important officers of the realm. There remained much, however, which the monarch could do only with the 'mature deliberation' of the members of parliament.

The most high and absolute power of the realme of Englande, consisteth in the Parliament. For as in warre where the king himselfe in person, nobilitie, the rest of the gentilitie, and the yeomanrie are, is y force and power of Englande: so in peace & consultation where the Prince is to giue life, and the last and highest commaundement, the Baronie for the nobilitie and highyer: the knightes, esquiers, gentlemen and commons for the lower part of the common wealth, the bishoppes for the clergie bee present to aduertise, consult and shew what is good and necessarie for the common wealthe'.[4]

---

[1] Ibid., p. 6.   [2] Ibid., p. 10.   [3] Ibid., p. 47.
[4] Ibid., p. 34.

Operating largely through law, parliament was entitled to interfere with private rights, alter the manner of monarchical succession, sanction taxes, issue pardons, establish a form of religion, and generally do whatever was necessary for the common benefit. For, parliament 'hath the power of the whole realme both the head and the bodie. For euerie Englishmen is entended to bee there present, either in person or by procuration and attornies . . . And the consent of Parliament is taken to be euerie mans consent.'[1]

It was suggested, then, that parliament was an adequate device for taking care of public matters. That which was dealt with there was 'the whole realmes deede: whereupon iustlie no man can complaine but must accommodate himselfe to finde it good and obey it'.

Obedience to law might well be conditional upon it being directed towards the common good. But the existence of parliament, Smith intimated, was the guarantee that this condition was met in England. Law could be presumed just and communally beneficial because it was framed by a representative assembly of the nation. Smith's work represents the maturation of that strain of thinking which sought limits to kingship through the combined wisdom of the community. Once it was accepted that a collective reason was incapable of damaging the general welfare, there was correspondingly less need to affirm that what parliament enacted was subject to supra-legal standards of rightness. Parliamentary infallibility ensured that the essential moral component of statutory law was secured.

With Smith, the theory of mixed government or limited monarchy reached its climax and from then until the eve of the Civil War, when it was resuscitated and used by both sides,[2] its appearance was sparse. Not that it was forgotten entirely. *De Repvblica Anglorvm* was reprinted several times. But fresh expressions of the theory were rare. The notable exception was James Whitelocke's famous parliamentary speech against impositions in 1610, in which he located regal authority within parliament where the king was 'assisted with the consent of the whole state'.[3] Other writers expounded the theory in a much more diluted form, and

[1] Ibid., p. 35.

[2] cf. C. C. Weston, 'The Theory of Mixed Monarchy Under Charles I and After', *English Historical Review*, LXXV (1960), pp. 426–43.

[3] T. B. Howell, *A Complete Collection of State Trials* (London, 1816), II, p. 482.

their rehearsal of familiar arguments ought not to blind us to the fact that they were no longer enunciating a doctrine of parliamentary omnicompetence.

William Camden referred to Fortescue in his *Discourse Concerning the Prerogative of the Crown*, written some time before 1623, in support of his claim that English government was mixed because law was made with the assent of king and community. Yet, besides stressing the monarch's exclusive prerogative in issuing proclamations, Camden effectively denied the supremacy of statute:

for if the law have not the use it should have, [and if] custom, general for a long time, finding it inconvenient hath decried it by it[s] practice, the law is utterly disanulled, and if it be a statute the penalty taken off; and it is very good reason that if the use of a law be not to the good of a commonwealth (whereby it wants that which should make it a law, for all law is justice and justice which the philosopher calls legal aimeth at the good of the commonwealth), I say then if that which is called law aimeth not at the end a law should aim at, it is good reason that a general and long continued custom should be sufficient testimony against it.[1]

Custom, it seems, was a more reliable indication of communal justice than the deliberations of the wise assembled in parliament.

This was a significant shift from the doctrine of parliamentary infallibility, and was by no means atypical.[2] The sixteenth-century advocates of limited monarchy had defended the authority of parliament more vigorously than this, and they had certainly not demoted its enactments to what, in effect, were enactments of common law. It was with a mixture of relief and delight that they had found none of the essential features of good government to be absent from the constitution, not only because the king had to legislate with the approval of the community in normal circumstances, but also because those joint determinations constituted the highest law in the land. What impressed them most about the political system was the existence of a monarch powerful enough

[1] Frank Smith Fussner, 'William Camden's "Discourse Concerning the Prerogative of the Crown"', *Procs. of the American Philosophical Society*, 101 (1957), pp. 212–13.

[2] 'In many cases,' according to Coke, 'the common law will control acts of Parliament and sometimes adjudge them to be utterly void: for when an act of Parliament is against common right and reason, or repugnant, or impossible to be performed, the common law will control it and adjudge such acts to be void.' Cited in J. W. Allen, *English Political Thought 1603–1660* (London, 1938), p. 63.

to provide for the common good, yet incapable of governing arbitrarily because he was practically restrained by the wisdom of the gathered nation. It was now being admitted that the latter, parliament, might err and that, when it did so, its members must be content to defer to a higher authority, that of custom.

This sanctification of custom was a far cry from the supposed infallibility of statute. To some of the sixteenth-century advocates of reform by statute, custom appeared as the embodiment of an unreason that required purification by means of parliamentary enactment. How could it be otherwise when they were supporting a disjuncture in the course of English history which, they believed, would lay the foundation for much needed social and economic reforms? In his tract on obedience, where his intention was to defend the break from Rome, Starkey emphasized the role of government in sweeping away the accumulated debris of the past, particularly outmoded ecclesiastical rites and customs. In the *Dialogue*, where his concern was to purge the body politic of its ailments, Starkey went much further in identifying custom as the depository of impediments to the general welfare. He wrote in reference to the law of primogeniture, and making use of the myth of the Norman Yoke that was to become so popular in the Civil War,[1] that, 'if we will restore our country to a perfit state with a true common weal, we must shake off all such tyrannical customs and unreasonable bonds institute by that tyran when he subdued our country and nation'.[2] This was an extreme statement, perhaps, even for the times. But neither Fortescue nor St. German, though certainly less radical than Starkey, spoke of the inviolability of custom. St. German argued that municipal customs were rationally defensible so long as they were shaped according to the precepts of natural law which, he felt, they usually were. But this did not entail a blanket justification of every single custom. One of the reasons preferred for the introduction of written law, for example, was that the law of reason 'was greatly lett and blinded by evil Customs'.[3] Even when not fully spelt out by the theorists of limited

---

[1] cf. Christopher Hill, *Puritanism and Revolution* (London, 1958), pp. 50–122; J. G. A. Pocock, *The Ancient Constitution and the Feudal Law; A Study of English Historical Thought in the Seventeenth Century* (Cambridge, 1957); Quentin Skinner, 'History and Ideology in the English Revolution', *Historical Journal*, VIII (1965), pp. 151–78.

[2] Starkey, *A Dialogue between Reginald Pole and Thomas Lupset*, pp. 110–11.

[3] St. German, *Doctor and Student*, p. 6.

monarchy, the implication was that, occasionally or frequently, custom had to bow before a more certain guide as the what was communally beneficial. And this was a communal wisdom channelled through parliament.

What had happened in the intervening period was that confidence in parliament, as the guarantee of the nation's welfare, had been eroded. The theory persisted so long as there was a reasonable degree of harmony between crown and parliament, and the former was not tempted by parliamentary intransigence to seek other sources of taxation. There was little point in continuing to represent parliament as the great bulwark against arbitrary monarchy when it was becoming increasingly apparent that a major slice of government business was being dealt with by such means as private petitioning to the privy council, and when parliament was emerging more and more as an expedient to be occasionally employed by the crown in an effort to overcome its financial straits. In these circumstances, the way to counter the arbitrary encroachments of the monarch was not to affirm the parliamentary basis of his prerogative, a double-edged weapon that could be used by the crown as an excuse to summon parliament at its pleasure to do its bidding, but to attribute supremacy to a law which neither king nor parliament, and especially the king, could make or abrogate. The theory of limited monarchy yielded before the presumed omnicomptency of common law.

The reverence which was accorded to common law in the seventeenth century has been adequately documented, especially in Professor Pocock's fine work, *The Ancient Constitution and the Feudal Law*. What, to my knowledge, has not been noticed is that custom was now viewed in the same perspective as parliament had been in the sixteenth century. For its admirers, custom testified to the capacity of social man to make provision for himself in the context of a rational universe, just as parliament had done for its supporters in the previous century. Custom provided concrete evidence that natural law could be lengthened out to meet the needs of each community,[1] distilled and secreted in local practices by generation upon generation of men as they sought a rational resolution to the problems of communal living. In his great eulogy to common law, Sir John Davies suggested that no other sort of

---

[1] For examples of how common law was understood to be an embodiment of natural law, see Judson, *The Crisis of the Constitution*, pp. 53–4.

human law had 'more harmonie of reason in it', none was such a perfect embodiment of natural law.[1] Unlike statute, which was superimposed upon the nation without having undergone a 'probationary' period, a custom became established only after some social practice had been found to be beneficial by repeated experience.

There was, too, the same patriotic conviction that England constituted the best of all existing worlds. It was no longer parliament which made England the envy of other nations but, so it was said, its possession of a system of law that had evolved to meet every contingency. England, said Davies, had been alone among European nations in declining to import the alien civil or Roman law, and he endowed his native custom with the same aura of infallibility which had previously shrouded parliamentary legislation: 'the iudgment and reason of [our Common Law] is more certain than of any other human Law in the world: as well because the grounds of our Common Law haue from the beginning bin laid with such deep wisdome, policie, and prouidence, as that they do prouide for and meet with, almost all places that can possibly fall out in our Common-wealth'.[2]

As parliament had been for an earlier generation, custom was now taken as evidence of the superiority of a collective wisdom in ensuring the justice of communal affairs. The divine wisdom was at work in the world, gradually revealing itself as men learned to live together by a process of trial and error, amending their arrangements when they were confronted by novel situations and depositing their accumulated experience in a uniquely complex, but none the less rational, system of regulations.

The difference between statute and custom, of course, was that the latter was created by the non-assembled members of the community. Even so, the Aristotelian idea that wisdom tended to be concentrated in a minority did not disappear. It had previously been expressed in Marsilius' distinction between the small number who framed proposals and the citizenry who endowed them with the status of law, and in the sixteenth-century belief that parliament represented the most refined wisdom of the community. The idea now reappeared in the guise of the judiciary. While the

[1] Sir John Davies, *A Discourse of Law and Lawyers*, in *The Works*, ed. A. B. Grosart (Printed for private circulation, 1876), II p. 255.
[2] Ibid., II, p. 261.

soundness of custom was proven by its tacit acceptance by the members of the community through time, it was animated by the practical wisdom of a small group which was equipped with the necessary expertise to make it operative on all relevant occasions. By their skill in applying common law to particular cases, the judges gave 'life and motion vnto Iustice'.[1]

An immediate effect of the decline of limited monarchy in the late sixteenth and early seventeenth centuries, therefore, was not the dissolution of the picture of society as a corporate entity with an internal identity and common purpose. The conceptualization of common law did not herald the arrival of bourgeois theory and the growth of individualist assumptions. By adding an historical dimension to the claims made on behalf of a collective wisdom, commentators gave weight to the belief that divine providence was unfolding itself in human affairs in a manner not immediately or directly amenable to fallible individual reason. Neither logic nor will, certainly not the arbitrary decisions of the single monarch, were adequate measures of the common good. Prescription, that which had been tried, tested, handed down by countless generations and synthesized in intricate social forms, was a sufficient guide to action. For the existence of custom signified that men had been co-operating with one another and with God in the rational order of the universe since time immemorial. It was to that order, or, rather, the peculiar English manifestation of it, that each individual had to accommodate his demands, because it contained a wisdom which he could never fully comprehend and against which his unaided judgement appeared feeble. We shall see that similar ideas had been used already in the sixteenth century, in Richard Hooker's great work, *Of the Laws of Ecclesiastical Polity*.

[1] Ibid., II, p. 273.

V

RICHARD HOOKER

Of the *Laws of Ecclesiastical Polity* is the most systematic and stylistically beautiful exploration in English of the theme of a rationally ordered universe. It was conceived in an effort to resolve the consciences of those who found certain contemporary arrangements defective, and so morally indefensible. Hooker's purpose was to undermine the case of those Puritans who condemned the practices of the established Church on the grounds that they were unscriptural. In opposition to an essentially unhistorical approach, which searched for evidence of human perversity in existing institutions and hoped to see the things of this world topple before the rigorous standards of the Almighty Word, Hooker endeavoured to 'portray the state as something inherently rational . . . To comprehend what is, this is the task of philosophy, because what is, is reason . . . To recognize reason as the rose in the cross of the present and thereby to enjoy the present, this is the rational insight which reconciles us to the actual.'[1] The words, of course, are Hegel's, but they would not be out of place in the preface to Hooker's treatise. Hegel sought to portray the State as the objective manifestation of its members, an historically evolved, concrete scheme of life in which the individual's striving for freedom was made actual. Likewise, Hooker's intention was to reveal the rational structure of the Elizabethan State in order that its members might consciously identify with it and willingly comply with its legal requirements.

Like many of the theorists of absolute monarchy, Hooker was preoccupied with the problem of dissidence and he, too, emphasized unity as a primary political value. Unlike them, he did not mystify political activity. He admitted that it fell within the scope of human reason which, from a political perspective, was a property of the corporate community. On the assumption that human laws and practices were morally defensible in so far as they

[1] F. Hegel, *Philosophy of Right*, trans. T. M. Knox (Oxford, 1952), pp. 11–12.

accorded with reason, Hooker argued that laws and practices which had been devised by the practical wisdom of many, and subsequently tried by experience, were indeed rational. In this way, the belief that that a collective wisdom was a more reliable guide than the fallible judgement of a small group of individuals in communal matters was invoked in order to cast suspicion on those who doubted the validity of existing practices.

By linking familiar arguments in defence of political stability with those affirming the competence of a communal reason in political matters, Hooker placed political society firmly within the context of a rationally ordered universe. God was working His purpose out through the practical operations of many men in history, so that the self-styled arbiters of godly rule who were unable 'to enjoy the present' were nothing less than impious. Moral dilemmas in public affairs could be settled by individuals deferring to the superior collective wisdom of the community to which they belonged, for any individual who despised its determinations and practices was making a fallacious judgement that arose because of the imperfections of his Adamic nature. Extending Hegelian terminology, from an historical perspective the two strains of thought with which we have been concerned may be regarded as two moments, incorporated by Hooker into a theory which, preserving integration in a State that contained safeguards against arbitrary government, transposed them to a higher level of philosophical coherence.

Hooker's work has deservedly attracted more attention than practically any other text of the period. In the first place, he stated very clearly the basic premises from which his thinking derived, and Christopher Morris observes that *Of the Laws of Ecclesiastical Polity* 'might well be called the earliest philosophical masterpiece written in the English language'.[1] Then, again, his style has what Somerset Maugham described as the quality of gorgeousness.[2] His work has a special interest for theologians and ecclesiastical historians, in so far as they view it as the major piece of writing through which the Anglican *via media* was transmitted to the

---

[1] Morris, *Political Thought in England*, p. 175.

[2] C. S. Lewis, *English Literature in the Sixteenth Century Excluding Drama* (Oxford, 1954), p. 462: 'The style is, for its purpose, perhaps the most perfect in English. In general it is far removed from the colloquial, yet it does not strike one as a decorated style.'

modern world.[1] A major source of interest has been the detective work required to establish the authenticity of the eight books which form the work. The sixth and eighth books were first published in 1648 and the seventh in 1662, sixty-two years after Hooker's death, and it was a long held opinion that they did not represent the views of their original author. It was believed, for example, that Book VII had been tampered with by the shady Bishop Gauden to suit the ideological needs of the Restoration Church. The controversy is now settled in favour of the authenticity of the whole work, with the qualification that the later books were left possibly unpolished and incomplete.[2]

But a debate continues regarding the internal consistency of the work, the argument being that Hooker was heir to too many philosophical strands to be able to construct a coherent theory. Indeed, Hooker has been cast frequently as a sort of intellectual schizophrenic who, vainly striving to reconcile the irreconcilable, merely managed to produce a collection of dislocated ideas. His reputation has suffered in this way for several reasons. Writing at a critical juncture in intellectual history, his work has been an open quarry for commentators who, eager to gather from it evidence for the changes in consciousness which they believe were occurring at this time, proclaim that it signifies an advance in some doctrine or other, regardless of the fact that Hooker would have been bewildered by the suggestion that this is what he was about.

In addition, he used concepts that were to become current among writers during the Civil War who operated with an individualist model of man. A typical assessment is that he was 'a

---

[1] e.g. Edward Dowden, *Puritan and Anglican: Studies in Literature* (London, 1900), p. 69: 'The Anglican position at the close of Elizabeth's reign is defined in the writings of Hooker . . . The spirit of the Renaissance is brought into harmony by him with the spirit of the Reformation.' V. H. H. Green, *From St. Augustine to William Temple* (London, 1948), p. 119: 'This is an astonishing and unique event; that a comparatively little-known and in many ways undistinguished man should have given the Anglican Church its most momentous apologia.' Gunnar Hillerdal, *Reason and Revelation in Richard Hooker* (Lund, 1962), p. 9: 'Richard Hooker's great work . . . has probably meant more than any other book in shaping a tradition peculiar to Anglicanism.' John S. Marshall, *Hooker and the Anglican Tradition* (London, 1963), p. 2: 'With Hooker we have at last a rational exposition of the doctrine and practice of what was to become the abiding form of the Anglican Church.'

[2] cf. C. J. Sisson, *The Judicious Marriage of Mr. Hooker and the Birth of the Laws of Ecclesiastical Polity* (Cambridge, 1940); W. Speed Hill, 'Hooker's Polity: The Problem of the "Three Last Books",' *Huntington Library Quarterly*, XXXIV (1971), pp. 317–36.

belated mediaevalist' who stood astride radically dissimilar
Weltanschauungen. 'Through him,' it is suggested, 'the Aristotelianism of the Middle Ages helped to found a theory of original
contract, utterly different from itself, and bitterly hostile to its
own teaching.'[1] It has been eminently respectable to misrepresent
Hooker ever since Locke juggled with some of his ideas in order to
lend credence to his own theory, though Locke showed himself
unacquainted with the substance of Hooker's thought and used it,
rather, as a stick with which to beat Anglican royalists. The result
has been that a long line of retrospective historians have had a
sound excuse for carving *Of the Laws of Ecclesiastical Polity* into
mutually incompatible segments. Even more sensitive commentators have been usually less intent on studying the work as a
sustained argument than with delving into it in order to discover
material illustrative of some general intellectual theme.[2]

Equipped with an armoury of concepts garnered from a later
epoch, historians have so distorted the work that, if we are to
believe them, Hooker can take credit for being the forerunner of
practically every modern doctrine and school of thought—a truly
Promethean accomplishment for one whose outlook on the world
had a strongly traditional flavour. Hooker's book has been regarded
as a precursor of contractualism, rationalism, positivism, even
mysticism, as well as of Whiggism, Liberalism and Conservatism.

Writing in the nineteenth century, Henry Hallam was so eager

---

[1] Ernest Barker, *The Political Thought of Plato and Aristotle* (New York,
1959), p. 509. D. W. Hanson, *From Kingdom to Commonwealth*, pp. 279–280,
finds in Hooker an expression of all the ambiguities of the medieval heritage
which were to erupt in civil war: 'It is clear, then, that Hooker's work is shot
through with ambiguities. Indeed, these are puzzling enough to make it impossible to say whether they amount to formal contradiction or not. It does seem
clear that he did not settle resolutely on any of the principles which might have
been employed to unify the system. Because this is so, his argument really drives
in four directions: towards royal sovereignty, the ultimate supremacy of the
national law of England, the sovereignty of the body politic, and the traditional
doctrine of the joint supremacy of king and parliament. He ought not to be condemned overmuch for this, however, for it was typical of the times. Indeed,
his very confusion is what makes us most indebted to him, for it serves at once
as a codification of past and present ambiguities and as a superb introduction to
the immediate future. For the several threads which were so intricately inter-
woven in Hooker's work could be unravelled and emphasized singly, and this is
substantially what happened in the pre-civil-war period.'
[2] Sheldon Wolin's, 'Richard Hooker and English Conservatism', *Western
Political Quarterly*, VI (1953), pp. 28–47, is a scholarly attempt to trace the origins of English conservatism to Hooker.

to force Hooker into the mould of an original Whig that he persuaded himself that Hooker's political theory was essentially the same as Locke's.[1] An even more bizarre interpretation was advanced by H. F. Kearney. Apparently bewitched by the conceptual distinction which Professor Oakeshott had recently made between the political traditions of Reason/Nature and Artifice/Will,[2] Kearney was content to cast Hooker in the role of a Hobbesian masquerading as a Thomist, on the grounds that he presented a voluntarist conception of human law within a Christian Aristotelian view of the universe.[3] Yet, not only is it manifestly clear that Hooker never suggested that a will uninformed by reason constituted a legitimate command,[4] all medieval thinkers believed that both reason and will were essential ingredients of a properly enacted law. Reason was necessary to ensure the substantive soundness of the proposal, and an authoritative will was required to convert the rational prescription into a legally enforceable command. Even more considered opinions, concluding that Hooker drew on such a rich storehouse of sources that his thought was bound to disintegrate into a mosaic of contradictory elements, concur in discerning an incipient dichotomy within the text. It is said, for instance, that there is a transition from Book I, where law is conceived as a rational determination, to Book VIII, in which law is conceived as command. The same point is made by arguing that Hooker began as a Thomist and ended as a Marsilian,[5] though it is now established that Hooker had no first-hand knowledge of Marsilius' writings.[6]

A favourite opinion is that Hooker superimposed the social

[1] Henry Hallam, *The Constitutional History of England from the Accession of Henry VII to the Death of George II* (London, 1854), I, p. 219: 'Nothing perhaps is more striking to a reader of the Ecclesiastical Polity than the constant and even excessive predilection of Hooker for those liberal principles of civil government, which are sometimes so just and always so attractive. Upon these subjects, his theory absolutely coincides with that of Locke. The origin of government, both in right and in fact, he explicitly derives from a primary contract.'

[2] cf. Hobbes, *Leviathan*, ed. Michael Oakeshott (Oxford, 1946), pp. xi–xii.

[3] H. F. Kearney, 'Richard Hooker: A Reconstruction', *Cambridge Journal*, 5 (1951–2), pp, 300–11.

[4] e.g. *E.P.* II. vii. 6: 'that authority of men should prevail with men either against or above Reason, is no part of our belief'.

[5] cf. Peter Munz, *The Place of Hooker in the History of Thought* (London, 1952).

[6] cf. W. D. J. Cargill Thompson, 'The Source of Hooker's Knowledge of Marsilius of Padua', *Journal of Ecclesiastical History*, XXXV (1974), pp. 75–81.

contract theory on an alien metaphysics.[1] This again seems to indicate an ignorance of medieval thought; for how else can we explain the inference that Hooker had in mind a model of the self-sufficient individual from the mere fact that he employed the concept of consent? The social contract theory is usually associated with writers of the seventeenth and eighteenth centuries who, operating with the notion of an autonomous and socially insulated individual, used the contract idea to justify the entrance of these essentially unconnected individuals into political society. The carriers of certain inalienable natural rights, men agreed to submit themselves to the requirements of a proposed legal structure on the understanding that certain rights, particularly those pertaining to life and property, would receive adequate recognition and protection. Now many medievalists envisaged the origin of political society in terms of some sort of agreement between men. Aquinas spoke of a *pactum* between a ruler and his subjects, and Spanish Thomists of the sixteenth century incorporated the contract idea into their thinking.[2] So far from adopting the premises of modern individualism, they were affirming the dignity of generic man as a being able to apprehend moral imperatives within the framework of the eternal law. The political order on this view was created by moral agents who, guided by right reason, sought appropriate institutional arrangements by which to express their natural impulse to communal living. The discretion which these thinkers allowed man in devising a polity was a token of their respect for him as a conscious agent who was able to take decisions that accorded with his natural desire for perfection. It was a teleological understanding of human nature that was far removed from the atomistic conception which was to supersede it. Exactly how political society originated was not a major problem for these writers because they did not assume the essential privacy and self-sufficiency of each human being. Nor was it a central problem for Hooker.

So much of the discussion of Hooker conveys a sense of unreality. It tells much about the games scholars like to play by

[1] e.g. F. J. Shirley, *Richard Hooker and Contemporary Political Ideas* (London, 1949), p. 227: 'Hooker is not one of the most consistent thinkers, and . . . there are two voices often to be heard . . . More than he realized, Hooker had his feet in two camps—that of Divine Right and that of Contractual Theory.'

[2] cf. Bernice Hamilton, *Political Thought in Sixteenth Century Spain: A Study of Vitoria, De Soto, Suarez and Molina* (Oxford, 1963).

employing arbitrary categories but it contains small evidence of any quest for historical understanding. There is no compelling reason to suppose that Hooker's thought is plagued with confusion simply because he was immensely learned and did not hesitate to elicit support from a host of authorities. For, apart from the all-important fact that those authorities shared the same universe of discourse, their basic ideas had been already mediated by a succession of lesser writers into coherent standpoints. Indeed, our approach has been to illustrate how the elements of the traditional world picture provided scope for intellectual versatility, enabling writers to mould them into differing, but none the less internally consistent theories.

Hooker differs from his contemporaries in degree rather than kind, in the great sweep of his knowledge and his flair for synthesis. In his work, the various strands of medieval thought that had been refined in the sixteenth century were woven into a philosophical tapestry that derived significance from the assumption that the world was permeated by the divine reason. Professor d'Entrèves' assessment is superbly accurate:

It is the role of some among the greatest sixteenth- and seventeenth-century thinkers to mark with unquestionable evidence the boundaries between medieval and modern thought. The merits of Hooker will appear to us only if we consider that his whole effort lies in the opposite direction. He endeavoured to gather up the threads of traditional speculation . . . He provides the formal continuity of doctrines and ideas which were to become formidable weapons in the hands of later writers and controversialists; a formal continuity which is of course no excuse for overlooking the deep change which their meaning underwent in the completely secularized political theory of modern times.[1]

By gathering up 'the threads of traditional speculation', Hooker was able to equip himself with the theoretical means of refuting a group of radical agitators. For he was supplied with a philosophical backcloth which enabled him to demonstrate the efficacy of a collective wisdom in making divine providence operative in human affairs, and also the deficiencies of individual reason when it cut itself off from that historically evolved totality.

By the time Hooker wrote, the Tudor State was sufficiently

---

[1] A. P. d'Entrèves, *The Medieval Contribution to Political Thought* (New York, 1959), pp. 115–16.

established to be represented as the traditional society. Hooker did just this. He disclosed the existence of the Elizabethan State as evidence of the cunning of divine reason at work in human history. For the various aspects of that State, though superficially disparate and without apparent justification, were revealed as cohering in a rational whole. The conviction that human society was a corporate entity within a universal framework of reason is the key to unravel the arguments *Of the Laws of Ecclesiastical Polity*, which unfolded in a perfectly consistent fashion from the first to the last book.[1]

Hooker made plain at the outset the structure that his work would have. In addition to revealing the threat to established ecclesiastical practices constituted by the Puritan challenge, the Preface to *Of the Laws of Ecclesiastical* outlined the form which the counter-argument would assume. Throughout the Elizabethan period there had been a noisy pressure group within the Church that was antagonistic to papal remnants such as clerical vestments and to features of ecclesiastical organization like episcopacy, an antipathy which stemmed from adherence to the fideistic doctrine of the total depravity of human nature.[2] For, correlative with

---

[1] Other commentators have also tried to establish the coherence of Hooker's thought by adopting an appropriate intellectual context. H. C. Porter, 'Hooker, the Tudor Constitution, and the Via Media', in W. Speed Hill (ed.), *Studies in Richard Hooker: Essays Preliminary to an Edition of his Works* (Cleveland and London, 1972), pp. 77–116, does so by comparing it with contemporary expressions of the Anglican *via media*, and with the views of common lawyers. W. D. J. Cargill Thompson, 'The Philosopher of the "Politic Society": Richard Hooker as a Political Thinker', in ed. cit., pp. 3–76, distinguishes him from his contemporaries by his method of argument, his understanding of the Church as a 'political society', and his attempt to relate 'things indifferent' to a general theory of law. Leslie Croxford, 'The Originality of Hooker's Work', *Procs, of the Leeds Philosophical and Literary Society: Literary and Historical Section*, XV (1973), pp. 15–57, argues, to my mind rather curiously, that the distinctive feature of Hooker was his intention to abandon argument by analogy, even though he was not conscious that he was doing what we are asked to believe was his intention! Arthur S. McGrade, 'The Coherence of Hooker's Polity: The Books on Power', *Journal of the History of Ideas*, XXIV (1963), pp. 163–82, makes it clear in a very intelligent way that the coherence of Hooker's work can be established if we bear in mind what he set out to accomplish.

[2] Hooker was not the first writer to defend the Church against Puritans. In his *Apology for the Church of England* (London, 1562), Bishop Jewel did so by claiming that the Church was essentially as it had always been, except that certain abuses had now been rectified. Following the two Puritan manifestos to parliament in 1571 and 1572, John Whitgift and others defended the Church along similar lines. But Hooker was the first to refute the Puritans at a philosophical level by illustrating how they misconstrued human nature.

denying that reason was competent to ascertain the norms of right conduct was the assertion that the Bible was an exclusive authority in all human affairs, including forms of church government. Aligned with this conviction, that anything for which scriptural validation could not be found was contrary to divine ordinance, was the believer's claim, deriving from some supposedly special insight into God's Word, to be the chosen interpreter and agent of divine injunctions. This meant that 'when the minds of men are once erroneously persuaded that it is the will of God to have those things done which they fancy, their opinions are as thorns in their sides, never suffering them to take rest till they have brought their speculations into practice' (Pref. viii. 12).

Hooker's argument was directed not so much against the practical demands of self-styled revolutionaries, for most of his opponents believed that they were making specific and limited proposals for reform from within the mainstream of the established Church. Rather, he detected in the zeal with which they demanded reform a latent but potent threat, an incipient ideology of individualism that was liable to erupt into a demand for the reception of a godly discipline, 'although the world by receiving it should be clean turned upside down' (Pref. viii. 5). In Hooker's opinion, their donning of a garb of purity and moderation barely concealed the fact that, potentially at least, his ideological rivals were a bunch of agitators who, convinced that they were in direct touch with the Holy Spirit, were eager to act out their conception of rightness in a public setting. He was, in other words, dealing with restless spirits whose peculiar epistemology stood, he imagined, as a direct challenge to the existing political structure.

The crux of the matter was that the Puritan doctrine sanctified the individual conscience, thus permitting the purified to question the established order at any point they desired. Yet no community might withstand the onslaught of some of its members actively campaigning to undermine the social fabric simply because they did not find certain features of public policy congenial. Recurrent throughout Hooker's work was the assumption that any society would disintegrate if it lacked authority to regulate the activities of its members through laws that were not directly enjoined by scripture, and he never missed an opportunity of exposing the seemingly harmless demands of his opponents. Commenting, for example, on the view that the Church was without authority to designate certain days as public holidays unless scriptural validation could be adduced, Hooker vigorously sketched the repercussions of such an opinion, for it,

shaketh universally the fabric of government, tendeth to anarchy and mere confusion, dissolveth families, dissipateth colleges, corporations, armies, overthroweth kingdoms, churches, and whatsoever is now through the providence of God by authority and power upheld . . . Those things which the law of God leaveth arbitrary and at liberty are all subject unto positive laws of men, which laws for the common benefit abridge particular men's liberty in such things as far as the rules of equity will suffer. This we must either maintain, or else overturn the world and make every man his own commander (V. lxxi. 4).

In outlining his intended approach, Hooker disclaimed any desire to persuade the radicals to act immorally. He made it abundantly clear that his arguments were designed to resolve the conscience.[1] At the same time, he refused to concede a right of withdrawing allegiance from ecclesiastical laws unless conclusive proof of their moral indefensibility was forthcoming. There was a presumption that publicly enacted law was morally sound, so that only definite and absolute proof to the contrary would suffice to override the *prima facie* obligation of obedience. To suppose otherwise was to destroy the possibility of social life.[2]

The following extract reveals what was to be the unifying theme of the eight books:

Be it that there are some reasons inducing you to think hardly of our laws. Are those reasons demonstrative, are they necessary, or but mere probabilities only? An argument necessary and demonstrative is such, as being proposed unto any man and understood, the mind cannot choose but inwardly assent. Any one such reason dischargeth, I grant,

[1] e.g. II. vii. 5: 'Now it is not required nor can be exacted at our hands, that we should yield unto any thing other assent, than such as doth answer the evidence which is to be had of that we assent unto . . . [I]n all things then are our consciences resolved, and in a most agreeable sort unto God and settled, when they are so far persuaded on those grounds of persuasion which are to be had will bear.'

[2] I. xvi. 5: 'The public power of all societies is above every soul contained in the same societies. And the principal use of that power is to give laws unto all that are under it; which laws in such case we must obey, unless there be reason shewed which may necessarily enforce that the Law of Reason or of God doth enjoin the contrary. Because except our own private and but probable resolutions be by the law of public determinations overruled, we take away all possibility of sociable life in the world.'

the conscience, and setteth it at full liberty. For the public approbation given by the body of this whole church unto those things which are established, doth make it but probable that they are good. And therefore unto a necessary proof that they are not good it must give place . . . As for probabilities, what thing was there ever set down so agreeable with sound reason, but some probable show against it might be made? . . . So that of peace and quietness there is not any way possible, unless the probable voice of every entire society or body politic overrule all private of like nature in the same body . . .

Nor is mine own intent any other in these several books of discourse, than to make it appear unto you, that for the ecclesiastical laws of this land, we are led by great reason to observe them, and ye by no necessity bound to impugn them (Pref. vi. 6–vii. 1).

What emerges from these prefatory remarks is that Hooker was concerned with the problem of political obligation in the sense, not of providing a justification of the entrance of atomistic individuals into a legal structure that would curtail certain rights, but of persons residing within an already established system being required to conform to legal commands which they felt to be morally unsound. Hooker was seeking to resolve the tension between two antithetical conceptions of right behaviour in a specified set of circumstances, that of the private individual as opposed to that of the legislative authority of the community to which he belonged.

Anticipating how the resolution was facilitated, Hooker argued that: i. the moral component of law was secured in so far as it was rationally derived, with the provisional clause that it was not contrary to scripture; ii. the reason of the corporately organized community was a more reliable indication of the moral acceptability of law than the judgement of a private person; iii. English laws and customs had been framed by the corporate wisdom of the community; iv. in the absence of demonstrative proof of the immorality of English laws, it was morally incumbent on every person to defer to the superior communal wisdom in public matters.

The Puritan desire to reshape the political structure in order to eradicate features unsupported by scripture derived from a confusion as to the available means of grasping the norms of correct behaviour. Thus, given that his intention was to establish the nonarbitrary nature of human activities which fell outside the scope of this narrow yardstick, Hooker's first task was to reaffirm the efficacy of reason within its proper sphere. This he did by describing the philoprogenitive deity of the Thomist tradition who had been moved to create a world that testified abundantly to his infinite goodness. The universe was saturated with reason because it was rationally designed and sustained, which Hooker expressed by saying that it was regulated in accordance with an eternal law that determined the path each created form must follow to actualize its potential for perfection. Human participation in this law was unique because only men had reason by which to apprehend their divinely appointed goal. Like their creator, they operated consciously and voluntarily, so that the law of human nature was 'the sentence of Reason, determining and setting down what is good to be done' (I. viii. 8). Desirous of perfection, through education and experience they were able to sharpen their rational faculty to the point where it could discriminate between good and evil and thus lead to a knowledge of the truth and an exercise of virtue. Reason, therefore, led to a discovery of those goods which pertained to sensible existence, such as food, health, wealth, and also those virtues which assisted intellectual development. Hooker believed that general moral precepts, that the greater good was to be preferred always, for example, that God was to be honoured, that men were to be mutually responsive, were so transparent to reason that all men might acknowledge them once they had been stated.

Beyond these a spiritual fulfilment was sought, for it was in union with God that the natural desire for perfection was ultimately satisfied.[1] Here, however, the natural means at men's disposal were insufficient to the end in view and works had to be supplemented by the scripturally revealed virtues of faith, hope and charity.[2] Yet, grace restoring and not destroying nature, reason was not rendered redundant in the quest for human felicity. Indeed, reason was needed to authenticate and interpret the scriptures themselves. 'Scripture teacheth us that saving truth

---

[1] 'A Learned Sermon of the Nature of Pride', in *The Works*, III, p. 599: 'That sovereign good, which is the eternal fruition of all good, being our last and chiefest felicity, there is no desparate despiser of God and godliness living which doth not wish for it.'

[2] Basil Willey, *The English Moralists* (London, 1964), p. 102, describes Hooker 'as a God-centered Humanist: that is, one who, while allowing due importance and scope to the human faculties of reason and the moral sense, yet never loses sight of the final orientation of man towards God, and his final completion on a supernatural level.'

which God hath discovered unto the world by revelation, and it presumeth us taught otherwise that itself is divine and sacred' (III. viii. 13). This was why the Puritans were so wrong in thinking that reason had been made worthless by the Fall.

In establishing the competence of human reason by sketching the familiar picture of a universe vibrant with the divine reason, Hooker had set the scene for appreciating the grounds of human law. He took social life to be rooted in the natural desire for perfection because, besides furnishing humankind with the necessities of existence, it facilitated the exchange of knowledge through the medium of speech. Here was the Aristotelian idea that the expansion of knowledge was a co-operative affair, men imparting 'mutually one to another the conceits of reasonable understanding' in a social context where 'this good of mutual participation is so much the larger than otherwise' (I. x. 12). Thus, the impetus to association was the inability of solitary living to provide the material and intellectual prerequisites of moral development. In justifying political organization, Hooker stressed its function in restraining the vicious tendencies of human nature, and thus maintaining society as a unity of order designed to foster that good which its members shared.[1] And, in a tone typical of all those thinkers who emphasized the overriding necessity of order, he envisaged the human community as an integral aspect of a hierarchically structured universe.

Without order there is no living in public society, because the want thereof is the mother of confusion, whereupon division of necessity followeth, and out of division, inevitable destruction . . . Order can have no place in things, unless it be settled amongst persons that shall by office be conversant about them. And if things or persons be ordered, this doth imply that they are distinguished by degrees. For order is a gradual disposition.

The whole world consisting of parts so many, so different, is by this only thing upheld; he which framed them hath set them in order. Yea,

---

[1] VIII. ii. 18: 'The good which is proper unto each man belongeth to the common good of all, as a part of the whole's perfection; but yet these two are things different; for men by that which is proper are severed, united they are by that which is common. Wherefore, besides that which moveth each man in particular to seek his private, there must of necessity in all public societies be also a general mover, directing unto the common good, and framing every man's particular to it. The end whereunto all government was instituted, was *bonum publicum*, the universal or common good.'

the very Deity itself both keepeth and requireth for ever this to be kept as a law, that wheresoever there is a coagmentation of many, the lowest to knit to the highest by that which being interjacent may cause each to cleave unto other, and so all to continue one.

This order of things and persons in public societies is the work of polity, and the proper instrument thereof in every degree is power (VIII. ii. 2).

Despite the natural inclination which men had to reside in society, and the necessity of government to prevent strife and promote the common good, Hooker insisted that no form of government was legitimate unless grounded upon the consent of those subject to it.

Several reasons appear to have been operative in persuading Hooker to attribute a crucial role to consent in legitimating government, none of which implied a rejection of traditional presuppositions. He dismissed the Aristotelian proposition that the natural supremacy of some was a sufficient justification of political power,[1] preferring to locate its genesis in a general recognition that the conflicts and inconveniences of pre-political society could be transcended by men 'ordaining some kind of government public, and by yielding themselves subject thereunto; that unto whom they granted authority to rule and govern, by them the peace, tranquillity, and happy estate of the rest might by pro-cured' (I. x. 4). In tracing the origins of political power to a consensus regarding its desirability, Hooker was highlighting the fact that men were conscious participants in the divine reason. Operating voluntarily, they were at liberty to choose a suitable form of government. Yet it was a choice conditional upon the necessity of there being some sort of government, especially in view of their fallen nature. Being the creation of a rationally

---

[1] I. x 4: 'without . . . consent there were no reason that one should take upon him to be lord or judge over another; because, although there be according to the opinion of some very great and judicious men a kind of natural right in the noble, wise and virtuous, to govern them which are of servile disposition; nevertheless for manifestation of this their right, and men's more peaceable contentment on both sides, the assent of them who are to be governed seemeth necessary. To fathers within their private families Nature hath given a supreme power; for which cause we see throughout the world even from the foundation thereof, all men have ever been taken as lords and lawfull kings in their houses. Howbeit over a whole grand multitude having no such dependency upon any one, and consisting of so many families as every politic society in the world doth, impossible it is that any should have complete lawful power, but by consent of men, or immediate appointment of God.'

informed will, government was sanctioned by divine approval. It was, therefore, ultimately of divine origin, though derived immediately from human co-operation.[1] Thus, by consenting to the emergence of political rule, men were responding to a moral imperative apprehended by the divinely implanted faculty of reason. Given that it was of the human essence to work consciously and voluntarily, there was no other way of conceiving the creation of a polity except by direct appointment of God.

Another reason why Hooker posited consent as the legitimating factor of political power was that he had been influenced by the medieval assimilation of political society to a corporation, where authority was held to reside with the collectivity of the members.[2] Government, therefore, must have arisen when the members of a pre-political society transferred their collective authority into some part of the whole. 'So that by comparing the body with the head, as touching power, it seemeth to reside in both, fundamentally or radically in the one, in the other derivatively' (VIII, ii. 10). Here Hooker was underpinning his explanation of the origins of government in terms of man's moral nature by tying it to a respectable line of political thinking.

Finally, the notion of consent was vital given Hooker's overall intention. For, apart from serving as a device justifying the right of any community to regulate the activities of its members through laws—as Hooker implied, even the actions of an absolute monarchy might be considered legitimate, on the grounds that his authority derived from an original transfer of power—the concept could be used to create the presumption that there was normally a collective dimension to public affairs. In defining political society as a corporately unfolding entity, he could imply that the approbation of its members to matters of polity was manifested by their accep-

---

[1] Thus, Hooker appears to have subsumed men's decision to form themselves into a political community under the general maxim that, 'Whatsoever is good, the same is also approved of God.' e.g. VIII. App. I, p. 458: 'Power is then of divine institution, when either God himself doth deliver, or men by light of nature find out the kind thereof. So that the power of parents over children, and of husbands over their wives, the power of all sorts of superiors, made by consent of commonwealths within themselves, or grown from agreement amongst nations, such power is of God's own institution in respect of the kind thereof.'

[2] VIII. ii. 5: 'every independent multitude, before any certain form of regiment established, hath, under God's supreme authority, full dominion over itself . . . God creating mankind did endue it naturally with full power to guide itself, in what kind of societies soever it should choose to live.'

tance of custom.[1] More specifically, he was able to employ the notion to explain how certain communities, reflecting on the disadvantages of unrestrained monarchy, had devised a form of government in which general and continuing consent was a feature of its legislative enactments. Originally, he argued, governments were probably unlimited monarchies, but men 'saw that to live by one man's will became the cause of all men's misery. This constrained them to come unto laws' (I. x. 5). As we shall see, this was to be essential in his defence of the English political system. By generally using the idea of consent to create the presumption that a communal wisdom was practically operative in social life and also to generate confidence in its efficacy, Hooker was preparing to undermine the claims made on behalf of individual conscience as a measure of political justice.

Having explained the right which societies had to make political provision for themselves, Hooker was in a position to consider the manner in which human laws were derived. And here he intended his remarks to encompass both civil and ecclesiastical legislation, in so far as a church, besides being a medium through which divine grace was bestowed upon believers, was a natural organization of men. It shared an affinity with any human group and was, therefore, authorized to construct a 'form for the outward administration of public duties in the service of God' (V. viii. 1), which included the administration of the sacraments, forms of public worship, and so forth. While properly enacted law was rationally framed, so that in his capacity as a lawmaker man was a coadjutant of God in the rational order of the universe,[2] its distinctive feature was command; for such laws 'do not only teach what is good, but they enjoin it, they have in them a certain constraining force' (I. x. 7). It was in explaining the necessity of the coercive aspect of human laws that Hooker described in detail how they were formulated in accordance with objective rational precepts.

[1] I. x. 8: 'And to be commanded we do consent, when that society whereof we are part hath at any time before consented, without revoking the same after by the like universal agreement. Wherefore as any man's deed is past as long as himself continueth; so the act of a public society of men done five hundred years sithence standeth as their who presently are of the same societies, because corporations are immortal; we were then alive in our predecessors, and they in their successors do live still, Laws therefore human, of what kind soever, are available by consent.'

[2] e.g. V. ix. 3: 'all good laws are the voices of right reason, which is the instrument wherewith God will have the world guided.' Cf. VII. xi. 10.

The need arose in the first instance because of the irrational and socially divisive behaviour of sinful men, which meant that certain actions 'which plain or necessary reason bindeth men unto may be in sundry considerations expedient to be ratified by human law' (I. x. 10). This was the old idea that an essential function of law was that of compelling men to conduct themselves in a morally acceptable manner, which they would do readily were it not for vicious lapses. Such laws, the prohibition of polygamy, for instance, simply persuaded men to comply with a moral obligation which already existed because it was enjoined directly by the eternal law. 'Which law in this case we term *mixed*, because the matter whereunto it bindeth is the same which reason necessarily doth require at our hands, and from the Law of Reason it differeth in the manner of binding only' (I. x. 10).

The need arose in the second instance because residence within a community demanded a degree of uniform behaviour as a means of preserving that unity which was the precondition of all goods accruing to social man. This category of law corresponded to that area of the moral life in which reason discerned several equally legitimate means to some good end. Prior to the enactment of law of this sort, there existed no necessary or compelling reason making performance of its requirements morally obligatory. Reason perceived the desirability of some rule defining rights of inheritance, for instance, but it was a matter of convenience that a particular society should enact the law of primogeniture. 'As for laws which are *merely* human, the matter of them is any thing which reason doth but probably teach to be fit and convenient; so that till such time as law hath passed amongst men about it, of itself it bindeth no man' (I. x. 10). The indifference was removed by enactment and it then became morally obligatory on each member of the community to frame his actions accordingly.

There was nothing peculiar in Hooker's subsumption of a large area of human law under this category. It reflected the conviction which we have seen to be generally held, that laws had to be fitting for time and place. But Hooker gave special emphasis to this category because he believed that the anti-social behaviour of the Puritans was due largely to their failure to appreciate the need for, and legitimacy of, such laws. Thus, 'by following the law of private reason, where the law of public should take place, they breed disturbance' (I. xvi. 6). Deferring to Aquinas in explaining the objective validity of these laws, Hooker made the usual distinction between the general precepts of natural law, and those particular determinations which were a specific embodiment of the more general principles (III. ix. 2; II. viii. 6). Such laws, therefore, were an extension of natural law at the point at which the particular needs of the community were taken into account. Hooker evidently believed that most ecclesiastical laws and forms of church polity were of this type. Just as speech could assume many different linguistic forms, so, too, church organization could take a variety of forms (III. ii. 1). Only possible or probable reasons might be adduced in support of such laws, for necessary or conclusive reasons were absent from that area of legislation in which discretion was required to choose from a number of available means to some morally desirable end. As Hooker explained in regard to ecclesiastical polity:

The first thing therefore which is of force to cause approbation with good conscience towards such customs or rites as publicly are established, is when there ariseth from the due consideration of those customs and rites in themselves apparent reason, although not always to prove them better than any other that might possibly be devised, (for who did ever require this in man's ordinances?) yet competent to shew their conveniency and fitness, in regard of the use for which they should serve (V. vi. 1).

Hooker had outlined the grounds of human law. The task now was to establish the coincidence of law and morality. In line with his intention, as stated in the *Preface*, he had to show that there were probable reasons existing in support of actual laws so that they commanded only that to which a rational agent could readily assent. Having done this, he would be able to argue that disobedience was provoked by a mistaken judgement on the part of dissidents.

Here Hooker's approach was double-edged. Negatively, he disputed the proposition that any private person was competent to assess the moral validity of existing laws. 'Men are blinded with ignorance and error; many things may escape them, and in many things they may be deceived' (II. vii. 3). Yet lawmaking was an exceedingly complex and hazardous process that was not to be entrusted to fools and amateurs. 'The secret lets and difficulties in public proceedings are innumerable and inevitable' (I. i. 1).

Multiple factors had to be considered in designing rules that took due account of the contingencies of social life, while retaining a view of the common good. Ordinary men were devoid of the requisite acumen for such matters because 'soundly to judge of a law is the weightiest thing which any man can take upon him' (I. xvi. 2; I. x. 7). This was the familiar idea, accepted by the advocates of both absolute and limited monarchy, that political matters demanded a degree of wisdom not contained in the fallible judgements of a single, imperfect individual.[1]

The more positive aspect of Hooker's approach was to identify a reliable indication of the moral acceptability of laws. He began by deferring to those with the requisite expertise in such matters. Lawmaking being such a difficult business, communities found it expedient to appoint some of their wisest members for the task of formulating suitable proposals. This, again, was the familiar idea that a particular group represented the refined or concentrated wisdom of the community in public affairs. He defended the idea with a quotation from Aristotle.

It is therefore the voice both of God and nature, not of learning only, that especially in matters of action and policy, 'The sentences and judgments of men experienced, aged and wise, yea though they speak without any proof or demonstration, are no less to be hearkened unto, than as being demonstrations in themselves; because such men's long observation is as an eye, wherewith they presently and plainly behold those principles which sway over all actions.' Whereby we are taught both the cause wherefore wise men's judgments should be credited, and the mean how to use their judgments to the increase of our own wisdom. That which sheweth them to be wise, is the gathering of principles out of their own particular experiments. And the framing of our particular experiments according to the rule of their principles shall make us such as they are (V. vii. 2).

---

[1] Hooker made this clear when arguing the need for equity to temper the strictness of existing law on occasion. Many, he said, failed to perceive the legitimacy of such exceptions. V. ix. 2: 'The cause of which error is ignorance what restraints and limitations all such principles have, in regard of so manifold varieties as the Matter whereunto they are applicable doth commonly afford. These varieties are not known but by much experience, from whence to draw the true bounds of all principles, to discern how far forth they take effect, to see where and why they fail, to apprehend by what degrees and means they lead to the practice of things in show though not in deed repugnant and contrary to one another, requireth more sharpness of wit, more intricate circuitions of discourse, more industry and depth of judgment, than common ability doth yield.'

It was sheer rashness for any individual to reject as worthless the experiences of such an enlightened gerontocracy, as those who desired to effect an alteration in established ecclesiastical practices evidently did.

In seeking for confirmation of the wisdom of laws so framed, Hooker resorted to the idea that a political society was a corporately unfolding entity.

If therefore even at the first so great account should be made of wise men's counsels touching things that are publicly done, as time shall add thereunto continuance and approbation of succeeding ages, their credit and authority must needs be greater . . . In which consideration there is cause why we should be slow and unwilling to change, without very urgent necessity, the ancient ordinances, rites, and long approved customs, of our venerable predecessors. The love of things ancient both argue stayedness, but levity and want of experience maketh apt unto innovations. That which wisdom did first begin, and hath been with good men long continued, challengeth allowance of them that succeed, although it plead for itself nothing. That which is new, if it promise not much, doth fear condemnation before trial; till trial, no man doth acquit or trust it, what good soever if pretend and promise. So that in this kind there are few things known to be good, till such time as they grow to be ancient. The vain pretence of those glorious names, where they could not be with any truth, neither in reason ought to have been so much alleged, hate wrought such a prejudice against them in the minds of the common sort, as if they had utterly no force at all; whereas (especially for these observances which concern our present question) antiquity, custom, and consent in the Church of God, making with that which law doth establish, are themselves most sufficient reasons to uphold the same, unless some notable public inconvenience enforce the contrary (V. vii. 3).

Hooker emerges here as a transitional figure between Reformation writers like Starkey, who could not but castigate a large number of inherited practices as irrational, and the common lawyers of the seventeenth century who sanctified the accumulated wisdom of the past, though he is closest to this second group. Basic to his argument, that laws would not have survived unless morally sound, was the assumption that a collective wisdom in its historical dimension was a valid test of moral acceptability. He had already posited general consensus as an indication of moral rightness, claiming that it was a means of identifying those duties enjoined by the law of reason,[1] God revealed himself in the course of human history and the concurrence of generations of minds was proof that the sinful veil of error and self-deception, which often obscured the truth from individual minds, could be pierced. He now placed human law, particularly laws pertaining to ecclesiastical matters, in this general perspective. 'What,' he enquired as he warned of the dangers of drastically altering England's ecclesiastical laws, 'have we to induce men unto the willing obedience and observation of laws, but the weight of so many men's judgement as have with deliberate advice assented thereunto; the weight of that long experience, which the world hath had thereof with consent and good liking?' (IV. xiv. 1). There was a presumption that laws which had been ratified by communal acceptance over a period of time were objectively sound and communally convenient. The real was rational because God was at work in the world, operating by means of human co-operation through the ages.[2]

This represented the kernel of his case against those who would detach themselves from the fabric of social life in order to question the legitimacy of practices which had stood the test of time. In effect, he had shifted the burden of proof to the would-be innovators—'that which the Church hath received and held so long for good, that which public approbation hath ratified, must carry the benefit of presumption with it to be accounted meet and convenient' (IV. iv. 2)—but in a way which left them practically without criteria for conducting their case. As a synthesis of lessons drawn from the past and made concrete, contemporary social practices were suffused with rationality. Yet their wisdom was often latent, to be adduced through immersion in what had been transmitted and not by some abstract logical process. But immersion in traditional practices would presumably induce a reasonable being to accept them, so that non-acceptance was a fair indication of the bigotry of those who rejected them. 'To them which ask why we thus hang our judgement on the Church's sleeve, I answer with

---

[1] I. viii. 3: 'Signs and tokens to know good by are of sundry kinds; some more certain and some less. The most certain token of goodness is, if the general persuasion of all men do so account it . . . The general and perpetual voice of men have at all times learned, Nature herself must needs have taught; and God being the author of Nature, her voice is but his instrument.'

[2] We ought, says Hooker, to 'admire the wisdom of God, which shineth in the beautiful variety of all things, but most in the manifold and yet harmonious dissimilitude of those ways, whereby his Church upon earth is guided from age to age, throughout all generations of men' (III. xi. 8).

Solomon, "because two are better than one". "Yea simply (saith Basil) and universally, whether it be in works of Nature, or of voluntary choice and counsel, I see not any thing done as it should be, if it be wrought by an agent singling itself from consorts" . . . The bare consent of the whole Church should itself in these things stop their mouths, who living under it, dare presume to bark against it. "There is (saith Cassianus) no place of audience left for them, by whom obedience is not yielded to that which all have agreed upon."' (V. viii. 2–3). Not that he claimed that the corporate wisdom of the Church guaranteed that its enactments were always perfect and never in need of amendment. Customs and enactments sometimes became obsolete. But, like any immortal corporation, the Church was adaptive, enacting new measures and abrogating old laws as occasion demanded (V. viii. 1; VII. xiv. 3). Politics being the pursuit of what was intimated by traditional practices, it was for the corporate Church through its public institutions to determine when the time was right for amendment. Individuals who set themselves apart from the Church were the least competent to judge of its requirements.

It might be assumed, therefore, that laws which had been expertly framed, and confirmed by communal approbation over a long period, were shaped by right reason to the common good. This was the assurance that probable reasons existed in their favour, for acceptance by the corporate community indicated that laws and practices simply endorsed that to which any reasonable being would assent. It followed that it was only foolish and arrogant individuals, motivated by the dogmatic assurance that their comparatively weak and unreliable judgement was infallible, who opposed them.

It was in the last book *Of the Laws of Ecclesiastical Polity*, where the specific intention was to defend the supremacy of the civil ruler in spiritual matters, that the arguments deployed so far were threaded together in order to illustrate the excellence of the English form of government. Displaying a familiarity with common law terminology that he probably learned as Master of the Temple Church from 1585–1591,[1] Hooker provided a defence of

---

[1] Raymond A. Houk, in his 'Introduction' to *Hooker's Ecclesiastical Polity Book VIII* (New York, 1931), p. 50, says that Hooker 'saturated himself in the legal atmosphere of the place'. It was there that he crossed swords with the Puritan minister, Walter Travers, and conceived the project of providing a refutation to the radicals.

limited monarchy which was based on the assumption that a collective wisdom was morally superior to any other kind of reason.

To begin with, he argued against dividing responsibility for
policy among several rulers, each supreme in his particular sphere
(VIII. ii. 18). To prevent the community from dispersing, there
had to be some locus of authority with overall responsibility for
co-ordinating the diverse activities of everyone to the common
good. In England, this was the function of the monarch and it was
absurd to suppose that he was incompetent to take care of the
spiritual aspect of life, 'as if God had ordained kings for no other
end and purpose but only to fat up men like hogs' (VIII. iii. 2). In
order to defend his prerogative in ecclesiastical matters, Hooker
resorted to the idea that the pre-political community was free to
bestow authority on some part of itself, a right of derivation that
extended to religious matters because, considered as a group of
Christians naturally inclined to association, a community constituted a Church. So that, 'the whole body of the Church . . . [was]
the first original subject of all mandatory and coercive power within
itself' (VIII. vi. 3). A ruler established in this manner was dependent upon the community as the original source of his authority.
He was, therefore, *major singulum universalis minor* (VIII. ii. 7),
which implied that the scope of his authority was communally
limited. It was determined according to what the people had originally agreed upon, or else according to what had been subsequently
consented to and embodied in positive law or custom (VIII. ii.
11).

Hooker's opinion was that monarchy was best when the king
was restrained by an 'indifferent rule; which rule is the law; I
mean not only the law of nature and of God, but very national or
muncipal law consonant thereunto' (VIII. ii. 12). The founders of
the English nation were to be commended for their wisdom in
confining the monarch according to the rule of law. This meant
that, while absolute in some respects, for example, in regard to the
making of war and peace, he was generally required to exercise his
legislative prerogative in conjunction with the assembled members
of the community.

The parliament of England together with the convocation annexed
thereunto, is that whereupon the very essence of all government within
this kingdom doth depend; it is even the body of the whole realm; it
consisteth of the king, and of all that within the land are subject unto

him: for they all are there present, either in person or by such as they voluntarily have derived their very personal right unto (VIII. vi. 11).

Apart from the fact that the monarch was excluded from doing certain things in the religious sphere—he could not, for instance, administer the sacraments—he was prevented by the rule of law from governing arbitrarily in that area in which he was empowered to act. As Bracton had said, he was under both God and the law, which meant in practical terms that he could only make laws for the ordering of the Church in conjunction with the whole body politic, assembled in parliament. Framed by the wisdom of those with the requisite expertise, that is, the clergy in convocation, and confirmed by the gathered community, the implication was that such laws were substantively sound. In England, the collective wisdom of the community was harnessed to deal with public matters. The nation, therefore, was possessed of an adequate institutional formula for deriving laws 'as conclusions from . . . divine and natural [law], serving for principle thereunto' (VIII. vi. 5). There was consequently no justification in disclaiming the right of monarchical supremacy in the ecclesiastical realm. For, given that he was enclosed by the wisdom of the community and that his legislative authority was restricted mainly to the power of veto, the king was not in a position to enact unreasonable measures.

It was also illogical, Hooker suggested, to deny him supremacy because it was a principle applicable to corporations that what touches all should be approved by all, and it was absurd to except the most important public figure from this maxim. In a university, for instance, only that which received the approval of the rector was valid, and the same held for the Church (VIII. vi. 9). Hooker was being ingenious here, for, whereas Marsilius and others had applied this Roman legal principle to political society as a means of establishing the legislative authority of the community, he was using it to affirm the right of the king as an essential member of the community. Moreover, historical precedent reinforced the conviction that the monarch should have legislative authority in spiritual affairs. When, by the *lex regia*, the Roman people had transferred their authority to the emperor, there had been no suggestion that the power of a ruler was confined to purely temporal matters (VIII. vi. 1). All the arguments converged to demonstrate the untenability of the Puritan position regarding the monarch's incompetence in religious affairs.

Hooker stated at the outset that he had 'endeavoured throughout the body of this whole discourse, that every former part might give strength unto all that follow, and every later bring some light unto all before' (I. i. 2). He had fulfilled his promise. The underlying thread lending coherence to the work is the belief that the corporate community is well able to make provision for the common good. On this basis, he had demonstrated the moral defensibility of English laws and practices, as well as the illogicality of denying monarchical supremacy in religious affairs. In doing so, he used arguments which could so easily have been adapted by his opponents. For, implicit in the idea of a corporate community, mobilized through its public institutions for political activity, was the assumption that political matters were accessible to human reason. Yet by emphasizing the overriding necessity of communal consolidation through functional differentiation, and the deference of each fallible individual to the decision-making processes of the whole, Hooker divested his theory of any suggestion of radical individualism or of any justification for a segment of society opposing itself to the whole. Linking arguments in support of order and unity with those which favoured the involvement of the organized community in public affairs, he had provided such a strong defence of the English State that the claims of his opponents seemed insubstantial.

It is nonsensical to suggest that *Of the Laws of Ecclesiastical Polity* is a premature expression of the type of thinking that was to become familiar during the Civil War. Hooker's entire enterprise was designed to establish the efficacy of a co-operative wisdom that had succeeded in constructing a viable set of institutional arrangements within which, and only within which, individual felicity and moral development were made possible. It was specifically directed against those who sought to establish the competence of individual reason or conscience. Hooker's work represents one of the last, certainly the finest, attempts to synthesize the various strands of medieval thought with which we have been concerned.

VI

CIVIL WAR

IN A SENSE, Hooker's account of the Tudor State was a piece of wishful thinking. His picture of a tidy hierarchy of stratified ranks, unified by adequate political institutions, lent philosophical weight to English society in a way which glossed over the dynamics of the social process. His endeavour to uncover the rational within the actual issued in a conception of how things ideally ought to be, rather than a portrayal of how they really were. Not that he was so out of touch with reality. His synthesis emanated from the measure of harmony which did exist at the political centre, though it was already strained when he wrote. His account was made possible by the Tudor experiment in power sharing, and the consequent satisfaction with political arrangements among a wide section of dominant groups.

Yet the very fact that Hooker felt provoked to articulate that satisfaction underlined the fragility of the structure he so earnestly sought to defend. His, essentially, was an attempt to stem the tide. 'The owl of Minerva spreads its wings with the falling of the dusk.' Hegel's famous aphorism suggests that the philosopher's success in weaving the achievements of his age into a coherent whole is clear indication that a new epoch is about to unfold. Hooker had recognized some of the incipient conflicts which possibly sounded the death-knell of his world. His intention was to preserve present accomplishments by undermining the case of those whose attitude constituted a running sore in the body politic. His tactic of isolating them, so as to represent them as a bunch of fanatics devoid of political sense and responsibility, might seem like taking a sledgehammer to crack a nut; for they were a ginger group within the Church whose proposals for reform were not all that drastic. But the tactic itself was part of Hooker's genius. He offered a prognosis of future development should a sufficiently large number lose faith in the legitimacy of the political process. His vision of a world turned upside down by discontent was to become a reality within less than a half century. And with it, the medieval synthesis so

clearly expressed by Hooker disintegrated into at least two opposing standpoints: the concern for order was channelled into a readiness to accept some form of arbitrary government as a means of
imposing discipline on a conflict-ridden society; the desire for
rationally defensible policies found expression in a justification of
representative government, the edicts of which were conceived as
mutually convenient rules for securing essentially private interests.
Both spelt the collapse of the medieval scaffolding which for so
long had sustained the theories of absolute and limited monarchy.
Signifying its breakdown was the rapidly assimilated assumption
that political reason was the property, not of a corporate community, but of each individual, assuring him of his particular
interests and supplying him with a readily accessible criterion by
which to assess the legitimacy of all government activity.

Between the time Hooker wrote and the onset of military
struggle, political thinking entered a sort of limbo. The theory of
absolute monarchy did not undergo drastic change. It was simply
appropriated by extremists. In the sixteenth century, the theory
had commanded a broad platform of support as a tactic adopted
by dominant groups when the nation was in the early and uneasy
stages of formation. It had served well enough in the strategy to
quell popular unrest and religious dissent, and had eventually
become a bandwagon from which to declare the growing confidence
which characterized the latter part of the century. When the political co-operation of the centre began to dissolve, its tendency to
enhance the personal qualities of the monarch made it a ready to
hand theory for his supporters. They developed the analogies of
the body politic and the natural world in order to demonstrate the
necessity of kingship. They detailed the qualities which set the
occupant of the throne apart from other men and which guaranteed
the public benevolence of his actions. There was no actual justification here of arbitrary government, nothing to indicate that political
rightness was a matter of will. Though the arguments were taken
at times to weird and incredible lengths, their pivot was the
unchallenged assumption that political activity was a means of
making God's rational order effective in human society. For, the
presence in society of a figure who was supposedly only a little
below God in wisdom and paternal affection was held to be a
divine instrument for eradicating human perversity from public
affairs.

If the theory of absolute monarchy was taken over by the defenders of an intransigent crown in the early decades of the seventeenth century, that of limited monarchy had all but disappeared. The proponents of the theory had never argued their case from the point of view of interest. They had not, that is, advocated power sharing on the grounds that access to the political process was a method by which those with something to lose might protect themselves. This might have been the reality of parliamentary government—as Henry Brinklow and others recognized—but it was never its justification. Limited government, rather, was seen as a means of combating partiality in politics by suppressing those passionate excesses which could incline even a king to be self-regarding in his official capacity. Once the monarch had chosen to disengage from the institutions which facilitated co-operation, and before the emergence of a group willing to assert itself as a more perfect embodiment than he of the national well-being, the need was for a theory which effectively curbed the royal prerogative. Hence, the attributes with which parliament had been formerly endowed were transferred to the common law. In this concrete collective wisdom, this finite testimony to the divine reason, the English nation had gradually overcome arbitrariness. No fallible, fickle and shortsighted individual, not even a king, was entitled to tamper with it.

The theory of absolute monarchy had become the stuff of rousing and fantastic sermons, that of limited monarchy had sunk beneath the eulogy of custom. Within the space of a few years following the beginning of the Civil War, the intellectual scene was to be altered almost beyond recognition by a deluge of political thinking. Initially, the theory of mixed government was elevated to unprecedented heights of popularity. For both sides it became a form of window-dressing, enabling them to cloak their respective demands in the garb of moderation and respectability. But, as constitutional stalemate gave way to military confrontation, the trotting out of familiar arguments barely concealed the radically transformed significance which they were assuming. Overnight, as it were, we move dramatically and irreversibly into a new world.

The problem is trying to explain this radical disjuncture in political thinking. Whig historiography has it that constitutional struggle generated a new civic consciousness; heightened recognition, that is, of the need for a set of public procedures for settling political disputes.[1] 'Civic consciousness' seems an unfortunate choice of phrase to characterize a style of thinking which, dissolving the ties of solidarity between people, was forced into defining the public realm as a system of external constraints to the activities of private individuals. The question is why individualist premises suddenly flooded the minds of people.

Clearly, long-term shifts in the pattern of socio-economic relations offer a fruitful line of investigation. In *The Political Theory of Possessive Individualism*, C. B. Macpherson suggests that the new model of civil society was extrapolated from an emerging market society. Dissolving the affective ties of traditional society into exchange values by bringing people into contact with the market, nascent capitalism fostered a conception of the acquisitive individual whose fellows stood as rivals in the scramble for limited commodities. The problem here is that we still have to explain why the revolution in political theory occurred at this particular historical juncture. The market society was not conjured out of a hat. The transformation to relations of exchange rather than ascription was a protracted process, neither begun nor completed in the 1640s. No commentator would be so naïve as to suggest that production for exchange as the primary mode of economic activity made a sudden and dramatic appearance on the historical scene.[2]

Moreover, the protagonists of those climactic years hardly saw themselves as the agents of a bourgeois revolution. Civil War may have disseminated what we now recognize as bourgeois ideology but it was not because productive relations were suddenly mediated to the consciousness in a simple and direct fashion. The parliamentarians, whom we might expect to have been the prime

---

[1] Hanson, *From Kingdom to Commonwealth*, p. 5: 'Both the argumentation and the institutional experiments and alterations of the civil war period give expression to the kind of recognition that is here being called civic consciousness. This is precisely consciousness of the existence of a uniquely public sphere, public in the sense that the issues are general to the political order and inescapably shared. It is the recognition that some matters, and these some of the most important ones, require the capacity and the willingness to focus political attention and sustained activity at the level of the central governmental institutions of the society.'

[2] Various explanations for the transition may be found in Eugene Kamenka and R. S. Neale (eds.), *Feudalism, Capitalism and Beyond* (London, 1975); and Rodney Hilton (ed.), *The Transition from Feudalism to Capitalism* (London, 1976).

carriers of a new spirit, tended to present themselves as heirs to
the Tudor State, reacting against the excesses of royal paternalism
by demanding a return to the political and economic *status quo
ante*. Many of them favoured a form of state regulation of the market
that would reverse the trend towards a consolidation of the privileges of a landed and commercial oligarchy.[1] While the issues
polarized along class lines as the Civil War sped its course and new
groups began to press their demands, the politics of confrontation
did not begin as a form of class warfare. Indeed, many members of
parliament were inhibited from assuming a clear-cut attitude by the
fact that their position embodied those very contradictions between
the court and local communities which helped to precipitate the
struggle.[2] There was no simple dichotomy between an 'aristocracy',
consisting of higher nobility and richer merchants cultivated by the
crown, and a 'bourgeoisie', but a tendency, no more, for some of
the gentry, mercantile interests, and the so-called middling sort to
unite in resistance to the unpalatable policies of royal absolutism.
A bourgeois revolution there may have been, but it was certainly
not initiated by men aggressively imbued with the spirit of individualism.

The revolution in political theory was nevertheless under way
in these early years. Significantly, one of the earliest statements of
radical individualism in the literary warfare of the time came not
from a parliamentarian, but from the pen of one who was to die for
the royalist cause, the young Dudley Digges. Not that there was
anything strikingly original in *The Unlawfulnesse of Subjects
taking up Armes against their Soveraigne*, because Digges plagiar-
ized the arguments of Hobbes's *De Cive*, the Latin version of
which had been printed privately in Paris the previous year, 1642.
More remarkable is the fact that the relevance to the ensuing
struggle of arguments so antithetical to the conventional wisdom
should have been perceived so quickly, and that these ideas should
have been assimilated into the debate without any attempt to
counter traditional beliefs and values by careful and sustained
refutation. It is as though a number of reputable scientists today
suddenly and baldly declared that the world is square. Whereas

---

[1] cf. Penelope Corfield, 'Economic Issues and Ideologies', in Russell (ed.),
The Origins of the English Civil War, pp. 197–218.
[2] cf. Conrad Russell, 'Parliamentary History in Perspective, 1604–1629',
History, 61 (1976), pp. 1–27.

they would be most likely certified insane by their peers, this was not the fate of Hobbes and Digges.

Until recently, it was assumed that Hobbes was universally disparaged as the *bête noire* of his generation, outraging public opinion by his supposed atheism and moral relativism.[1] Careful scholarship by Quentin Skinner has now established, not only that Hobbes was generally understood to be grounding political obligation in self-interest, the obligation emanating from a prudential calculation by the obligee that government would secure his protection, but also that 'Hobbist' arguments were employed by a number of writers after 1649 as a means of justifying the Commonwealth.[2] This is not hard to appreciate, for, apart from the need to validate a regime without historical precedent, by 1649 there was a sense of war-weariness which resulted in a predilection to accept practically any form of government. Expediential justifications for what emerged were almost inevitable.

This was not the case in 1643, which did not prevent the unacknowledged absorption of the radical premises expounded by Hobbes into more immediately combative literature. In effect, this entailed an undermining of the traditional view that political reason was a property of the community, to be exercised on its behalf by one man or some group. It implied, correlatively, the self-sufficiency of individual reason, of which the test was a willingness by each individual to restrain his activities for the sake of self-preservation rather than from acknowledgement of the superior claims of a supra-individual common good. No one has successfully fathomed the depths of Hobbes's unique genius and I am not competent to contribute to the continuing debate as to whether

[1] cf. John Bowle, *Hobbes and his Critics: a Study in Seventeenth Century Constitutionalism* (London, 1951); Samuel I. Mintz, *The Hunting of Leviathan: Seventeenth-Century Reactions to the Materialism and Moral Philosophy of Thomas Hobbes* (Cambridge, 1962).

[2] Quentin Skinner, 'The Context of Hobbes's Theory of Political Obligation', in Maurice Cranston and Richard S. Peters (eds.) *Hobbes and Rousseau* (New York, 1972), pp. 109–42. In view of Skinner's findings, it is strange to find the author of a recent book on Hobbes perpetrating the idea that his reception was almost entirely negative. Thomas A. Spragens, *The Politics of Motion: The World of Thomas Hobbes* (London, 1973), p. 21: 'Hobbes's own contemporaries reacted to his thought with virtually unanimous horror . . . His alleged atheism, his materialism, his political absolutism, his alleged libertinism all were perceived as bound up in one frightening package, potent but wholly unacceptable, worthy of being taken seriously but only as an adversary.'

his thinking was inspired mainly by scientific naturalism, the operations of a market society, or philosophical nominalism.[1] But it is perhaps possible to venture an explanation as to why the individualism, of which he was the most rigorous and magnificent exponent, was so rapidly distilled into political thinking.

I have suggested that the theories of absolute and limited monarchy reflected the moderate success of Tudor government in satisfying the expectations of a broad section of dominant groups. The theory of absolute monarchy was a vehicle which served to convey their desire for national unity, while that of limited monarchy originated in the political developments by which a degree of unity was achieved. So long as the literate members of society were reasonably convinced that justice was being dispensed to all corners of the realm, they were content to articulate a conception of the common good which transcended particular interests. While their interests were relatively secure, they were prepared to declare the moral acceptability of existing institutions. Hence the persistence of the traditional view of society as a functional and corporate entity whose political actors were presumed to have special access to a system of objective moral standards. Either a uniquely favoured monarch, or the combined wisdom of the king in parliament, was held to be the medium through which a shared and objective well-being was made tangible in the community. Both theories judged the rational capacity of each ordinary individual to be deficient, arguing that ungoverned passion or undue regard for self-interest were individually detrimental and socially disastrous. Both, that is, were predicated on the necessity of curtailing individual volition through a public representation of the good life in objectively rational policies.

While the nation remained politically integrated its spokesmen were ready to acknowledge that its authority structures embodied a kind of wisdom not found in each member of the community considered individually. Even when the crown began to act in a way which excluded certain groups from the political process and so disappointed expectations, its opponents could provide theoretical resistance by deploying the notion of a superior communal wisdom in the form of custom. By 1640, however, disappointment

---

[1] For a cogent survey of the different interpretations, see W. H. Greenleaf, 'Hobbes: The Problem of Interpretation', in Cranston and Peters (eds.), *Hobbes and Rousseau*, pp. 5–36.

had turned to hostility, and many members of dominant social groups found it impossible to believe that government was in any sense the repository of a higher wisdom. It was intra-class strife, not inter-class warfare, which acted as a catharsis on political thinking.[1]

Established institutions had lost their credibility. Just as in religion various sects were challenging the monopoly of truth claimed by the Church of England, so the once proclaimed infallibility of traditional political institutions was now denied by a broad segment of the community. In the absence of a general consensus regarding the efficacy of those structures, it became increasingly difficult to sustain the view that there was some group naturally entitled to govern by virtue of its privileged knowledge of communal requirements. Some ground for political authority other than a supposedly special linkage to the divine reason had to be sought once parliament had vigorously asserted its claim to be an alternative, and more authentic, custodian of the common good than the crown.

The market society did not impinge itself on men's consciousness because they suddenly became aware of the economic formations of nascent capitalism. Long-term socio-economic trends were mediated to the consciousness in the form of a political confrontation that shattered the conventional conception of an integrated society in which the well-being of everyone was politically secured. Once the belief that political wisdom was an exclusive property of those who traditionally wielded political power had been destroyed, and the assumption that this wisdom entailed a special type of expertise had been consequently eroded, it was only a short step to defining political reason as a capacity exercised by individuals. The uncertainty which preceded and accompanied the Civil War bred a sort of anarchy of private opinion in which numerous people felt entitled to proffer their own solutions to the nation's ills. As one writer, reflecting the welter of debate that accompanied

[1] Stone, *The causes of the English Revolution 1529–1642*. pp. 56–7: 'Before civil war could break out, it was necessary for the major institutions of central government to lose credibility and to collapse. Although the crisis only becomes intelligible in the light of social and economic change, what has to be explained in the first place is not a crisis within the society, but rather a crisis within the regime, the alienation of very large segments of the élites from the established political and religious institutions . . . [T]he war began as a power struggle between competing elements of the pre-existing structure of authority.'

the breakdown of traditional patterns of practice and belief, put it in 1642: 'Conscience is that new name which no man knowes but hee that hath it.'[1] Once the legitimacy of conscience or private reason had been acknowledged, it was inevitable that political debate should focus on that which concerned each particularly, and of which he had immediate knowledge, his security and self-interest. Whereas reason had always been respected as a means of transcending particularity, it was now linked to it. Whereas government had been viewed as a device for combating self-interest and partiality, the actual wants of each particular man were now treated as goals worthy of political pursuit. It was not that political activity prompted men towards an otherwise unattainable level of moral and spiritual perfection, but that it supplied an ordered framework within which interests might be pursued. Government was no longer the embodiment of a higher form of wisdom, but a convenient arrangement that removed some of the obstacles to volition amongst men whose mutually exclusive concerns made them potential rivals.

The traditional world picture disintegrated with remarkable speed. Old notions nevertheless lingered, and sometimes they were cogently expressed. On the parliamentary side, a careful classification of the various forms of constitution was provided in Philip Hunton's, *A Treatise of Monarchy*. Hunton's intention was to curb the excesses of the crown by outlining the legitimate restraints to its prerogative. He did not, however, offer a statement of the philosophical assumptions underlining his definition of English government as a monarchy which was both limited and mixed.

This was done in a series of works by Henry Parker, the most persistent and able advocate of the parliamentary cause, who specifically invoked the idea of a superior collective reason in order to reveal the moral poverty of absolute monarchy and the necessity, therefore, of a politically mobilized community to restrain the activities of an irrational king.[2] Parker's thinking hinged on the conventional belief that the common possession of reason was politically relevant. He condemned those who mystified political

---

[1] Charles Herle, *A Fuller Answer to a Treatise written by Doctor Ferne* (London, 1642), sig. A. 2.

[2] For this reason, I can make no sense of the assessment by Jordan, *Men of Substance*, p. 86: 'Parker sketched in clear and precise outlines the political theory which Hobbes, with one of the most lucid and powerful minds that England has ever known, was to expand into a systematic and documented structure.'

activity with their suggestion that the king was qualitatively
different from his subjects and was possessed, therefore, with a
monopoly of political wisdom. This, said Parker, was a recipe for
servility and tyranny.[1] Whereas all individuals, including the king,
'have but their own particular set limits of perfection, and have
judgements besides apt to bee darkened by their owne severall
interests and passions', their combined wisdom 'injoynes a con-
fluence of severall perfections'. It was, therefore, capable of de-
ciphering and operating a norm of justice which defeated partiality.[2]
If a collective reason was a competent filter of objective standards,
it followed that its political expression, parliament, was an infallible
dispenser of communal justice.[3] As a 'collective uniuersality, whose
rayes like the Suns, are every where dispersed', it was inconceivable that any parliament would enact measures which were detrimental to the common good.[4] Hence, Parker repeated the old
maxim that a good king would spurn his frail, unaided judgement
by surrounding himself with the wisdom of many, whose eyes
perceived with greater clarity and impartiality the requirements
of the community. Parker, who had read both Fortescue and
Hooker, elaborated a theory of consent with the intention of illustrating how a community might make political provision for itself.
Power being inherently and originally in the community, the
latter delegated authority to some agency with responsibility for
executing laws made in regard to the common benefit. When
those entrusted with this task began to abuse their office, most
nations had found it expedient to combat arbitrariness by adopting
procedures which made legislation the joint responsibility of the
king and elected representatives of the community.

   There was nothing very new in this, no hint of individualism.
Parker was not using the notion of consent to explain how an
artificial political unity might be created out of an agglomeration

   [1] Henry Parker, *Jus Populi* (London, 1644), p. 8.
   [2] Henry Parker, *A Discourse Concerning Puritans* (London, 1641), p. 49.
   [3] Ibid., p. 48: 'The Courts of Parliament, and their unquestionable Acts, and
Ordinances, and their infallible avisoes, are now in all well-governed Countries;
the very Oracles of all Policy, and Law, they are the fountaines of civill bloud,
spirits, and life; and the soveraigne antidotes of publike mischiefes.'
   [4] Henry Parker, *Observations upon some of his Majesties Late Answers and
Expresses* (1642), in Haller (ed.), *Tracts on Liberty in the Puritan Revolution*, II,
p. 188: 'no age will furnish us with one story of any Parliament freely elected,
and held, that ever did injure a whole Kingdome, or exercise any tyranny, nor
is there any possibility how it should'.

of private, thus anti-social interests. It was for him, as it had been
for Hooker, a device by which to explain how the individual will of
the monarch could be restrained to good effect, facilitating a unity
of action according to a standard other than the interests of any
segment of the community. What was new was the context in
which the theory was expressed. By choosing to ignore the
machinery created to achieve political co-operation, the king had
contravened the Roman legal principle, what touches all must
be approved by all.[1] In this situation, parliament became the
custodian of the common good. For it represented the pooled, thus
objectively valid, wisdom of the community, in contrast to the inferior
determinations of a fallible individual. Parliament might legitimately do, therefore, whatever was necessary to prevent national
ruin.

Parker had revived the theory of limited monarchy by appealing
to an institutionally expressed corporate rationality, rather than
to custom or historical precedent. The representative voice of the
people as it now expressed itself assumed priority over the inscrutable activities of a king out of parliament.[2] Parker's premises may
have been traditional. Yet he was inadvertently clearing the way
for those who, in the name of the people, would press demands
which, they held, any ordinary person might immediately acknowledge to be self-evidently just.

On the royalist side, old notions lingered longer. After Charles
had made a belated effort in 1642 to salvage the situation by admitting in a series of propositions that English government consisted
of a nice balance of the three estates, some royalists appropriated
the theory of mixed government in order to portray themselves as
the true heirs of the English constitution. It was parliament, they
held, which had destroyed the balance by arrogating functions not
properly belonging to it. Replying to one of Parker's pamphlets,
Sir John Spelman said that it had always been recognized that
English government was a limited monarchy in which the king
was the pre-eminent partner. The bulk of the body politic related

---

[1] Ibid., p. 171.
[2] Parliament's claim to represent the people was less incredulous when Parker
wrote than it might have seemed a century earlier. For the decades preceding
civil war witnessed a rise in the number of contested elections, an expansion in
the size of the electorate, and greater responsiveness by members to demands
emanating from their electoral bases. cf. Derek Hirst, *The Representative of the
People? Voters and Voting in England under the Early Stuarts* (Cambridge, 1975).

to him in a consultative capacity, and the initiative in summoning representatives lay with him. Spelman adapted Fortescue's definition of English society as 'a body mysticall governed by one man', arguing that the conception of a body politic in which the monarch stood in an inferior relation to his subjects was as absurd as that of a natural body governed by a member other than the head.[1] Henry Ferne, a favourite target for parliamentarians, also stressed the advisory role of parliament. He insinuated, somewhat feebly in the light of preceding events, that parliament had misjudged events because there will 'be always sufficient reason to withhold the King from a wilful deniall of his Consent to the free and unanimous Vote of his Houses: he cannot but see there will always be some necessary good accrewing to him by his Parliament, that will keep him in all reason from doing so'.[2]

The appeal to history was reinforced by the need to counter the argument that government had originated in communal consent and was, consequently, endowed only with as much authority as the whole community deemed appropriate. Thus, assertions of the king's direct responsibility to God were supported by Old Testament examples of monarchical government, and by the assimilation of political society to the most natural unity of authority, the family. There was more than an analogy between the authority of a father and that of a king, suggested Ferne, for the one had been the historical successor to the other. 'Fatherly rule' enlarged 'it selfe into a Kingly power, which bore and used the sword'.[3]

Appeals to history and half-hearted admissions of the limited nature of English monarchy were overshadowed by a more familiar style of argument, the invocation of a hierarchically organized universe. John Maxwell used it to ridicule the supposition that human consent had a part to play in making political power legitimate, or in laying unnatural restrictions on the royal prerogative. 'How can it then be conceived, that God hath left it to the simple consent and composition of man, to make and establish a herauldry of *Sub* and *Supra*, of one above another, which neither Nature nor the Gospel doth warrant?'[4] The appropriate pattern of order had

---

[1] Sir John Spelman, *A view of a printed book Intituled Observations upon His Majesties Late Answers and Expresses* (Oxford, 1642) p. 8.

[2] Henry Ferne, *The Resolving of Conscience* (Cambridge, 1642), p. 27.

[3] Henry Ferne, *Conscience Satisfied* (Oxford, 1643), p. 8.

[4] John Maxwell, *Sacro-Sancta Regum Majestas: or, the Sacred and Royall Prerogative of Christian Kings* (Oxford, 1644), p. 83.

been divinely established, and was everywhere visible for those who cared to look.

The analogies existing between human society and the universal structure were most fully developed in an ornate, rambling work, full of fine distinctions which suggest that its author had time on his hands. He had, indeed, for Michael Hudson wrote *The Divine Right of Government* in the Tower, which must have given him ample opportunity, as he put it, to wander through 'obscure and uncouch pathes'.[1] Hudson traced the origins of regal authority to Adam's paternity, and drew attention to the degrees of subordination and superiority exhibited in the natural world, in order to demonstrate the absurdity of a multi-headed political community, which he termed 'polarchy . . . For though the body of man, which is the most exact Model of Nature, consists of two hands and Armes, and two feet and legs, and though each of them also have five toes and fingers, yet doth one head direct the actions and motions of all these.'[2] Order in human society depended upon the preservation of the pre-existing pattern of the universe. The mass of men were naturally excluded from engaging in political activity by an immutable principle of inequality.

In fact, despite concessions to the theory of limited monarchy, the types of argument used by royalists—the appeal to history, the analogy with the family, as well as a reiteration of the world view of order—were intended to perpetuate a tendency we have previously considered, that of mystifying politics by propagating the idea that ordinary mortals were somehow incapacitated from taking an active role in directing the nation.

Filmer's reputation probably derives from the rather clever way in which he blended various levels of argument into an affirmation of the prerogative of a uniquely competent monarch. 'Sir Robert Filmer's patriarchal theory was, if anything, an exaltation of history, a mythical history, to be sure, but real enough to him and some of his contemporaries.'[3] It was evidently this. Yet the tracing of political authority to its Adamic origins was itself part

[1] Michael Hudson, *The Divine Right of Government* (London, 1647), p. 65.
[2] Ibid., p. 93.
[3] Perez Zagorin, *A History of Political Thought in the English Revolution* (London, 1954), p. 28. Patriachalism is the subject of a recent comprehensive study: Gordon J. Schochet, *Patriarchalism in Political Thought: The Authoritarian Family and Political Speculation and Attitudes Especially in Seventeenth-Century England* (Oxford, 1975).

of a broader strategy intended to undermine the case of those seeking to place politics on a more rational, more immediately accessible basis than formerly. *Patriarcha*, essentially, was an attempt to stem the tide by destroying the emerging assumption, implicit in parliament's claim to be a more reliable repository of the common good than the crown, that the exercise of political authority entailed skills of which ordinary men were not totally devoid. Filmer began his treatise by modestly disavowing any intention,

to meddle with mysteries of the present state. Such arcana imperii, or cabinet councils, the vulgar may not pry into. An implicit faith is given to the meanest artificer in his own craft; how much more is it, then, due to a Prince in the profound secrets of government: the causes and ends of the greatest politic actions and motions of state dazzle the eyes and exceed the capacities of all men, save only those that are hourly versed in managing public affairs.[1]

Here was the traditional idea that politics was properly a business for experts. And it was linked with the belief that God retained effective, though oft-times inscrutable, control of public affairs. Not only did He appoint and remove rulers at will,[2] but took a continuing fatherly interest in the welfare of His people, though the purpose of His actions was not always immediately apparent to them. By comparing the duties of a king with those of a natural father, Filmer was hoping to create the impression that, like his heavenly father, the monarch incessantly cared for the well-being of his subjects and was incapable of harming them. Like good children, model subjects would implicitly trust and obey their ruler's commands, presenting petitions through parliament but never daring to question the wisdom of his decisions. It was a form of royalist propaganda that had been effective in previous times, but was less credible now that a significant chunk of the nation felt at least as well qualified as the crown to determine the community's political destiny.

Their self-confidence in this direction was manifested in the growing conviction that politics had to do with that which affected each directly and immediately, that is, self-interest. It was rather

[1] Sir Robert Filmer, *Patriarcha and Other Political Works,* ed. Peter Laslett (Oxford, 1949), p. 54.
[2] Ibid., p. 62.

less an activity for eradicating sin from public affairs than a mundane mechanism for adjusting competing claims between individuals. While Henry Parker was busily defending parliament as a trustee and interpreter of a universal norm of justice, others were doing so on the less esoteric basis that it was a forum enabling sufficient units of interest to be taken into account.[1] Self-interest was now judged to be a proper end of government, and parliament was valued because it was better structured than the crown to safeguard the properties and privileges of a wide section of society.

This, for instance, was the manner in which Charles Herle sought to refute the claims of Henry Ferne. Herle began, unremarkably enough, by defining English government as a temperate mixture of the three estates. Like Parker, he held that the duty of preserving the nation devolved on parliament now that the monarch was acting arbitrarily. This, he said, accorded with fundamental law or custom, and was proven by the corporate character of the English constitution. For corporations being immortal, it followed that concern for the nation's safety was not obliterated by the king's refusal to fulfil his traditional functions. That concern was preserved in parliament whose ordinances were equivalent to the 'wisdom of State'.

Herle broke new ground, however, when explaining why parliament was less likely than the monarch to make bad laws:

experience shews that most mens activities are swayed most what by their ends and interests: those of Kings (for the most part) *absolutenesse of rule*, inlargement of Revenue by Monopolyes, Patents, &c. are altogether incompatible and crosse centred to those of Subjects, as *Property*, *Priviledge*, &. with which the Parliaments either ends or interest cannot thus dash and interfer, the Members are all subjects themselves, not onely *intrusted* with, but self *interested* in those very *priviledges*, and properties: besides they are many, and so not only see more, but are lesse swayable; as not easily reducible to *one* head of private *interest*; but by a neer equality of *Votes*, (you'l say) in Parliament it may come to an odde man to cast by, and then the whole trust and interest both lyes in him wholy. I answer, no such matter . . . the last odde sand doth not make the hourglasse *empty* more then any of the rest, it doth but tell us when 'tis *empty*, suppose 200 of one side and 201 of the other, the odde

---

[1] For an account of the emergence of the concept of interest, see J. A. W. Gunn, *Politics and the Public Interest in the Seventeenth Century* (London, 1969).

is carryed by the one, but the *Vote* by the whole 201; the odde one tells us 'tis the major part, but 'tis all the rest that make it so: so that we have (however) the judgement; trust and interest of 201 chosen men engaged in the equity and fitnesse of the *Vote :* this is it that that greate Father of the Law, so much magnifies the wisdom of this government.[1]

In spite of the fact that Fortescue was the great Father of the law referred to, and the familiar ring of some of the language, fundamentally different claims were now being made on behalf of parliament. Gone was the idea that arbitrariness was overcome by a gathering of the wise whose enactments defeated caprice and selfishness by connecting with eternal standards of justice. Impartiality was achieved, rather, by an assembling of interested parties whose representation ensured that their interests were accommodated. Rationality was now made equivalent to the promotion of self-interest, and political activity judged to be rational in so far as it maximized the individual units of interest found in society. Arbitrariness was said to be combated by 'number, trust, self interest', not by raising men's sight towards a qualitatively distinct common good which demanded a restraint of individual desires.

Herle disclaimed the conventional principle of parliamentary infallibility. Parliament, he said, was no pope, for, as a collection of self-regarding individuals, it might err. He could hardly claim otherwise because a political mechanism intended to sort out interests that were mutually exclusive would be unlikely to facilitate complete adjustment. There would always be some losers, some interests would receive recognition at the expense of others. The assertion of infallibility remained credible only so long as parliament was supposed to rise above the clash of particular interests in search of a universal norm where ultimate reconciliation and harmony were conceivable. Nevertheless, Herle held that parliament was better informed than any individual and its enactments, therefore, more likely to be 'peeces of quick and walking reason'.[2] Despite this deference to Aristotle's definition of an impartial law, it clearly amounted in Herle's view to a rule which successfully mediated between competing private interests. Impartiality was achieved when political support was given to the various interests at large in society, not by the suppression

---

[1] Herle, *A Fuller Answer to a Treatise,* pp. 16–17.
[2] Ibid., p. 19.

of self-interest through the substitution of a higher standard of rightness.

The justification of parliament had assumed a quantitative dimension. It was judged superior to absolute monarchy on the grounds that it represented a wider range of interests. Once this line of argument had been adopted, it was inevitable that certain groups should attack the exclusiveness of parliament and demand representation of an even larger number of interests. While parliament was envisaged as a trustee of an objective reason, it was irrelevant that certain sections of the community were not directly involved in the political process. What mattered, so it was said, was that parliament should channel the refined wisdom of the community towards the realization of a good in which particulars were included. Now that parliament had been proclaimed a market-place where those with interests at stake might gather and sort out their respective claims, it could only be a matter of time before attention was drawn to its unrepresentative nature.

This was an argument which even royalists found useful. In *The Anarchy of a Limited or Mixed Monarchy*, Filmer gave the concept of representation this connotation as a means of undermining Hunton's defence of mixed government. The Commons, said Filmer, was not entitled to thrust itself forward as the trustee of the nation's welfare because it represented the interests of a minority only. It did not speak on behalf of the king and nobility and, moreover, the major part of the common people were excluded from it.[1] So it was nonsensical to argue that the Commons might intervene in the appointment and regulation of kings. Even Filmer was not above using the idea of representation in its current individualist sense when it suited his purpose.

---

[1] Filmer, *Patriarcha and Other Political Works*, p. 290: 'The Commons in Parliament are not the representative body of the whole kingdom: they do not represent the King, who is the head and principal member of the kingdom; nor do they represent the Lords, who are the nobler and higher part of the body of the realm, and are personally present in Parliament, and therefore need no representation. The Commons only represent a part of the lower or inferior part of the body of the people, which are freeholders worth 40s. by the year, and the Commons or freemen of cities and boroughs, or the major part of them. All which are not one-quarter, nay, not a tenth part of the Commons of the kingdom; for in every parish, for one freeholder there may be found ten that are no freeholders: and anciently before rents were improved, there nothing so near so many freeholders of 40s. by the year as now are to be found.'

Others accepted Filmer's assessment of the unrepresentative
nature of parliament, though not his conclusions. They sought a
redress through a shift in the balance of political power from its
concentration in gentry hands towards the middling sort. En-
shrined in the Leveller programme was a set of demands intended
to make parliament more responsive to the interests of a wider
section of the community and which, intentionally or not, gave an
added thrust to the unfolding of individualist assumptions. For in
order to validate their demands, the Levellers were compelled to
devalue history by rewriting it as a tale of oppression and institutionalized domination. In spite of several years of intensive fighting, parliament had failed to secure the rights of Englishmen and
the fault lay, it seemed, in the English political tradition itself.
Hence the Levellers' celebration of a pristine political form, pre-
dating the arrival of the Norman Conqueror, was a call for radical
reconstruction. Custom was conceived as the dross of ages and
contemporary institutions castigated as the sediment of an historical unreason. What was required, therefore, was a cleansing
operation that would sweep away the debris of past errors to begin
afresh in the light of rationally apprehended principles. For, men
might reshape history in a way that would enable their communal
arrangements to embody those human rights which were apparent
to any rational being.

The Levellers denied the charge that they wished to level men's
estates. Their intention, they said, was to see 'the Commonwealth
. . . reduced to such a passe that every man may with as much
security as may be enjoy his propriety'.[1] It was a straightforward
and relatively modest intention. Nevertheless, it was grounded in
the radical assertion of the self-sufficiency of individual reason, a
faculty which allegedly enlightened its possessor as to the institutional prerequisites of self-preservation, and equipped him with
an eternally valid and easily applied yardstick by which to assess
the efficacy of existing political structures. Richard Overton expressed the doctrine clearly:

All forms of laws and governments may fall and pass away, but right
reason (the fountain of all justice and mercy to the creature) shall and
will endure for ever. It is that by which in all our actions we must stand

[1] William Haller and Godfrey Davies (eds.), *The Leveller Tracts 1647–1653*
(New York, 1944), p. 279.

or fall, be justified or condemned; for neither morality nor divinity amongst men can or may transgress the limits of right reason . . . Therefore from hence is conveyed to all men in general, and to every man in particular, an undoubted principle of reason: by all rational and just ways and means possibly he may, to save, defend, and deliver himself from all oppression, violence and cruelty whatsoever, and (in duty to his own safety and being) to leave no just expedient unattempted for his delivery therefrom. And this is rational and just. To deny it is to overturn the law of nature, yea and of religion too; for the contrary lets in nothing but self-murder, violence and cruelty . . . For all just human powers are but betrusted, conferred, and conveyed by joint and common consent; for to every individual in nature is given an individual propriety by nature, not to be invaded or usurped by any . . . for every one as he is himself hath a self propriety—else could he not be himself— and on this no second may presume without consent; and by natural birth all men are equal, and alike born to like propriety and freedom, every man by natural instinct aiming at his own safety and weal.[1]

It was no longer a divinely favoured monarch or the collective wisdom of the community that was endowed with infallibility, but the unaided judgement of each individual. The appeal might be still to natural law, but it was a far cry from the days when the higher law was shrouded in mystery, ultimately accessible to reason but uncovered only gradually by the practical wisdom of generations of men. Reason no longer taught the individual to immerse himself in traditional social practices, but to be vigilant in seeking out the flaws in those practices. It no longer informed him of his own imperfections and his need of political direction, but advised him that he was as competent as anyone to assess the legitimacy of all temporal arrangements. It no longer persuaded him that he would be nothing apart from an intricate hierarchy of socio-political relationships, but revealed to him those natural rights which no political structure might legitimately jeopardize. The modest aim of the Levellers issued, therefore, in the radical demand for a new constitution that would emanate from the consent of each rational being and which would safeguard those self-evident rights belonging to all.

Since reason was now regarded less as a communal property than as an individual capacity, the concept of order could not but assume transformed significance. It had been held that a rational

[1] Richard Overton, *An Appeal from the Commons to the Free People* (1647), in A. S. P. Woodhouse, *Puritanism and Liberty* (London, 1938), pp. 323–7.

human order consisted in preserving that pattern revealed throughout the universe. Political relationships merely confirmed the natural inequality of men, providing a context for the good life in terms of a functional structure that gave to each the opportunity of moral development within the confines of his station. It was now being said that men were equal by virtue of a rational faculty which prompted each to pursue his interests in whatever way he considered appropriate. But interests being exclusive and mutually incompatible, rational behaviour was calculated to lead to political conflict and not, as had been thought previously, to a duplication of the ordered structure of the universe.[1] The practically solipsistic understanding of the rational human being, as a self-regarding and self-sufficient creature, transformed the problem of political order into that of contriving an artificial unity that would impose a degree of uniformity upon diverse human behaviour. If order did not already exist in society, it had to be created *ex nihilo* and objectified in a form which was external to the agglomeration of conflicting private interests. Political power was now envisaged in a much more innovatory sense. The ruler had to be truly sovereign in devising and enforcing rules that would prevent communal fragmentation. It was this theme which preoccupied royalists, and they pursued it vigorously.

It emerged, for instance, in the changing imagery used to describe the sort of order that existed in political society. Whereas some continued to liken the human community to the microcosm and other ordered wholes, others began to speak of the State as a ship that would flounder without a pilot. This was the language employed by Robert Grosse in his *Royalty and Loyalty*.[2] Grosse attributed to the king sufficient power to do whatever was necessary to preserve national unity. The king, he suggested, making use of a civil law maxim, had '*The power of making and abrogating Laws at pleasure*, as the necessity of the Common wealth shall require'.[3] Necessity rather than objective reason had become the measure of

---

[1] As Engels put it, Karl Marx and Frederick Engels, *Articles on Britain* (Moscow, 1971), p. 16: 'Since interest is essentially subjective, egoistic, individualistic . . . the setting up of interest as the bond among men, so long as this interest remains directly subjective, quite simply egoistic, inevitably leads to universal disunity, the preoccupation of individuals with themselves, mankind's isolation and transformation into a heap of mutually repelling atoms.'

[2] Robert Grosse, *Royalty and Loyalty* (London, 1647), p. 2.

[3] Ibid., p. 26.

legitimate government activity. It was a barely disguised justification of arbitrary government and a radical departure from earlier defences of absolute monarchy.

The theme also emerged in the use made of the social contract. By reading the instability around them back into a hypothetical state of nature, royalists were able to explain precisely why civil society required a suspension of individual reason. A modicum of peace and security would be attained only if men agreed not to be self-determining in a political sense, only, that is, if they consented not to make their rational faculty politically operative. Following Hobbes, Digges described the state of nature as a condition where insatiable desires were continually confronted and thwarted by the inescapable fact of scarcity. Men being mutually suspicious and envious, no one was strong enough to be free of the fear that his possessions would be snatched and his life brutally terminated. In this situation, characterized by the absence of agreed rules for settling disputes, the law of nature amounted to a right of nature, the liberty of each to do whatever he reasoned to be necessary for preserving himself. But, the law of nature consisting of an injunction to self-preservation, men came to recognize that conflicts would be finally eradicated only through a mutual renunciation of the right to do whatever each pleased.

There being no way to effect this naturally, they reduce themselves into a civill unitie, by placing over them one head, and by making his will the will of them all, to the end there might be no gap left open by schisme to returne to their former confusion . . . [This] signifies the giving up of every mans particular power into his disposall, so that he may be inabled to force those who are unwilling upon some private ends, to be obedient for the common good.[1]

So civil society originated in the prudential calculation of each that an ordered framework might be created if he transferred to a sovereign his right of self-defence. He did not confer upon the sovereign the power of formulating and enforcing a system of laws because he perceived him to be of greater intelligence or wisdom than other members of the community. The sovereign had not been granted keener insight into objective norms which defined the common good: he was no wiser in the classical sense, no more

---

[1] Dudley Digges, *The Unlawfulnesse of Subjects taking up Armes against their Soveraigne* (London, 1643), p. 4.

altruistic than those subject to his commands. The only effective limitation to his legislative activity was his own self-interest because no sovereign would be foolish enough to impose the kind of edicts likely to incite his subjects to rebel. As Digges put it in another work, in which his intention was to defend the English monarch against the accusations of Parker:

if the People hearken to reason they must needes thinke, His Majestie will be more ready to prevent all reall danger, then any Subject whatsoever, because He is sure to beare the greatest share in the losse. It alwaies was the Master-pollicy amongst the wisest Legislators to grant to them the greatest power of Government, to whom the preservation of the present State would be most beneficiall; because their private Interests were the same with the Publique, from which if they swerv'd by error or mis-information, their owne disadvantage did soone appeare.[1]

In this way, natural law was pushed back to the margins of civil society. No longer was it conceived as a system of norms intended to infuse daily life with a moral flavour through the mediating activity of government. It was envisaged, rather, as an injunction to self-preservation which dictated to each the necessity of holding his political reason in abeyance once the initial act of creating political society had taken place, and which advised the sovereign that he would do well to secure the lives and properties of his subjects if he wished to retain his position. Exactly how he did this, the content of the laws which he made, was left to his discretion. Sovereign will rather than objective reason had become the standard of political legitimacy.

The force of these arguments was not lost on those who were not especially inclined to the royalist cause. From 1648 a number of writers were prepared to accept peace at any price. Anthony Ascham referred to 'the transcendent right which wee naturally have in the preservation of ourselves, and of those things without which wee cannot be preserved'.[2] Ascham did not find any form of government particularly attractive but he was prepared to accept any coercive power which was likely to heal divisions and thereby create an ordered framework within which the overriding goal of

---

[1] Dudley Digges, *An Answer to a printed book, intituled, Observations upon some of his Majesties late answers and expresses* (Oxford, 1642), p. 53.

[2] Anthony Ascham, *A Discourse: wherein is examined, what is particularly lawfull during the Confusions and Revolutions of Government* (London, 1648), pp. 36–7.

self-preservation might be attained. Marchamont Nedham was struck by the inherent corruption and impermanence of all forms of government. England, he said in 1650, had adopted a new form of government but this, too, would eventually decay. Meanwhile, it was peevish to resist the new government because this would serve to intensify strife and spread confusion. It was all a matter of admitting invariable political facts, of recognizing that all government depended upon the sword and expediently submitting to its commands. 'It is ground enough for the submission of particular persons in things of political equity that those which have gotten the power are irresistible and able to force it if they refuse.'[1] Might had become right and the last vestiges of the world view of a rationally ordered universe had been swept away.

Those whose values derived significance from that ideational structure believed that the function of political activity was to make an objective moral order communally operative, though they disagreed as to the most effective means of fulfilling this task. It was now being said that men were united by little else besides a common desire for self-preservation and advancement, that they were driven grudgingly by considerations of self-interest to create an ordered political structure. Reason had been transformed from a capacity capable of yielding universal norms into a subjective process that sought suitable means to particular utilitarian ends. It now sanctified that which separated men, legitimating their engagement in a competitive struggle for the limited goods available. In so far as the existence of objective standards was acknowledged, they were now held to consist of a few basic rights which were accessible to any private person through a simple process of deduction. Political organization being a device for striking some sort of compromise between multiple and conflicting interests, laws were now conceived as conventional rules validated by common agreement, or else as the arbitrary commands of a sovereign who was authorized to intimidate everyone into a submissive conformity. There was nothing natural about a rational human order because it had to be contrived, artificially created, and its lamentable absence from the nexus of social life was now made into a primary justification of political authority. Government was made necessary by the lack of any recognizable or reliable

---

[1] Marchamont Nedham, *The Case of the Commonwealth of England Stated*, ed. Philip A. Knachel (Charlottesville, Virg., 1969), p. 31.

bonds of human solidarity and its function was to formally construct and enforce that sense of community of which men in their
daily lives were deprived.

Social atomism was a poor substitute for a community of mutually responsive beings where the human potential of each was
actualized and harnessed for the benefit of everyone. This, at any
rate, was the opinion of some who made what Dr. Hill terms the
revolt within the revolution.[1] In the ideas of the Diggers, and in
their communitarian experiment on St. George's Hill in 1649, was
outlined a programme intended to construct a human order on the
basis of the natural reason each man was presumed to possess.
Gerrard Winstanley, the chief theoretician of this movement of the
dispossessed, turned the now conventional justification of civil
authority on its head by portraying government as a confirmation
of alienated social relationships. Political power was identified as
a form of institutionalized greed, the extension and confirmation
of a class struggle whereby dominant groups consolidated those
gains which they had made since the introduction of private
property.

Much of Winstanley's language has a familiar ring because the
medieval world had furnished ample affirmations of the entitle-
ment of all men to the fruits of the earth; a form of social criticism
which, we have noticed, culminated in attacks by commentators
such as Robert Crowley and Henry Brinklow upon the English
parliament as a thinly disguised institutional mechanism of economic exploitation. But Winstanley's writings, for all their sense
of urgency and millenarian expectancy, explored these themes in a
much more extensive and systematic fashion. Indeed, it was the
charged millenarian ingredient in his thinking which prompted
Winstanley to postulate a pristine human condition where all
were infused with the divine spirit of reconciliation. In doing so he
rejected, more fully and explicitly than any previous writer, the
assumption that human nature was a fixed datum of which the
established political system was the natural and invariable counter-
part. Human nature as it was now constituted was an historical
artifact, contrived by the unfortunate series of social relations in
which individuals were intricated.

Men were not naturally avaricious and aggressive. This was a
myth induced by the bad form of socialization to which people

[1] Christopher Hill, *The World Turned Upside Down* (London, 1972).

had been subjected throughout the course of human history. The myth was perpetrated by the wielders of political power whose interests were served by an ideological cloak that was designed to conceal the fact that communal wealth was distributed unjustly. In this way, Winstanley postulated an historically modifiable human nature in which men as they were now, with all their faults and limitations, were portrayed as the victims of a contingent constellation of social and political forces. There was nothing inevitable or indispensable about coercive political structures: they merely endorsed and entrenched the unacceptable features of the contemporary human condition by legitimating a sin which was far from being inherent in human nature:

And hereupon the earth (which was made to be a common treasury of relief for all, both beasts and men) was hedged into enclosures by the teachers and rulers, and the others were made servants and slaves: and that earth, that is within this creation made a common storehouse for all, is bought and sold and kept in the hands of a few, whereby the great creator is mightily dishonoured, as if he were a respecter of persons, delighting in the comfortable livelihood of some, and rejoicing in the miserable poverty and straits of others. From the beginning it was not so . . . But this coming in of bondage is called A-dam, because this ruling and teaching power without doth dam up the spirit of peace and liberty, first within the heart, by filling it with slavish fears of others; secondly without, by giving the bodies of one to be imprisoned, punished and oppressed by the outward power of another. And this evil was brought upon us through his own convetousness, whereby he is blinded and made weak, and sees not the law of righteousness in his heart, which is the pure light of reason, but looks abroad for it, and thereby the creation is cast under bondage and curse, and the creator is slighted.[1]

Eradicate the cause of human misery and imperfection, abolish the institution of private property by making communal wealth equally available to all, 'and mankind will not only become single-hearted again, but will walk in the light of pure reason and love, and never fall again into divisions'.[2]

Winstanley projected a community of non-competitive beings where ties of solidarity emanated from the self-regulating capacity

[1] Christopher Hill (ed.) *Winstanley: The Law of Freedom and other writings* (London, 1973), p. 78.
[2] Ibid., p. 268.

of each. It was a society which issued from the rationality inherent in each and where, therefore, the coercive apparatus of the state withered away because it was redundant.[1] The wheel had come full circle. A rational human order was natural after all. But its foundation was not the divine hierarchy of the universe. Nor was its political expression the exclusive responsibility of a king or a particular group of men. It was grounded, rather, in the potential of all men to conduct themselves in an orderly fashion, with an eye to that common good in which particulars were truly integrated. Needless to say, the poor did not become the revolutionary agents of a new world. The society which was in the process of formation, and for which the Civil War engendered theoretical spokesmen in abundance, was radically different from that which Winstanley envisaged. It was different, too, from the society which had encouraged its members to think in terms of a rationally ordered universe.

[1] Though it has to be admitted that, especially in his last and more programmatically orientated work, *The Law of Freedom*, Winstanley is unwilling to rely entirely on internalized norms of right conduct as a basis of social cohesion. There must be institutional guarantees of communal justice in that men have to be actively discouraged from behaving anti-socially. cf. J. C. Davis, 'Gerrard Winstanley and the Restoration of True Magistracy', *Past and Present*, 70 (1976), pp. 76–93. Even so, the bulk of Winstanley's writings do articulate a conception radically at odds with the emergent view of the state; as the public interest objectified in an external form precisely because the nexus of social relations was seen to consist of an arena of conflicting private interests.

BIBLIOGRAPHY

PRIMARY SOURCES

AQUINAS, ST. THOMAS, *In Libros Politicorum Aristotelis Expositio*, ed.
R. M. Spiazzi, Rome, 1951.
Selected Political Writings, ed. A. P. d'Entrèves, Oxford, 1965.

ARISTOTLE, *Politics*, trans. Benjamin Jowett, Oxford, 1920.

ASCHAM, ANTHONY, *A Discourse: wherein is examined, what is particularly lawfull during the Confusions and Revolutions of Government*,
London, 1648.

AUGUSTINE, ST., *The City of God*, ed. R. V. G. Tasker, 2 vols., London,
1967.

AYLMER, JOHN, *An Harborowe for Faithfull and Trewe Svbiectes*,
Strasbourg, 1559.

BACON, NATHANIEL, *An Historicall Discourse of the Uniformity of the
Government of England*, London, 1647–51.

BRACTON, HENRY DE, *On the Laws and Customs of England*, trans. S. E.
Thorne, Cambridge, Mass., 1968.

BRETON, NICHOLAS, *A Murmurer*, in *The Works*, II, ed. A. B. Grosart,
New York, 1966.

BRINKLOW, HENRY, *Complaynt of Roderyck More*, ed. J. M. Cowper,
Early English Text Society, London, 1874.

BRINTON, THOMAS, *The Sermons*, ed. Sister Mary Aquinas Devlin, 2
vols., Camden Society, 3rd series, LXXXV–LXXXVI, 1954.

BUCKERIDGE, JOHN, *A Sermon Preached at Hampton Court before the
Kings Maiestie*, London, 1606.

CAMDEN, WILLIAM, 'William Camden's "Discourse Concerning the
Prerogative of the Crown",' intro. and ed. Frank Smith Fussner,
Proceedings of the American Philosophical Society, 101, 1957.

CAMPBELL, LILY B., ed., *The Mirror for Magistrates*, New York, 1938.

CARPENTER, JOHN, *A Preparatiue to Contentation*, London, 1597.

CHEKE, SIR JOHN, *The hurt of sedition how greeuous it is to a commonwealth*, in Holinshed, *Chronicles*, III, London, 1808.

CHRISTOPHERSON, JOHN, *An Exhortation to all menne to take hede and
beware of rebellion*, London, 1554.

CLEMENT, *The First Epistle of Clement to the Corinthians*, in *The Apostolic Fathers*, I, trans. Kirsopp Lake, London and New York, 1912.

CRAIG, SIR THOMAS, *The Right of Succession to the Kingdom of England*,
London, 1703.

CRAKANTHORPE, RICHARD, *A Sermon at the Solemnizing of the Happie
Inauguration of . . . King Iames*, London, 1609.

CROMPTON, RICHARD, *A short Declaration of the ende of Traytors*, London, 1587.

CROWLEY, ROBERT, *The Select Works*, ed. J. M. Cowper, Early English Text Society, extra series, XV, London, 1872.

DANTE, *De Monarchia*, in *A Translation of the Latin Works of Dante Alighieri*, I, The Temple Classics, London, 1904.

DAVIES, SIR JOHN, *A Discourse of Law and Lawyers*, in *The Works*, II ed. A. B. Grosart, Privately Printed, 1876.

DIGGES, DUDLEY, *An Answer to a printed book, intituled, Observations upon some of his Majesties late answers and expresses*, Oxford, 1642.
The Unlawfulnesse of Subjects taking up Armes against their Soveraigne, London, 1643.

DUDLEY, EDMUND, *The Tree of Commonwealth*, ed. D. M. Brodie, Cambridge, 1948.

ELYOT, SIR THOMAS, *The Boke named the Gouernour*, London, 1907.

FAWKNER, ANTONY, *Nicodemus for Christ, or the Religiovs Moote of an Honest Lawyer*, London, 1630.

FERNE, HENRY, *The Resolving of Conscience*, Cambridge, 1642.
Conscience Satisfied, Oxford, 1643.

FERNE, JOHN, *The Blazon of Gentrie*, London, 1586.

FILMER, SIR ROBERT, *Patriarcha, and Other Political Works*, ed. Peter Laslett, Oxford, 1949.

FISTON, WILLIAM, *The Schoole of good Manners: or, a new Schoole of Vertue*, London, 1609.

FLETCHER, PHINEAS, *The Purple Island, Or The Isle of Man*, in Giles and Phineas Fletcher, *Poetical Works*, II, ed. F. S. Boas, Cambridge, 1909.

FLOYD, THOMAS, *The Picture of a perfit Common wealth*, London, 1600.

FORREST, SIR WILLIAM, *Pleasaunt Poesye of Princelie Practise*, ed. Sidney H. Herrtage, Early English Text Society, extra series, XXXII, London, 1878.

FORSET, EDWARD, *A Comparative Discovrse of the Bodies Natvral and Politiqve*, London, 1606.

FORTESCUE, SIR JOHN, *The Works*, ed. Lord Clermont, London: Privately Printed, 1869.
The Governance of England, ed. Charles Plummer, London, 1926.
De Laudibus Legum Angliae, ed. and trans. S. B. Chrimes, Cambridge, 1949.

FULBECKE, WILLIAM, *The Pandectes of the law of Nations*, London, 1602.

GARDINER, STEPHEN, *De Vera Obedientia*, Leeds, 1966.

GOODMAN, CHRISTOPHER, *How Superior Powers Ought to be Obeyed*, Facsimile Text Society, New York, 1931.

GROSSE, ROBERT, *Royalty and Loyalty*, London, 1647.

HALLER, WILLIAM ed., *Tracts on Liberty in the Puritan Revolution 1638–1647*, 3 vols., New York, 1965.

HALLER, WILLIAM and DAVIES, GODFREY eds., *The Leveller Tracts 1647–1653*, New York, 1944.

HARRISON, WILLIAM, *The Description of England*, in Holinshed, *Chronicles*, I, London, 1807.

HERLE, CHARLES, *A Fuller Answer to a Treatise written by Doctor Ferne*, London, 1642.

HOBBES, THOMAS, *Leviathan*, ed. Michael Oakeshott, Oxford, 1946.

HOOKER, RICHARD, *The Works*, ed. John Keble, 3 vols., Oxford, 1845.

Homilies Appointed to be Read in Churches, Oxford, 1814.

HOWELL, T. B., *A Complete Collection of State Trials*, II, London, 1816.

HUDSON, MICHAEL, *The Divine Right of Government*, London, 1647.

HUNTON, PHILIP, *A Treatise of Monarchy*, London, 1643.

JAMES I, *The Political Works*, ed. C. H. McIlwain, New York, 1965.

JEWEL, JOHN, *The Works*, ed. John Ayre, Cambridge, 1845–50.

KAIL, J. ed., *Twenty-Six Political and Other Poems*, Early English Text Society, London, 1904.

KING, HENRY, *A Sermon Preached at Pavls Crosse, The 25, Of November, 1621*, London, 1621.

A Sermon Preached at St. Pavls March 27. 1640 : Being the Anniversary of His Maiesties Happy Inauguration to His Crowne, London, 1640.

KNOX, JOHN, *The First Blast of the Trumpet against the monstrvos regiment of women*, Geneva, 1558.

LILLY, JOSEPH ed., *A Collection of Seventy-Nine Black-Letter Ballads and Broadsides, Printed in the Reign of Queen Elizabeth, Between the Years 1559 and 1597*, London, 1870.

MAXWELL, JOHN, *Sacro-Sancta Regum Majestas : or, the Sacred and Royall Prerogative of Christian Kings*, Oxford, 1644.

MAYNWARING, ROGER, *Religion and Allegiance : in two sermons preached before the Kings Maiestie*, London, 1627.

MERBURY, CHARLES, *A Briefe Discovrse of Royall Monarchie, as of the Best Common Weale*, London, 1581.

MORISON, SIR RICHARD, *A Remedy for Sedition*, ed. E. M. Cox, London, 1933.

NEDHAM, MARCHAMONT, *The Case of the Commonwealth of England Stated*, ed. Philip A. Knachel, Charlottesville, Virg., 1969.

PADUA, MARSILIUS OF, *The Defender of Peace*, trans. Alan Gewirth, New York, 1967.

PARKER, HENRY, *A Discourse Concerning Puritans*, London, 1641.

Jus Populi, London, 1644.

PARIS, JOHN OF, *Tractatus de regia potestate et papali*, ed. Fritz Bleienstein, Stuttgart, 1969.

[PARSONS, ROBERT], *A Conference Abovt the Next Svccession to the Crowne of Ingland,* 1594.

PELLING, JOHN, *A Sermon of the Providence of God,* London, 1607.

PONET, JOHN, *A Shorte Treatise of politike pouuer,* facsimile reprint in Winthrop S. Hudson, *John Ponet (1516?–1556) Advocate of Limited Monarchy,* Chicago, 1942.

RAWLINSON, JOHN, *Vivat Rex,* Oxford, 1619.

ROMANUS, AEGIDIUS, *De Regimine Principum,* ed. Samuel P. Molenaer, New York, 1899.

SACKVILLE, THOMAS and NORTON, THOMAS, *Gorboduc,* Menston, 1968.

ST. GERMAN, CHRISTOPHER, *An answere to a letter,* London, 1535? *Doctor and Student: or Dialogues Between a Doctor of Divinity, and a Student in the Laws of England,* 15th ed., London, 1751.

SALISBURY, JOHN OF, *The Statesman's Book,* trans. John Dickinson, New York, 1963.

SANDYS, EDWIN, *The Sermons,* ed. John Ayre, Cambridge, 1842.

SMITH, SIR THOMAS, *A Discourse of the Commonweal of This Realm of England,* ed. Mary Dewar, Charlottesville, Virg., 1969. *De Repvblica Anglorvm,* Menston, 1970.

SPELMAN, SIR JOHN, *A view of a printed book Intituled Observations upon His Majesties Late Answers and Expresses,* Oxford, 1642.

STARKEY, THOMAS, *An exhortation to the people instructynge theym to vnitie and obedience,* London, 1534. *Starkey's Life and Letters in England in the reign of King Henry the Eighth,* ed. Sidney H. Herrtage, Early English Text Society, extra series, XXXII, London, 1878. *A Dialogue between Reginald Pole and Thomas Lupset,* ed. Kathleen M. Burton, London, 1948.

SYDENHAM, HUMPHRY, *Five Sermons Preached upon Severall Occasions,* London, 1637.

TWYSDEN, SIR ROGER, *Certaine Considerations upon the Government of England,* ed. J. M. Kemble, Camden Society, 1849.

TYNDALE, WILLIAM, *Doctrinal Treatises,* ed. H. Walter, Cambridge, 1848.

VALENTINE, HENRY, *God Save the King. A Sermon Preached in St. Pauls Church the 27th of March 1639,* London, 1639.

VENNARD, RICHARD, *An Exhortacion to continew all Subiects in their dew obedience, together with the reward of a faithfull subject to his Prince,* in *The Right Way to Heauen: and the true testimonie of a faithfull and loyall subiect,* London, 1601.

WINSTANLEY, GERRARD, *The Law of Freedom and other writings,* ed. Christopher Hill, London, 1973.

SECONDARY SOURCES

ALLEN, J. W., *English Political Thought 1603–1660*, London, 1938.
A History of Political Thought in the Sixteenth Century, London, 1960.
ALLERS, RUDOLF, 'Microcosmus: From Anaximandros to Paracelsus', *Traditio*, II, 1944.
ANDERSON, PERRY, *Lineages of the Absolutist State*, London, 1974.
ARMSTRONG, R. A., *Primary and Secondary Precepts in Thomistic Natural Law Teaching*, The Hague, 1966.
ARMSTRONG, W. A., 'The Elizabethan Conception of the Tyrant', *Review of English Studies*, XXII, 1946.
BABB, LAWRENCE, *The Elizabethan Malady: A Study of Melancholia in English Literature from 1580 to 1642*, East Lansing, 1951.
BARKAN, LEONARD, *Nature's Work of Art: The Human Body as Image of the World:* New Haven and London, 1975.
BARKER, ERNEST, *The Political Thought of Plato and Aristotle*, New York, 1959.
BAUMER, FRANKLIN LE VAN, *The Early Tudor Theory of Kingship*, New York, 1966.
'Christopher St. German: The Political Philosophy of a Tudor Lawyer', *American Historical Review*, XLII, 1936–7.
'Thomas Starkey and Marsilius of Padua', *Politica*, 2, 1936–7.
BETHELL, S. L. *The Cultural Revolution of the Seventeenth Century*, London, 1951.
BLACK, ANTONY, *Monarchy and Community: Political Ideas in the Later Conciliar Controversy, 1430–1450*, Cambridge, 1970.
BOWLE, JOHN, *Hobbes and his Critics: a Study in Seventeenth Century Constitutionalism*, London, 1951.
CASPARI, FRITZ, *Humanism and the Social Order in Tudor England*, Chicago, 1954.
CHRIMES, S. B., *English Constitutional Ideas in the Fifteenth Century*, New York, 1966.
CHROUST, A-H., 'The Corporate Idea and the Body Politic in the Middle Ages', *Review of Politics*, 9, 1947.
CHURCH, R. W., intro. to *Hooker, Book I Of the Laws of Ecclesiastical Polity*, Oxford, 1882.
CLEBSCH, WILLIAM A., *England's Earliest Protestants, 1520–1535*, New Haven, 1964.
COHN, NORMAN, *The Pursuit of the Millenium: Revolutionary millenarians and mystical anarchists of the Middle Ages*, London, 1970.
COLLINSON, PATRICK, *The Elizabethan Puritan Movement*, London, 1967.
CONGER, G. P., *Theories of Macrocosms and Microcosms in the History of Philosophy*, New York, 1922.

CRAIG, HARDIN, *The Enchanted Glass*, Oxford, 1960.

CROXFORD, LESLIE, 'The Originality of Hooker's Work', *Proceedings of the Leeds Philosophical and Literary Society : Literary and Historical Section*, XV, 1973.

DAVIES, E. T., *The Political Ideas of Richard Hooker*, London, 1946.

DAVIS, J. C., 'Gerrard Winstanley and the Restoration of True Magistracy', *Past and Present*, 70, 1976.

DEANE, HERBERT A., *The Political and Social Ideas of St. Augustine*, New York and London, 1963.

D'ENTRÈVES, A. P., *Richard Hooker, a study in the history of political philosophy*, D.Phil., Oxford, 1932.

The Medieval Contribution to Political Thought, New York, 1959.

Natural Law: An Introduction to Legal Philosophy, London, 1967.

DEWAR, MARY, *Sir Thomas Smith: a Tudor Intellectual in Office*, London, 1964.

DE WULF, MAURICE, *Mediaeval Philosophy Illustrated from the System of Thomas Aquinas*, Harvard, 1922.

Philosophy and Civilization in the Middle Ages, Princeton, 1922.

DIRKSEN, CLETUS F., *A Critical Analysis of Richard Hooker's Theory of the Relation of Church and State*, Ph.D., Notre Dame, Indiana, 1947.

DOWDEN, EDWARD, *Puritan and Anglican: Studies in Literature*, London, 1900.

ECCLESHALL, ROBERT, 'Richard Hooker's Synthesis and the Problem of Allegiance', *Journal of the History of Ideas*, XXXVIII, 1976.

ELTON, G. R., *England under the Tudors*, London, 1959.

The Tudor Constitution: Documents and Commentary, Cambridge, 1960.

The Body of the Whole Realm: Parliament and Representation in Medieval and Tudor England, Charlottesville, Virg., 1969.

Policy and Police: The Enforcement of the Reformation in the Age of Thomas Cromwell, Cambridge, 1972.

Reform and Renewal: Thomas Cromwell and the Common Weal, Cambridge, 1973.

'The Tudor Revolution: A Reply', *Past and Present*, 29, 1964.

'Reform by Statute: Thomas Starkey's Dialogue and Thomas Cromwell's Policy', *Proceedings of the British Academy*, LIV, 1968.

ESCHMANN, 'Studies on the Notion of Society in St. Thomas Aquinas: I. St. Thomas and the Decretal of Innocent IV *Romana Ecclesia: Caterum*', *Mediaeval Studies*, VIII, 1946.

'Studies on the Notion of Society in St. Thomas Aquinas: II. Thomistic Social Philosophy and the Theology of Original Sin', *Mediaeval Studies*, IX, 1947.

EVERITT, ALAN, 'Social Mobility in Early Modern England', *Past and Present*, 33, 1966.

FERGUSON, ARTHUR B., *The Articulate Citizen and the English Renaissance*, Durham, N.C., 1965.

'Fortescue and the Renaissance: a Study in Transition', *Studies in the Renaissance*, VI, 1959.

'The Tudor Commonweal and the Sense of Change', *Journal of British Studies*, III, 1963–4.

FRIEDRICH, C. J., *Transcendent Justice: The Religious Dimension of Constitutionalism*, Durham, N.C., 1964.

GIERKE, OTTO, *Political Theories of the Middle Age*, trans. F. W. Maitland, Cambridge, 1900.

Natural Law and the Theory of Society, 1500–1800, trans. Ernest Barker, Cambridge, 1958.

GILBERT, FELIX, 'Sir John Fortescue's "Dominium Regale et Politicum"', *Mediavalia et Humanistica*, II, 1943.

GILSON, ETIENNE, *Reason and Revelation in the Middle Ages*, London, 1954.

GORE, CHARLES ed., *Property: its Duties and Rights*, London, 1913.

GOUGH, J. W., *Fundamental Law in English History*, Oxford, 1955.

The Social Contract, Oxford, 1963.

GREEN, V. H. H., *From St. Augustine to William Temple*, London, 1948.

GREENLEAF, W. H., *Order, Empiricism and Politics: Two Traditions of English Political Thought 1500–1700*, London, 1964.

'The Divine Right of Kings', *History Today*, XIV, 1964.

'The Thomasian Tradition and the Theory of Absolute Monarchy', *English Historical Review*, LXXIX, 1964.

'Hobbes: The Problem of Interpretation', in *Hobbes and Rousseau*, eds. Maurice Cranston and R. S. Peters, New York, 1972.

GRISLIS, EGIL, 'Richard Hooker's Method of Theological Inquiry', *Anglican Theological Review*, XLV, 1963.

GUNN, J. A. W., *Politics and the Public Interest in the Seventeenth Century*, London, 1969.

HALE, DAVID G., *The Body Politic: A Political Metaphor in Renaissance English Literature*, Ph.D., Duke University, 1965.

HALLAM, HENRY, *The Constitutional History of England from the Accession of Henry VII to the Death of George II*, I, London, 1854.

HANSON, DONALD W., *From Kingdom to Commonwealth: The Development of Civic Consciousness in English Political Thought*, Cambridge, Mass., 1970.

HAMILTON, BERNICE, *Political Thought in Sixteenth-Century Spain: A Study of the political ideas of Vitoria, De Soto, Suarez, and Molina*, Oxford, 1963.

HEARNSHAW, F. J. C. ed., *The Social and Political Ideas of Some Great Medieval Thinkers,* London, 1932.

HEGEL, F., *Philosophy of Right,* trans. T. M. Knox, Oxford, 1952.

HEXTER, J. H., *Reappraisals in History,* London, 1961.

HILL, CHRISTOPHER, *Puritanism and Revolution,* London, 1958.
Intellectual Origins of the English Revolution, Oxford, 1965.
The World Turned Upside Down, London, 1972.
Change and Continuity in Seventeenth Century England, London, 1974.

HILL, W. SPEED ed., *Studies in Richard Hooker: Essays Preliminary to an Edition of his Works,* Cleveland and London, 1972.
'Hooker's Polity: The Problem of the "Three Last Books"', *Huntington Library Quarterly,* XXXIV, 1971.

HILLERDAL, GUNNAR, *Reason and Revelation in Richard Hooker,* Lund, 1962.

HILTON, RODNEY, *Bond Men Made Free: Medieval Peasant Movements and the English Rising of 1381,* London, 1973.
ed., *The Transition from Feudalism to Capitalism,* London, 1976.

HINTON, R. W. K., 'Government and Liberty Under James I', *Cambridge Historical Journal,* XI, 1953.
'The Decline of Parliamentary Government under Elizabeth I and the Early Stuarts', *Cambridge Historical Journal,* XIII, 1957.
'English Constitutional Theories from Sir John Fortescue to Sir John Eliot', *English Historical Review,* LXXV, 1960.

HIRST, DEREK, *The Representative of the People? Voters and Voting in England under the Early Stuarts,* Cambridge, 1975.

HOLDSWORTH, W. S., *Essays in Law and History,* eds. A. L. Goodhart and H. G. Hanbury, Oxford, 1946.

HOOPES, ROBERT, *Right Reason in the English Renaissance,* Cambridge, Mass., 1962.

HORKHEIMER, MAX, *Eclipse of Reason,* New York, 1947.

HOUK, RAYMOND A., *Hooker's Ecclesiastical Polity Book VIII,* New York, 1931.

HURSTFIELD, JOEL, *Freedom, Corruption and Government in Elizabethan England,* London, 1973.

JAMES, M. E., 'Obedience and Dissent in Henrician England: The Lincolnshire Rebellion 1536', *Past and Present,* 48, 1970.

JESSUP, FRANK W., *Sir Roger Twysden 1597–1672,* London, 1965.

JONES, WHITNEY, R. D., *The Tudor Commonwealth 1529–1559,* London, 1970.

JORDAN, W. K., *Men of Substance: A Study of the Thought of Two English Revolutionaries, Henry Parker and Henry Robinson,* New York, 1967.

JUDSON, MARGARET A., *The Crisis of the Constitution: An Essay in*

Constitutional and Political Thought in England 1603–1645, New Brunswick, N.J., 1949.

KAMENKA, EUGENE and NEALE, R. S. eds., *Feudalism, Capitalism and Beyond,* London, 1975.

KANTOROWICZ, ERNST H., *The King's Two Bodies. A Study in Mediaeval Political Theology,* Princeton, N.J., 1957.

KEARNEY, H. F., 'Richard Hooker: a Reconstruction', *Cambridge Journal,* 5, 1951–2.

KNAPPEN, M. M., *Tudor Puritanism,* Chicago, 1939.

LEHMBERG, S. E., *The Reformation Parliament 1529–1536,* Cambridge, 1970.

LEWIS, EWART, *Medieval Political Ideas,* 2 vols., London, 1954.
'Organic Tendencies in Medieval Political Thought', *American Political Science Review,* XXXII, 1938.
'Natural Law and Expediency in Medieval Political Theory', *Ethics,* L, 1939–40.
'The "Positivism" of Marsiglio of Padua', *Speculum,* XXXVIII, 1963.

LEWIS, C. S., *English Literature in the Sixteenth Century Excluding Drama,* Oxford, 1954.

LIEBESCHUTZ, HANS, *Medieval Humanism in the Life and Writings of John of Salisbury,* London, 1950.

LOVEJOY, A. O., *The Great Chain of Being,* New York, 1960.

LOWERS, JAMES K., *Mirrors for Rebels: A Study of Polemical Literature Relating to the Northern Rebellion 1569,* Berkeley and Los Angeles, 1953.

MACLURE, MILLAR, *The Paul's Cross Sermons, 1534–1642,* Toronto, 1958.

McGRADE, ARTHUR S., 'The Coherence of Hooker's Polity: The Books on Power', *Journal of the History of Ideas,* XXIV, 1963.

MACPHERSON, C. B., *The Political Theory of Possessive Individualism: from Hobbes to Locke,* Oxford, 1962.

MAJOR, JOHN M., *Sir Thomas Elyot and Renaissance Humanism,* Nebraska, 1964.

MARKUS, R. A., *Saeculum: History and Society in the Theology of St. Augustine,* Cambridge, 1967.

MARSHALL, JOHN S., *Hooker and the Anglican Tradition,* London, 1963.

MARX, KARL and ENGELS, FREDERICK, *Articles on Britain,* Moscow, 1971.

MILLER, EDWARD, *The Origins of Parliament,* Historical Association Pamphlet, London, 1960.

MINTZ, SAMUEL I., *The Hunting of Leviathan: Seventeenth-Century Reactions to the Materialism and Moral Philosophy of Thomas Hobbes,* Cambridge, 1962.

MOHL, RUTH, *The Three Estates in Medieval and Renaissance Literature*, New York, 1962.

MORRALL, J. B., *Political Thought in Medieval Times*, London, 1958.

MORRIS, CHRISTOPHER, *Political Thought in England : Tyndale to Hooker*, London, 1953.

MOSSE, GEORGE L., *The Struggle for Sovereignty in England from the Reign of Queen Elizabeth to the Petition of Right*, East Lansing, 1950.

'Change and Continuity in the Tudor Constitution', *Speculum*, XXII, 1947.

MULLER, J. A., *Stephen Gardiner and the Tudor Reaction*, London, 1926.

MUNZ, PETER, *The Place of Hooker in the History of Thought*, London, 1952.

NEALE, J. E., *The Elizabethan House of Commons*, London, 1949.

NEW, JOHN F. H., *Anglican and Puritan : The Basis of Their Opposition, 1558–1640*, London, 1964.

NICHOLSON, MARJORIE HOPE, *The Breaking of the Circle : Studies in the effect of the 'New Science' upon seventeenth-century poetry*, London, 1960.

OWST, G. R., *Literature and Pulpit in Medieval England*, Cambridge, 1933.

PAGET, F. R., *An Introduction to the Fifth Book of Hooker's Treatise of the Laws of Ecclesiastical Polity*, Oxford, 1899.

PARSONS, WILFRID, 'The Medieval Theory of the Tyrant', *Review of Politics*, 4, 1942.

PHILLIPS, J. E., *The State in Shakespeare's Greek and Roman Plays*, New York, 1940.

POCOCK, J. G. A., *The Ancient Constitution and the Feudal Law : A Study of English Historical Thought in the Seventeenth Century*, Cambridge, 1957.

The Machiavellian Moment : Florentine Political Thought and the Atlantic Republican Tradition, Princeton, N.J., 1975.

POST, GAINES, *Studies in Medieval Legal Thought : Public Law and the State, 1100–1322*, Princeton, N.J., 1964.

'Parisian Masters as a Corporation, 1200–1246', *Speculum*, IX, 1934.

'*Plena Potestas* and Consent in Medieval Assemblies', *Traditio*, I, 1943.

'A Roman Legal Theory of Consent, *Quod Omnes Tangit*, in Medieval Representation', *Wisconsin Law Review*, 1950.

PREVITE-ORTON, C. W., 'Marsilius of Padua', *Proceedings of the British Academy*, XXI, 1935.

ROGERS, ALAN, 'Henry IV, the Commons and Taxation', *Mediaeval Studies*, XXXI, 1969.

ROSE-TROUP, FRANCES, *The Western Rebellion of 1549*, London 1913.
ROSKELL, J. S., 'Perspectives in English Parliamentary History', *Bulletin of the John Rylands Library*, 46, 1963–4.
ROUSE, RICHARD H. and MARY A., 'John of Salisbury and the Doctrine of Tyrannicide', *Speculum*, XLII, 1967.
RUSSELL, CONRAD ed., *The Origins of the English Civil War*, London, 1973.
'Arguments for Religious Unity in England, 1530–1650', *Journal of Ecclesiastical History*, XVIII, 1967.
'Parliamentary History in Perspective, 1604–1629', *History*, 61, 1976.
RUSSELL, F. W., *Ket's Rebellion in Norfolk*, London, 1859.
SAYLES, G. O., *The King's Parliament of England*, London, 1975.
SCARISBRICK, J. J., *Henry VIII*, London, 1968.
SCHLATTER, RICHARD, *Private Property : The History of an Idea*, London, 1951.
SCHOCHET, GORDON J., *Patriarchalism in Political Thought: The Authoritarian Family and Political Speculation and Attitudes Especially in Seventeenth-Century England*, Oxford, 1975.
SHEPARD, MAX A., 'The Political and Constitutional Theory of Sir John Fortescue', in *Essays in History and Political Theory in Honor of Charles Howard McIlwain*, Cambridge, Mass., 1936.
SHIRLEY, F. J., *Richard Hooker and Contemporary Political Ideas*, London, 1949.
SIEGEL, PAUL N., 'English Humanism and the New Tudor Aristocracy', *Journal of the History of Ideas*, XIII, 1952.
SIGMUND, PAUL E., *Nicholas of Cusa and Medieval Political Thought*, Harvard, 1963.
SISSON, C. J., *The Judicious Marriage of Mr. Hooker and the Birth of The Laws of Ecclesiastical Polity*, Cambridge, 1940.
SKEEL, CAROLINE A. J., 'The Influence of the Writings of Sir John Fortescue', *Transactions of the Royal Historical Society*, 3rd series, X, 1916.
SKINNER, QUENTIN, 'History and Ideology in the English Revolution', *Historical Journal*, VIII, 1965.
'The Context of Hobbes's Theory of Political Obligation', in *Hobbes and Rousseau*, eds. Maurice Cranston and R. S. Peters, New York, 1972.
SMALLEY, BERYL ed., *Trends in Medieval Political Thought*, Oxford, 1965.
The Becket Conflict and the Schools : A Study of Intellectuals in Politics, Oxford, 1973.
SMITH, EDWARD O., JNR., 'The Royal Mystique and the Elizabethan Liturgy', *Historical Magazine of the Protestant Episcopal Church*, XXXI, 1962.

'The Doctrine of the Prince and the Elizabethan Episcopal Sermon: 1559–1603', *Anglican Theological Review*, XLV, 1963.

'The Elizabethan Doctrine of the Prince as Reflected in the Sermons of Episcopacy, 1559–1603', *The Huntington Library Quarterly*, XXVIII, 1964–5.

SPENCER, THEODORE, *Shakespeare and the Nature of Man*, New York, 1951.

SPRAGENS, THOMAS A., *The Politics of Motion : The World of Thomas Hobbes,* London, 1973.

STONE, LAWRENCE, *The causes of the English Revolution 1529–1642*, London, 1972.

'Social Mobility in England, 1500–1700', *Past and Present*, 33, 1966.

STRONG, ROY C., 'The Popular Celebration of the Accession Day of Queen Elizabeth I', *Journal of the Warburg and Courtauld Institutes*, XXI, 1958.

TALBERT, E. W., *The Problem of Order : Elizabethan Political Commonplaces and an Example of Shakespeare's Art*, N. Carolina., 1962.

THOMAS, KEITH, *Religion and the Decline of Magic : Studies in popular beliefs in sixteenth and seventeenth century England*, London, 1971.

THOMPSON, W. D. J. CARGILL, 'The Source of Hooker's Knowledge of Marsilius of Padua', *Journal of Ecclesiastical History*, XXXV, 1974.

TIERNEY, BRIAN, *Foundations of the Conciliar Theory : The Contribution of the Medieval Canonists from Gratian to the Great Schism,* Cambridge, 1955.

'Bracton on Government', *Speculum*, XXXVIII, 1963.

TILLYARD, E. M. W., *Shakespeare's History Plays*, London, 1944.

The Elizabethan World Picture, London, 1963.

ULLMANN, W. H., *The Medieval Idea of Law as Represented by Lucas de Penna*, London, 1946.

Principles of Government and Politics in the Middle Ages, London, 1961.

The Individual and Society in the Middle Ages, London, 1967.

VINOGRADOFF, PAUL, 'Reason and Conscience in Sixteenth-Century Jurisprudence', *Law Quarterly Review*, XXIV, 1908.

WALZER, MICHAEL, *The Revolution of the Saints : A Study in the Origins of Radical Politics,* London, 1966.

WESTON, C. C., 'The Theory of Mixed Monarchy Under Charles I and After', *English Historical Review*, LXXV, 1960.

WHITE, HELEN C., *Social Criticism in Popular Religious Literature of the Sixteenth Century*, New York, 1965.

WILKINSON, B., *Constitutional History of Medieval England, 1216–1399*, 3 vols., London, 1958.

Constitutional History of England in the Fifteenth Century, London, 1964.

'The "Political Revolution" of the Thirteenth and Fourteenth Centuries in England', *Speculum*, XXIV, 1949.

WILKS, M. J., *The Problem of Sovereignty in the Later Middle Ages*, Cambridge, 1963.

WILLEY, BASIL, *The English Moralists*, London, 1964.

WILLIAMS, PENRY and HARRISS, G. L., 'A Revolution in Tudor History?' *Past and Present*, 25, 1963.

WILMER, RICHARD B., JNR., 'Hooker on Authority', *Anglican Theological Review*, XXXIII, 1951.

WINNY, JAMES ed., *The Frame of Order*, London, 1957.

WOLIN, SHELDON S., 'Richard Hooker and English Conservatism', *Western Political Quarterly*, VI, 1953.

WOODHOUSE, A. S. P., *Puritanism and Liberty*, London, 1938.

'Religion and Some Foundations of English Democracy', *Philosophical Review*, 61, 1952.

WORMUTH, FRANCIS D., *The Royal Prerogative 1603–1649*, New York, 1939.

YATES, FRANCES, *Astrae : The Imperial Theme in the Sixteenth Century*, London, 1975.

ZAGORIN, PEREZ, *A History of Political Thought in the English Revolution*, London, 1954.

ZEEVELD, W. G., *Foundations of Tudor Policy*, Cambridge, Mass., 1948.

INDEX